Crisis Communications:
A Casebook Approach

Crisis Communications:
A Casebook Approach

Kathleen Fearn-Banks
University of Washington

LEA **LAWRENCE ERLBAUM ASSOCIATES, PUBLISHERS**
1996   Mahwah, New Jersey

Lawrence Erlbaum Associates, Inc., Publishers
10 Industrial Avenue
Mahwah, NJ 07430

Cover design by Gail Silverman

Frontespiece illustrated by Leonard Rifas

Library of Congress Cataloging-in-Publication Data

Fearn-Banks, Kathleen.
    Crisis communications : a casebook approach / by Kathleen
Fearn-Banks.
        p. cm.
    Includes bibliographical references and indexes.
    ISBN 0-8058-1921-5 (alk. paper). — ISBN 0-8058-1922-3 (pbk.
: alk. paper)
    1. Public relations—Management—Case studies.   2. Crisis
management—Case studies. 3. Advertising—Case studies. I. Title.
HD59.F37 1995
659.2—dc20   95-41222
                                                          CIP

Books published by Lawrence Erlbaum Associates are printed on
acid-free paper, and their bindings are chosen for strength and durability.

Printed in the United States of America
10 9 8 7 6 5 4 3 2

This book is dedicated to my parents,
Dr. Kayte M. Fearn and Dr. James E. Fearn,
who made it unnecessary for me to look
outside of home for role models.

Contents

Preface

"I experience a crisis every day." That's a declaration made by numerous public relations professionals. Pity those who actually do. Even organizations that thrive on disasters, conflicts, tragedies—like the American Red Cross, fire departments, police departments, and child abuse agencies—are not necessarily organizations in crisis. Their ordinary tasks are other people's crises.

This volume presents case studies of problems that can turn into crises, and crises, if not handled effectively, that can become catastrophes.

Cases included in public relations (PR) textbooks are frequently written in the formats of public relations campaign plans. Particularly popular are the plans in which the steps of the campaign are abbreviated by the acronyms RACE or ROPE. RACE, for some, stands for Research, Action, Communication, Evaluation. Others make the "A" in RACE stand for Adaptation. ROPE stands for Research, Objectives, Program, Evaluation. The formulas are a process of management by objectives (MBO), a system that focuses on desired results rather than performance activities.

I do not argue the value of such systems in public relations planning. Nevertheless, in a crisis, an organization is frequently forced to perform the third step—which is Communication in RACE or Program in ROPE—without having gone through the other steps.

A crisis, by definition, presents a great deal of uncertainty and immediacy. You, the PR professional, may not make the decision of when to take action;

outside forces demand it. You cannot tell the media or other key publics, "We're doing our objectives now, we'll call you back."

There are other outside influences affecting what is and is not done, even if there is a precrisis plan. The research data changes constantly. New research done by outsiders can come crashing down on you. Issues and adversaries that you may have never expected may appear. Strategies and tactics may change from day to day, hour to hour. You hope that a day will come when you can evaluate your plan; it may not.

Therefore, a study of organizations in crisis cannot be a simple matter of describing the steps in RACE or ROPE. Most of the cases in this book are, consequently, written in narrative form so that the reader can feel the tensions, stress, uncertainty, fear, and all the emotions that go along with coping with crises.

Chapters 1 through 4 describe the skills needed to communicate effectively in a crisis. Chapter 1 defines "crisis" as opposed to "problem" and describes the normal stages of a crisis and theories pertaining to crisis communications.

Chapter 2 is a how-to manual on developing and implementing a crisis communications plan.

Chapter 3 deals with some causes of crises—rumor, sensationalized, and irresponsible news coverage (including a relatively new horror, the nonexpert expert). This chapter also includes three case studies of crisis communications campaigns responding to these crisis makers.

Chapter 4 features tips on how to work with, rather than in conflict with, the media and lawyers. This chapter includes two case studies of how public relations operations, affected by the same crisis, dealt very differently with the media, along with a third case describing an innovative media relations program.

Chapters 5 through 9 are narrated case studies of how public relations professionals used communication in several kinds of crises. Most, but not all, of the professionals featured are not the heads of public relations departments, but the people who actually do the hands-on work, people with whom students of public relations may easily identify.

A decision was made to include examples of the primary types of places where public relations professionals work. There are crises managed by giant companies with large public relations staffs (like the U.S. Postal Service and the Southern California Gas Company) as well as companies with small staffs (like the Swedish Medical Center and the Pepsi/Seven-Up Beverage Group), and public relations agencies (the EvansGroup, Dick Gruenwald Associates). There are also nonprofit agencies, government agencies, hospitals, and universities as well as companies.

There are the two "textbook cases"—Tylenol and Exxon—but more recent cases of product tampering and environmental issues are also treated. In each chapter, there are two or more cases of organizations suffering crises similar in some respects, but vastly different in others.

Although the cases are organized in the volume by types of crises, they are also adaptable to instructors teaching basic public relations principles as examples of media relations, consumer relations, community relations, government relations, internal relations, emergency public relations, and relations with special publics. There are lessons to be learned from each case, no matter what type of crisis is described—lessons in strategizing, tactics, and so on.

The appendices are sample documents that will prove useful to practitioners and students of public relations preparing for crises. Appendix A is a generic crisis communications plan for a large multi-site corporation. Appendix B is a a crisis communications plan contributed by Big Brothers/Big Sisters of America, headquartered in Philadelphia, Pennsylvania. Appendix C is a crisis communications plan contributed by News & Public Affairs at the University of Florida.

An instructor's manual and a student workbook are also available to supplement the textbook for classroom use.

ACKNOWLEDGMENTS

The executives and public relations professionals mentioned in most of the cases studies unselfishly agreed to interviews in person, by telephone, by fax, by E-mail, or by mail. In addition to helping with the information-gathering process, each of them took a step further by fact-checking drafts of the cases. All of these people and the "mystery editor" at Johnson & Johnson are especially appreciated.

I am grateful to my colleagues, the faculty of the School of Communications, University of Washington, especially Director Edward P. Bassett and Professors Anthony Giffard, Gerald Baldasty, Lawrence Bowen, Don Pember, and Albert Sampson. Staff members Ann Condon, Jodi Naas, Kellus Stone, Karen Nagai, and Pat Denning were especially helpful.

I thank the students in the public relations sequence, especially those in Communications 430: Crisis Communications, who conducted preliminary research on the StarKist and U.S. Postal Service cases.

I applaud the persons who proved that the theory of "three degrees of separation" is true. They all, at least, knew somebody who knew somebody I needed to interview. They are the following: Charlayne Hunter-Gault, Rich McKando, Ofield Dukes, Erik Peterson, Dave Endicott, Betsy Aaron, Wally Pfister, Danner Graves, Rhonda Bailey Staton, Michael Tidwell, Tanya Rhone, Cynthia Adams and Catherine Hindrichsen.

People of great assistance were Anne Burford-Johnson, Osie Thornton, Mickey Fearn, Allison Fearn, Nicholas Fearn, Barbara Hughey, Mary Ryan and her trusty computers at Wordcrafters, Dr. Marilyn Kern-Foxwworth, Dr. Richard-Alan Nelson, Judy Schleske, Evelyn Stampley, Gina Arnold, Lani Jones, Peter Kahle, Mike Noblet, Karen Noblet, Vivian Phillips-Scott, Lani Jacobson, and especially, my mother, Dr. Kayte Marsh Fearn, the sweetest combination of supporter and critic imaginable.

I thank my friends, Hal Williams and Flip Wilson, and my father and stepmother, Dr. James Fearn and Rheba Galloway Fearn, who all provided me with idyllic retreats for writing.

Finally, if there is any person I did not think of when writing this acknowledgment, you are appreciated too.

Kathleen Fearn-Banks

The Nature of Crises

WHAT IS A CRISIS?

"If something can go wrong, it will."

This expression, popularly called Murphy's Law, takes on real meaning for crisis planners. In the mid-1990s, many large corporations still have no crisis management or crisis communications plans. Management and public relations personnel in these companies are likely to say they acknowledge the need for such a plan; they realize that Murphy's Law is right. However, they either lack the manpower or the expertise to develop a crisis plan, so they think positively and hope that the inevitable will never occur until the economy improves and they can hire someone with crisis planning expertise.

Many organizations and individuals go through life saying that they are thinking positively, that somehow if they never have a negative thought, nothing negative will happen. This is absolute balderdash! The slogan should be "Think Negatively."

A crisis can and will happen. "When?" is the question. Thinking negatively is more appropriate than positive thinking in crisis management. This book will show that if an organization's leaders think and plan for the worst-case scenario, they will come out of a crisis in better condition than they would otherwise.

A *crisis* is a major occurrence with a potentially negative outcome affecting an organization, company, or industry, as well as its publics, products, services, or good name. It interrupts normal business transactions and can sometimes threaten the existence of the organization. A crisis can be terrorism, fire, a boycott, product tampering, product failure, a strike, or numerous other events (see the list on page 19).

1

The size of the organization is irrelevant. It can be a multinational corporation, a one-person business, or even an individual.

Public relations professionals often say, "I have a crisis every day." This is an exaggeration, of course. The term "crisis" denotes something more serious than a "problem." Public relations people deal with problems—solving them, avoiding them. By definition, however, a crisis interrupts the normal flow of business, so a crisis cannot be a *normal* part of this flow.

On the other hand, a crisis is not necessarily so catastrophic that the life of the organization is destroyed. Exxon suffered the crisis of crises after its oil spill in 1989. It still suffers from a bad image, but it thrives in business. According to the 1994 Fortune 500 list of the top corporations in the United States, Exxon was first in profit, third in sales (The Fortune 500, 1994).

In the 1995 Fortune 500 list, Exxon was again ranked third in sales, but second in profit. Ranked within the petroleum industry, it was ranked first in sales, nearly doubling its nearest competitor, Mobil Oil (Fortune 500, 1995, May 15).

In Fortune's list of most admired companies, Exxon was 70th out of the 395 companies ranked, a respectable position. Its corporate reputation was ranked fourth in the petroleum industry (Jacob, 1995, March 6).

Toying with definitions is actually unnecessary. This book advises you to plan for the worst that can happen, whether crises or problems. This brings us to another expression: "Be prepared."

Even if you have never been a Boy Scout, this is good advice. This book shows you how to prepare yourself and your organizations to cope with crises that may occur. It deals with preparations made far in advance, as well as with strategies and tactics to be used during a crisis. It examines the experiences of public relations professionals in crises, describing what they did, what they wished they had done, and what hampered their progress. We can learn from their successes and failures.

In a crisis, unlike in a problem, emotions are on edge, brains are not fully functioning, and events are occurring so rapidly that drafting a plan during a crisis is unthinkable. Simply following one is difficult.

Crisis management is a process of strategic planning for a crisis or negative turning point, a process that removes some of the risk and uncertainty from the negative occurrence and thereby allows the organization to be in greater control of its own destiny.

Crisis communications is the communication between the organization and its publics prior to, during, and after the negative occurrence. The communications are designed to minimize damage to the image of the organization.

Effective crisis management includes crisis communications that not only can alleviate or eliminate the crisis, but can sometimes bring the organization a more positive reputation than before the crisis.

Public relations deals with *publics*. Publics are the specific audience targeted by programs. People frequently use the term "general public," but public relations professionals usually are more specific in their targeting. Examples of corporation publics would be the following:

Employees
Customers
Stockholders
Community members
Board members
Unions
Retirees

There can be numerous others. An organization depends upon these publics for survival because they have some stake in the organization.

Public relations is concerned with reputation. It exists to avoid a negative image and to create or enhance a positive reputation. It is largely the fear of a negative image that causes organizations to develop public relations departments, hire public relations agencies, or both.

Too often, an organization does not consider utilizing public relations until it is in a crisis. Then it wants a speedy recovery.

Research shows (see Crisis Communications Theory, p. 10) that companies with ongoing two-way communications often avoid crises or endure crises of shorter duration or of lesser magnitude. Research also shows that companies with a crisis management plan come out of a crisis with a more positive image.

Whether an organization is a large multinational company or very small, a crisis communications plan is needed. A crisis communications plan is preferably a part of a company-wide crisis management plan that would include sections on evacuation, work sites, equipment, and so on. If a company does not have a crisis management plan, a crisis communications plan is still advisable, even urgent.

The media that you have tried to pitch ideas for news stories, the media that toss "perfect" news releases in the trash, the media that never return phone calls—THAT MEDIA will call on you in a crisis. They will probably not telephone in advance. They will show up on your premises—"in your face." The media, seeing themselves as advocates for the people, can be the principal adversaries in a crisis.

This is a time when public relations (PR) takes front and center—in a very crucial way. This is not to say that public relations will operate independently—that might be a greater disaster. It is a time, however, when the chief executive officer (CEO) may listen to the PR guy whose name he can never remember.

Even in a crisis, sometimes, the CEO does not listen because business schools often teach CEOs to make their own decisions. There are many documented cases of disasters when CEOs acted independently.

The Exxon crisis, again, is an example. Exxon's CEO, Lawrence Rawl, did not respond as the media and environmentalists would have preferred. He did not accept responsibility as rapidly as critics felt he should. He did not fly to Valdez to express concern. All the moves that public relations experts would advise, Rawl ignored. Rawl is not alone in his response among corporate heads, but the number of bad responses is declining as business learns the effects of public opinion.

In a crisis when everyone else is in a state of panic, public relations practitioners must have a calming attitude of "This is not as bad as it seems," or "This could be worse. We cannot turn crises into catastrophes. This is what we do. . . ."

FIVE STAGES OF A CRISIS

A crisis has five stages:

1. Detection.
2. Prevention/Preparation.
3. Containment.
4. Recovery.
5. Learning.

Detection

The detection phase may begin with noting the warning signs, what Barton (1993) referred to as *prodromes* or the *prodromal stage*. Some crises have no noticeable prodromes, but many do.

When an organization in the same business as yours suffers a crisis, it is a warning to your organization. The 1982 Tylenol tampering case was a prodrome to other manufacturers of over-the-counter drugs. Most companies heeded that warning and now use tamper-proof containers. Imagine how many crises were avoided by noticing that what happened to Tylenol could happen to other companies.

On the other hand, Johnson & Johnson itself had little warning before it was hit with this crisis. No one had ever poisoned over-the-counter pain-killers; it was not a crisis Johnson & Johnson had anticipated.

The only warning the company had was a phone call from a journalist taken by a public relations staff member. The journalist asked questions about the company's holdings, the spelling of names, and so forth. The employee reported the call to supervisors who called the newspaper and found out that there were deaths attributed to Tylenol (see chap. 5, Johnson & Johnson and the Tylenol Murders).

The Exxon Valdez oil spill was a prodrome to other companies as well as to Exxon itself. Oil companies now know better how to prevent spills, how to clean up spills, and how to react to the public after spills.

There are other less obvious prodromes. Employee discontent over any issue is a sign of a brewing crisis. Perhaps there is an increase in complaints about work hours, work conditions, or unreasonable supervisors. Any one of these and many more issues can be an early sign of a work stoppage. The same prodromes can be early signs of workplace violence.

If you know that your chief executive's salary is especially exorbitant, you also know that this can be fuel for public concern, especially if you are a nonprofit organization.

This was a prodrome for the United Way of America when its chief executive, William Aramony, was criticized for his salary and perks (see chap. 4, United Way of America and the CEO).

An organization should watch for prodromes and make attempts to stop a crisis at that stage before it develops into a full-blown crisis.

To detect those early signs, organizations form employee committees that function like lighthouse keepers watching for vessels at sea, watchdogs, or whistle-blowers. These whistle-blowers report these signs to organization officials who can implement plans to avoid the impending crisis or at least have time to prepare to address the media or other publics.

Roy Betts, media representative for the U.S. Postal Service, speaking of the postal workers' violence prevention program, said, "You should be aware of your surroundings. There *are* warning signs if you look for them and consider them carefully." The U.S. Postal Service installed hotline telephones so workers can report odd or potentially violent behavior. Each call to the hotline is seriously considered.

Crisis detection also refers to a system within the organization in which key personnel are immediately notified of a crisis. An organization has a considerable advantage if it knows about a crisis before its publics do, especially before the news media gets the tip. It gives the organization time to draft a statement, make preparations for a news conference, notify the crisis team, and call spokespersons.

As mentioned earlier, the phone call from the *Chicago Tribune* gave Johnson & Johnson some lead time before the public knew about the Tylenol murders.

Crisis Prevention

Continuous, ongoing public relations programs and regular two-way communications build relationships with key publics and thereby prevent crises, lessen the blows of crises, or limit the duration of crises.

The establishment of a corporate culture conducive to the positive and open interaction of members also minimizes crises as does including crisis management in the strategic planning process (see Crisis Communications Theory, p. 10).

There are other specific tactics and actions that an organization may adopt to prevent crises. These tactics must be communicated to appropriate publics. A company must not only do what is right; it must tell its publics that it is doing so. Some of the tactics are the following:

1. Fostering the continued development of organizational policies allowing for updates and changes based on variances of publics and mission.
2. Reducing the use of hazardous material and processes.
3. Initiating safety training and rewards for employees with stellar safety records.
4. Allowing the free flow of information from employees to management with no punishment of employees or members who deliver bad news.
5. Following-up on past crises or problems.
6. Attending community meetings.
7. Developing a community board with key outside members who are public opinion leaders.
8. Circulating a newsletter to frequent consumers.
9. Offering scholarships for employees and their children as well as to other children in community.
10. Hosting community or employee picnics.
11. Sponsoring community activities, like Little League teams or community charities.

In communications, diligence can sometimes prevent crises. A public relations executive in the Midwest told of a telephone call from a West Coast journalist at 5 p.m., just as she was leaving for the weekend. She could easily have refused the call, but she decided to take it.

The reporter was preparing to write a story for a big-city newspaper about the failure of a product manufactured by the PR executive's company. The story was one that could have sparked a full-scale crisis. The PR person took the time to locate information that proved the information to be baseless. The reporter was satisfied and the crisis-that-could-have-been was averted.

If all members of the management staff are trained to be media savvy, numerous crises can be prevented. Using the same story, the PR executive could have consulted a respected expert on the issue to refute the charges and nip them in the bud. Public relations personnel and key organizational leaders should always be aware of who these experts are and how to reach them in emergencies. Prompt responses to media inquiries are also a plus.

Crisis Preparation

There are crises that cannot be prevented. Pepsi-Cola had no way of anticipating a scare in which hypodermic syringes were found in cans of Diet Pepsi. The presence of these syringes in the cans cried "AIDS," and fear of the illness and death far surpassed brand loyalty. Pepsi could not have prevented the crisis, but it was prepared for it (see chap. 5, Pepsi and the National Syringe-in-the-Can Scare).

The crisis communications plan is the primary tool of preparedness (see The Crisis Communications Plan, p. 18). This plan is a manual telling each key person on the crisis team what his or her role is, whom to notify, how to reach people, what to say, and so on. The crisis communications plan (CCP) provides a functioning collective brain for all persons involved in a crisis, persons who may not operate at normal capacity due to the shock or emotions of the crisis event.

Containment

Containment refers to the effort to limit the duration of the crisis or keep it from spreading to other areas affecting the organization.

Pepsi used an ad to end its own crisis. After several hoaxes had been exposed without the discovery of one documented case of a syringe in a can after the original incident, the company decided the crisis was over and told the world so. And it was.

Local United Way agencies managed to contain the effect of the headquarters crisis with the CEO by publicizing the local organizations as separate entities that are totally autonomous (see chap. 4, United Way of King County and the CEO).

Foodmaker, parent company of the Jack-in-the-Box fast-food chain, was charged by PR critics with delaying resolution of the *E. coli* crisis that killed several children and one adult because the company did not take responsibility for the tainted meat soon enough.

On the other hand, as long as people, especially children, were sick and dying, there was no way Foodmaker could curtail the crisis. It was contained to certain geographical areas and did not affect all outlets of the chain. Also, Jack-in-the-Box communicated to consumers that other food products in the restaurants were not tainted.

Recovery

Recovery refers to efforts to return the company to business as usual. Organizations will want to leave the crisis behind and restore normalcy as soon as possible. It may mean restoring the confidence of key publics, which means communicating this return to normal business.

Snapps, a fast-food restaurant in Fort Pierce, Florida, suffered from a rumor that one of its managers had AIDS and had infected hamburgers. To implement recovery, health department officials participated in a news conference telling the public that all managers had been tested, that none had the AIDS virus, and that the virus could not be transmitted through hamburgers.

Exxon attempted to recover from the Valdez oil spill by efforts to persuade tourists that Alaska was still a beautiful place to visit. It is particularly interesting that Exxon looked beyond its own recovery to the way its crisis had affected the tourism industry.

Learning

The learning phase is a process of examining the crisis and determining what was lost, what was gained, and how the organization performed in the crisis. It is an evaluative procedure also designed to make the crisis a prodrome for the future.

One might think that this is like closing the barn door after the cows have escaped. Any farmer will tell you that once the cows are back in the barn, they will escape again. Just because a company has suffered one crisis is no indication that it will not happen again.

Johnson & Johnson, after its second tampering crisis, learned its lesson by selling over-the-counter medications in tamper-proof containers. Other companies followed suit. Public relations personnel set about the task of telling the public about the new safety containers.

Johnson & Johnson's neck was placed on the block again in late 1994 when data revealed that long-term use of Tylenol may cause kidney ailments. Although it is now facing a different kind of crisis, Johnson & Johnson—because of its stellar reputation during the tampering crises—will be expected to follow its own prodrome and maintain an open and honest policy with the media and its key publics in dealing with this latest crisis. (This volume was written prior to the resolution of that crisis.)

Another example of this learning process is illustrated by the case of U.S. airlines, which had been plagued with hijackings during the 1960s and 1970s. The airlines set up metal detectors at the airports for persons boarding planes. The procedure was extended to cover employees after an irate employee boarded a plane with a gun, shot a supervisor onboard, and caused a fatal crash. The airlines' public relations personnel informed passengers of the new safety procedures.

The learning phase brings about change that helps prevent future crises.

Public Opinion

In a crisis, the public perceives truth to be whatever public opinion says. An organization in a crisis must prove to its publics, and often to the general public, that the prevailing opinion is not factual. In the court of public opinion, a person or organization is guilty until proven innocent. This is the reverse of experience in a court of law where a person is innocent until proven guilty.

Public opinion is difficult to define, but it is based on attitudes of individuals toward specific issues. These attitudes are based on age, educational level, religion, country, state, city, neighborhood, family background and traditions, social class, or racial background. All of these help to form each individual's attitudes, and a predominance of similar attitudes make up public opinion.

On any given issue people find themselves in favor of it, against it, neutral, or so disinterested that they could not care less. Most people, unfortunately, fall into the last category. Public relations reinforces positive attitudes, attempts to change the negative attitudes, and tries to provide information—and provide it in a way that causes the unopinionated and neutral to form the opinion most conducive to the organization's function.

The last category of people is sometimes called the silent majority. In politics, it is called the "swing vote."

An organization has no choice in accepting a crisis. A crisis is forced upon it, and the organization must deal with it. Organizations can ignore a crisis and hope it will go away. Occasionally, it does. More often, it does not. A crisis ignored is an organization failing.

The essential role of crisis communications is to affect the public opinion process and to be instrumental in establishing and communicating proof that the prevailing "truth" is not factual or not wholly factual.

The news media is a prime tool for changing public opinion. It can reach the masses in a short period of time because most Americans utilize some form of news media, primarily television and radio during prime traffic hours. Public relations experts are trained in knowing how to reach the media, when and how to call a news conference, when and how to do one-on-one interviews, and when and how to disseminate written material.

Crisis communications, like public relations, is not merely the distribution of news releases. Neither is it only media relations. Frequently community relations, consumer relations, employee relations, investor relations, government relations, as well as many other kinds of public relations, are involved.

Writing skills are not the only key to success in crisis communications. The next section explains theories of what characteristics cause organizations to fare well in crises.

CRISIS COMMUNICATIONS THEORY

Corporation "A" owns a chain of clothing stores in a major United States city with catalog sales to other cities out of state. Its sales total in the millions of dollars. All of its public relations activities are accomplished by one 15-person department, which has as its primary task the writing and distribution of news releases about new products, trends in fashion, and so forth. Each PR practitioner—with a degree in journalism or public relations and a minimum of five years of experience—spends 80% of his or her workday writing news releases. There are quotas each must meet in numbers of well-written news releases.

Corporation "B" also has a chain of clothing stories in the same city. Its sales total only about one third of the sales of Company "A," and it has no catalog sales out of town. The five people in the public relations department write news releases, but they also spend just as much time internally publicizing the "Employees Talk Back" closed-circuit television show shown in the cafeteria and writing brochures and letters for a program through which the best customers get 25% discounts on their birthdays.

Which corporation is likely to suffer most from a crisis? Crisis communications theories tell us the answer (see the end of the chapter).

Public relations professionals, prior to a crisis or during a crisis, need to know why they perform various strategies and tactics as well as the benefits from research revealing what strategies and basic organizational practices are successful. Public relations theories explain this.

Unfortunately, few public relations professionals realize which theories they actually follow or should follow. As the profession matures, there will be more theorists as well as an increased knowledge of existing theories and how they fit into the framework of public relations programs.

For many years, practitioners entered the field with a knowledge of journalistic or communications theories if they had academic backgrounds in journalism. Frequently, however, in the past, and to a certain degree today, public relations professionals could be drafted from any position in a company and be anybody from a capable secretary to a frustrated executive. In volunteer organizations, public relations is often the task of the person who says loudest, "That sounds interesting."

As more university students study public relations and enter the field, a knowledge of public relations theory will slowly pervade the profession.

Theories on crisis communication basically explain why various techniques and tactics are successful or not, whether the same techniques would be expected to work in future crises, and how the techniques could be altered to produce the desired success.

Grunig and Grunig

Most of the crisis communications theories build on the public relations excellence theory developed by J. Grunig and Hunt and later expanded by J. Grunig and L. Grunig (1992). The *excellence theory* is based on types of public relations practices called "models." The four models defined by J. Grunig and Hunt (1984) provide a way of classifying the types of public relations that individuals and organizations may practice.

In a spectrum of *excellence* of public relations programs, Model 1 would be the least desirable. Model 4 would be the most desirable, or could be said to be the most *excellent*. Models 2 and 3 are between the two extremes.

Model 1—Press Agentry/Publicity Model. In this model, the public relations practitioner is interested in making his organization or product known. He may or may not use truthful statements. Falsehoods, half-truths, and incomplete facts are all permissible. The practitioner's abiding slogan is "All publicity is good publicity." It is a one-way transfer of information from the organization to the publics. Little or no research is required. There is no feedback.

Grunig and Hunt (1984) revealed that this model was used by 15 percent of public relations practice. Later, Grunig and Grunig (1992) found the earlier data to be inaccurate and reported that most public relations practice, unfortunately, still falls into this category.

As practitioners become more knowledgeable, and the profession of public relations grows in respect, the number of practitioners using this model should decrease.

Model 2—Public Information Model. This model is characterized by the desire to report information journalistically. It is different from Model 1 in that truth is essential. Most public relations practice in government agencies today falls into this category. Companies that simply distribute news releases are examples of this model.

This model also involves a one-way transfer of information from the organization to the publics. Little or no research is required. There may be some type of evaluation, such as readership surveys or the counting of news clips. This model is most common in corporations.

Model 3—Two-Way Asymmetric Model. In this model, also called the scientific persuasion model, the public relations practitioner uses social science theory and research, such as surveys and polls, to help persuade publics to accept the organization's point of view. There is some feedback, but the organization does not change as a result of communications management. In asymmetric public relations programs of this type, the organization rules. It always knows best. Its attitude is that publics should adhere to the organization's viewpoints. Examples of asymmetric actions are a letter informing a public of a new policy or a recorded telephone message with no technology available for returning messages.

Model 4—Two-Way Symmetric Model. The public relations practitioner in this model, the mutual understanding model, is an intermediary between the organizations and its publics. The practitioner tries to achieve a dialogue, not a monologue as in the other models. Either management or the publics may make changes in behavior as a result of the communications program.

Research and social science theory are used, not to persuade, but to communicate. Effective public relations programs based on this model are said to be *excellent* programs.

Symmetrical public relations programs negotiate, compromise, bargain, listen, and engage in dialogue. As a result, the organization knows what the publics want and need, and the publics understand the organization's needs and desires. An example is talking to consumers by telephone or at a public meeting in which the consumers can talk back.

In crises, organizations are frequently forced, by circumstances, to practice symmetrical communications with adversarial publics. Although most organizations practice Models 1 and 2, research by Grunig and Grunig (1992) revealed that PR practitioners would prefer to practice Model 4 if they had the expertise to do so and if the organizations were receptive to that practice.

The classifications are not precise. An organization, for example, may practice Model 2 and Model 4. If the organization practices Model 2 more than Model 4, it is considered a Model 2 public relations operation.

Before an in-depth discussion of theories, there are a few terms that require definition:

strategy—an approach, how one handles a problem.

stakeholders—people who are linked to an organization or who have an interest in an organization and are affected by the decisions made by that organization. Examples of company stakeholders are employees, stockholders, communities, and government officials.

strategic publics—stakeholders who are crucial to an organization. The organization cannot function without them. Examples are boards of directors, investors, and unions.

strategically managed public relations—communications programs designed to build relationships with strategic publics, the crucial stakeholders of an organization.

segmentation—the division of a market, population, or a large public into groups whose members are bound by mutual interests, concerns, and characteristics.

risk communications—an ongoing program of informing and educating various publics (usually external publics) about issues that can affect, negatively or positively, an organization's success. It builds solid relationships between an organization and its key publics, the publics on which its survival depends. These relationships must be established prior to a crisis. It is too late after a crisis erupts.

organizational ideology—an organization's philosophy, its working climate, its corporate culture. Each person's experience with organizations— no matter how small or large—puts him in contact with that organization's ideology, its corporate culture. There are norms of dress, formal rules, informal codes of conduct, taboos, jokes, language, and more.

These are the elements of organizational culture. They make up an invisible, internalized whip that cracks and tells us what we can do, what we cannot do, what we can say, and what we cannot say in our dealings with the organization.

Researchers disagree on whether organizational culture is harmonious or conflicting, consistent or inconsistent. Nevertheless, it is inescapable that the culture determines to some degree how people within the organization behave.

Popular examples of organizational ideology are, "Look busy whether you are or not," and "The boss is always right."

Johnson & Johnson (see chap. 5) relied on its organizational ideology in 1982 when, without a crisis management or communications plan, it followed its credo after several people died from poisoned Tylenol capsules.

The company's executives credit the credo with getting it through the crisis. Unlike most organizational ideologies, it was written—although very brief. More importantly, it was felt and practiced by employees and executives alike. The basic message was this. The company has responsibilities to four groups: 1) consumers, 2) employees, 3) communities served by the company, and 4) stockholders.

communications ideology—the organization's philosophy and attitudes of behavior in communicating with publics.

Again, Johnson & Johnson's public relations program during the tampering case is an example. The company's basic rule in dealing with the media, and thereby with the consuming public, was "open and honest information." It is difficult for a public relations department of a major corporation to have a communications ideology different from the organizational ideology. A productive public relations operation necessarily suffers from an unproductive organizational ideology and vice versa. (This is further examined in the discussion of the Exxon–Valdez crisis in chap. 6.)

Grunig and Repper

J. Grunig and F. Repper (1992) identified theories on strategic management, publics, and issues as having two primary propositions. Both are conducive to a study of crisis communications programs:

1. Public relations is most likely to be excellent—will contribute to organizational effectiveness—when it is an integral part of an organization's strategic management process and when public relations is managed strategically.
2. Public relations is managed strategically when it identifies stakeholders—separates active publics from stakeholder categories—and resolves issues created by the interaction of organization and publics through symmetrical communications programs early in the development of issues.

These propositions mean that *excellent* public relations programs, as well as *excellent* crisis communications programs, have the following characteristics:

1. The public relations' head is an important part of the top management of the organization.

2. Programs are designed to build relationships with all key stakeholders of an organization or company.

3. Public relations, through research, identifies who the organization's key stakeholders are and ranks them in order of importance. They may be customers, media, employees, competitors, unions, special interest groups, vendors, suppliers, environmental groups, consumer advocates, and critics, to name a few.

4. An ongoing public relations plan is developed for each key stakeholder. This necessarily goes beyond media relations into a Model 4 program (two-way symmetrical program). These programs can sometimes prevent crises. At other times, they lessen the severity of crises.

5. In *segmentation*, public relations breaks down large publics into smaller subpublics with which it can communicate more effectively about issues or problems. These publics are usually, but not always, active rather than passive. Active publics seek out information and are more likely than

passive publics to act on an issue. For example, if an organization wanted to gear a program to all public school children, it might direct its program to the National Education Association or the American Federation of Teachers, organizations consisting of members, educators, who can reach all school children. Organizations that do not segment their stakeholders might send a news release to metropolitan newspapers *hoping* that teachers will read the subsequent article and communicate with children.

6. *Issues Management* is part of a two-way symmetrical program handled by the public relations department. A public makes an issue when it perceives that a problem is brewing or has happened. In issues management, the public relations department anticipates the issues that are potential crises and ranks them in order of possible damage to the organization. Then strategies and tactics are developed and implemented to lessen the likelihood of crises. The crucial element here is early identification of potential crises, like treating a sniffle before it comes the flu. The treatment might involve making allies of potential adversaries or meeting with a community activist to explain a procedure that might be construed as damaging to consumers. Consequently, the odds are enhanced that an issue can benefit the organization rather than hamper it.

Many times, issues management is handled by public affairs or corporate communications departments, which are separate and apart from public relations departments that only handle media relations. Grunig and Repper's theory does not advise this separation.

Marra

Marra (1992), in an attempt to build and validate a model of excellent crisis public relations, suggested that organizations develop a theoretically based crisis public relations model that would allow practitioners to identify which variables can be adjusted to make a crisis communications plan work and which variables, if not adjusted, make it fail. He says this knowledge will allow the public relations practitioners to know before a crisis what will or will not work. Marra identifies strategies and techniques common to *excellent* responses to crises with the following hypotheses:

1. An organization having strong and well-developed relationships with its key publics prior to a crisis will suffer less financial, emotional, or perceptive damage than organizations with weak and poorly developed relationships with its key publics prior to a crisis. Key publics would not only be media, but employees, customers, community, and so forth.

2. Marra believes, as the Grunigs and Repper do, that organizations with weak precrisis relationships are those with asymmetrical practices, Models

1, 2, and 3. Therefore, an organizations that uses two-way symmetrical crisis communications procedures will suffer less financial, emotional, or perceptual damage than the Model 1, 2, or 3 organizations or those who use silence as a response to crises.

3. An organization that establishes and puts into effect continuing risk communications activities and prepares crisis communications plans prior to crises will have stronger relationships with key publics, use two-way symmetrical crisis public relations practices and, as a result, will suffer less financial, emotional, and perceptual damage than the organization that does not.

4. An organization with communication ideologies that encourage, support, and champion crisis management preparations, crisis communications plans and actions, and two-way symmetrical communications practices will suffer less financial, emotional, and perceptual damage than the organization that does not.

SUMMARY

Various public relations and crisis communciations theories suggest attributes and characteristics of programs that are likely either to prevent crises or enable organizations to recover from crises more swiftly than organizations without those charactertics.

Among these characteristics are strong relationhips with publics (including media), prominence of public relations within the organization, sound organizational culture, and preplanning for crises.

Persons with public relations savvy are likely to say, "This is obvious. People who are prepared should withstand a crisis better." Neverthless, the likelihood of a crisis is not seen as obvious by many organizational heads. Most companies still do not plan for crises and take the attitude, "It hasn't happened, so it won't happen."

*   *   *

Answer to question on page 10: Crisis communications theories, so far, do not relate total sales, numbers of employees, education and experience of PR practitioners, and quantity or quality of news releases to the probability of successful and swift conclusion of a crisis. Company "B" has ongoing two-way relationships with employees, customers who are key stakeholders. Considering that the PR department of Company "A" spends 80 percent of its time on news releases, it is unlikely that there is a two-way symmetrical relationship with strategic publics. Therefore, Company "A," according to theorists studied in this chapter, is more likely to suffer a sustained crisis.

REFERENCES

Barton, L. (1993). *Crisis in organizations.* Cincinnati: South-Western Publishing Co.

The Fortune 500. (1995, May 15). *Fortune, 131*(9), 1–58.

The Fortune 500. (1994, April 18). *Fortune, 129*(8), 220.

Grunig, J. E., & Grunig, L. A. (1992). Models of public relations and communications. In J. E. Grunig (Ed.), *Excellence in public relations and communication management* (pp. 285–326). Hillsdale, NJ: Lawrence Erlbaum Associates.

Grunig, J. E., & Hunt, T. (1984). *Managing public relations.* New York: Holt, Rinehart & Winston.

Grunig, J. E., & Repper, F. C. (1992). Strategic management, publics, and issues. In J. E. Grunig (Ed.), *Excellence in public relations and communication management* (pp. 117–157). Hillsdale, NJ: Lawrence Erlbaum Associates.

Jacob, R. (1995, March 6). Corporate reputations: How all 395 companies rank. *Fortune, 131*(4), 54–94.

Marra, F. J. (1992). *Crisis public relations: A theoretical model.* Unpublished doctoral dissertation, University of Maryland, College Park, MD.

The Crisis Communications Plan

CRISIS INVENTORY

Before an organization can develop a crisis management plan (CMP) or a crisis communications plan (CCP), it must determine which crisis or crises the organization is likely to face. A crisis communications plan's usefulness is directly associated with how specific it is to a particular type of crisis.

Although there are several items in a crisis communications plan that are mutual to all types of crises, varying information is needed for each type of crisis for maximum effectiveness. For example, a restaurant chain may decide that food poisoning and fire are its most probable crises. If a food poisoning crisis occurs, the media will want, and the public relations department can have, the following items readily available and in its crisis communications plan: Its recipes, a list of ingredients stocked, a list of vendors used, kitchen precautions and procedures, names and contact numbers of chefs and all personnel handling food, and a list of medical experts for consultation and for spokespersons.

If a fire occurs, the public relations department would require, in a specific plan, its evacuation procedures, its policy of using nonflammable decor items (such as window coverings and tablecloths), the floor plan of the structure, and fire experts for spokespersons.

The following list enumerates common types of crises. There are, of course, numerous others. Companies and organizations would be advised to consider the list carefully and add types of crises specific to their operations.

Frequent Types of Crises

acquisition
age discrimination
alcohol abuse
bankruptcy
boycott
bribery
chemical spill or leak
contamination
drug abuse
drug trafficking
earthquake
embezzlement
explosion
fatality
fire
flood
hurricane
kickbacks
kidnapping
lawsuits
layoffs
merger
murder
negative legislation
plant closing
product failure
protest demonstrations
racial issues
robbery
sexual discrimination
sexual harassment
strikes
suicide
takeover
tax problems
terrorism
tornado
toxic waste
transportation accident
transportation failure
workplace violence

Some crises will involve more than one of the types listed, such as "work-place violence" and "fatality," or "boycott" and "sexual discrimination."

Perhaps the involvement of the entire company or representatives of each department can determine the crises the company is likely to face. Then each unit's selections could be compared and compiled into a company-wide list.

Done properly, this can be an effective proactive employee relations program, a way of creating "we-ness," a way of including all of the employees in the company's decision making. Janitors, secretaries, blue-collar and white-collar workers, and midlevel executives, as well as top executives, can have a say. After all, each employee stands to suffer if the company should go under after the most serious of crises.

Employees in each position classification have a unique perspective on things that can go wrong. Janitors are more aware of heating and cooling equipment, possible gas leaks, and so on. Workers on an auto assembly line know more about the quality of cars than managers in their carpeted offices.

If the company-wide crisis identification program is not feasible, a meeting of key employees familiar with all facets of the operation can determine the crises the company is likely to face. Such a meeting should certainly include more than public relations staff members. You do not want the company blaming the public relations staff for failure to recognize a possible crisis.

Frequently, ascertaining probable crises can point out problems that prevent crises from occurring. This is the best reason for company-wide involvement. The second best reason is to be able to manage a crisis once it occurs.

You will find that every company and organization *can* experience many types of crises. The questions that must be answered are, "How likely is this crisis?" and "How devastating can the crisis be?" Crisis communications plans should be developed for the crises believed to be both most probable and most devastating. To do this, the public relations department, with its key executives, must take an inventory. Each possible crisis must be ranked as follows:

0—Impossible, has basically no chance of occurring

1—Nearly impossible

2—Remotely possible

3—Possible

4—More than possible, somewhat probable, has happened to competitors or similar companies

5—Highly probable, may or may not have previously occurred in company, warning signs are evident

Each crisis should be ranked according to its potential damage to the company. The rankings in this category are as follows:

0—No damage, not a serious consequence

1—Little damage, can be handled without much difficulty, not serious enough for media concern

2—Some damage, a slight chance that media will be involved

3 —Considerable damage, but still will not be a major media issue

4—Considerable damage, would definitely be a major media issue

5—Devastating, front page news, can put company out of business

For added security, when in doubt, rank a crisis in the next higher category.

Company Z determines that there are five crises it could face: workplace violence, fire, protest demonstrations, negative legislation, and tax problems. Each might be ranked as follows:

Crisis Type	Probability	Damage
workplace violence	4	5
fire	3	4
protest demonstrations	2	5
negative legislation	5	2
tax problems	2	3

Keep in mind that what you determine to be unlikely because it never happened before, can happen tomorrow. Both human nature and nature are very unpredictable, so natural disasters (e.g., earthquakes, floods, and hurricanes) and human failure (e.g., workplace violence, embezzlement, drug trafficking, and all kinds of discrimination) can all be expected to some degree. Frequently, there is no warning.

After rankings for probability and damage are made, it will be effective for you to make bar graphs to clearly see and consider each crisis and compare it to others. (Bar graphing can be done on various computer programs or by hand.)

At the base of each graph, write the type of crisis (see Fig. 2.1). Plot the height of each bar according to numbers attributed to each crisis in the probability and damage rankings. Choose different colors or shadings for probability bars and damage bars.

When Company Z plots its data on a bar graph, it will resemble Figure 2.1. Considering Company Z's graph, we see that the probability and seriousness of a crisis relating to *tax problems* is not as crucial as in the other crises. This does not mean that crisis plans are not important for tax problems, just not as important as for other issues, and not priorities.

Company Z's Crisis Inventory

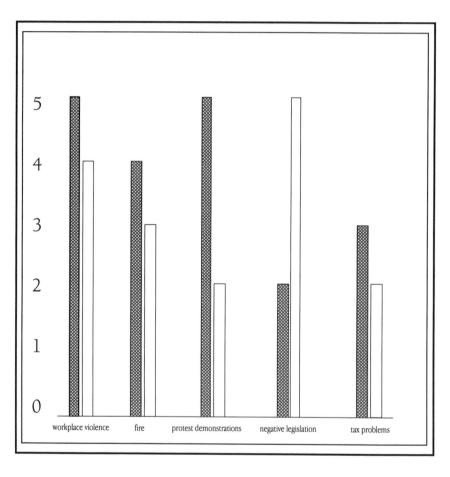

FIG. 2.1. A sample graph of how an organization or company might assess probability of various types of crises and degrees of damage resulting from crises.

According to the graph, the possibility of Company Z suffering a crisis resulting from *negative legislation* is likely, though not particularly critical. On the other hand, *protest demonstrations* are critical, although not very likely. *Workplace violence* and *fire* seem both likely and critical.

Most organizations plan for crises ranked high in both probability and damage. In this case, Company Z would probably develop crisis management and crisis communications plans for workplace violence first, then the following in descending order of importance: fire, protest demonstrations, negative legislation, and tax problems.

Sometimes organizations make crisis plans for the most devastating crises no matter how probable or improbable they are. In this case, Company Z would develop plans for *workplace violence* first, followed by *protest demonstrations*, then *fire*. Naturally, a version of Murphy's Law can be expected. That crisis for which you have no plan will likely happen. Moreover, you will find that any plan, and the process of developing that plan, will make you more prepared for crises generally.

Some organizations, having several crises classified with similar rankings in all categories, make general crisis communications plans with detailed information for all types of crises, although sometimes the detailed information is omitted.

Many companies fearing all possibilities of crises equally, merely adopt a policy of "open and honest response" with the media and all publics and plan to be in a total reactive mode during a crisis.

The importance of the crisis inventory is to force organizations to think about the possibilities. Sometimes the most ridiculous crisis occurs, something no one in the company could predict. Pepsi probably never dreamed that it would have a crisis of hypodermic syringes in its cans. On the other hand, Foodmaker and Jack-in-the Box could certainly have anticipated children dying from eating hamburgers. Exxon could have anticipated the worst oil slick in America.

The ranking procedure may introduce ideas for prevention programs. You also may realize that your organization is more vulnerable than you anticipated.

Considering that the toll of stress and emotion during a crisis necessarily affects one's thought processes, a carefully developed crisis communications plan is the best substitute for a fully functioning brain. Even if you are cool and calm under pressure, others are not. The crisis communications plan alleviates that problem too.

DEVELOPING THE CRISIS COMMUNICATIONS PLAN

Once likely crises have been identified, a crisis communications plan (CCP) can be written. A CCP can be part of a larger crisis management plan (CMP), or it may stand alone as a document to help public relations practitioners handle crises more effectively.

The CMP will include information such as evacuation procedures; emergency staffing of various departments of a company; and places to purchase or rent emergency equipment, tools, or vehicles—all the things a company may need in a crisis.

Public relations during a crisis focuses on *communications* with the company's publics during the crisis, for the most part, the same publics to which normal PR activities are directed.

The CMP is sometimes a large volume of instructions, whereas a CCP should be a more manageable, easier to read document. After a crisis has erupted, employees are likely to look at a large volume and think, "We don't have time to read this now," and then proceed to handle the crisis by "winging" it.

The CCP should be organized in such a way that the practitioners can hastily turn to each section. Some professionals use tabs in a notebook; others use tables of contents. Some are on computer, but that is dangerous because many crises prevent access to offices (fire, earthquakes, explosives, etc.).

Many companies (like Johnson & Johnson after the Tylenol crisis) urge employees to keep copies of the plan in various key spots—the office, at home, near the night stand, or in the car. That way, the odds are that at least one will be available, when crisis or disaster occurs.

If a crisis inventory determines, for example, that there are three likely crises, the organization should draft a CCP for each type. A plan for an earthquake must be different from a plan for product failure. The publics may be different; the media may be different. The messages must be different.

The CCP states purposes, policies, and goals, then assigns employees to various duties. It generally makes communication with publics faster and more effective and should help end the crisis more swiftly than without a plan.

When a CCP is ineffective, it is usually because the type of crisis was not anticipated or because variables arose that were not anticipated: For example, spokespersons or supplies may not be available. The CCP sometimes fails because it is an ancient document, so plans should be updated regularly.

Even if unanticipated variables do arise, the CCP should be more effective than no plan at all. Still, it must be remembered that a CCP is not a manual guaranteeing success, with everything done "by the book," but, rather, a guide that must be flexible.

An effective crisis communication plan should have various components arranged in an order that best suits the organization and the crisis or disaster. The components, discussed in detail later, are the following:

Cover Page
Introduction
Acknowledgments
Rehearsal Dates
Purpose and Objectives
List of Key Publics
Notifying Publics
Identifying the Crisis Communication Team
Crisis Directory
Identifying the Media Spokesperson
List of Emergency Personnel, Local Officials
List of Key Media
Crisis Control Center
Equipment and Supplies
Pregathered Information
Key Messages

Cover Page

The cover page will be similar to the cover page of a term paper. There are as many ways of doing one as there are ways of doing crisis communications plans. It should include the date when the plan was written, as well as revision dates.

Introduction

The head of the company or organization usually writes this introduction (or the PR practitioner ghost writes it for the CEO with his or her approval). The purpose of this component is to persuade employees to take the CCP seriously. It stresses the necessity and importance of the plan and also emphasizes the dire results possible when a plan is not followed.

Acknowledgments

This takes the form of an affidavit signed by all crisis personnel as well as by key executives, indicating that they have read the plan and are prepared to put it into effect. The signatures assure management that its personnel have read the plan.

Rehearsal Dates

Dates of rehearsals for the crisis are recorded here. Crises should be practiced for the most likely crisis at least annually if not every six months. Rehearsal for any crisis is helpful no matter if the eventual crisis may be somewhat different.

d Objectives

statement details the organization's policies toward its publics. ...,...,. In a crisis, an open and honest disclosure with the media shall be stressed."

The purpose is an expressed hope for a recovery and return to normalcy, to get out of the media. Similarly, the objectives are responses to the question, "What do you hope to achieve with this plan?" Objectives should not be overly ambitious in difficulty or number. For example, a company may adopt the following goals:

1. To be seen in the media as a company that cares about its customers and employees.
2. To make certain that all communications are accurate.

List of Key Publics

The key publics listed should include all the publics, both external and internal, with which the organization must communicate during the crisis. The list will vary with organizations, but may include the following as well as others:

board members,
shareholders,
financial partners,
investors,
community leaders,
customers,
clients,
suppliers,
vendors,
neighbors of physical plant(s),
competitors,
key management,
employees,
legal representation,
media,
union officials,
retirees, and
government officials (city, state, county, federal).

Not every public needs to be notified in each crisis, but the list should be comprehensive; unneeded publics can be eliminated at the time of crisis.

This is easier than trying to think of all the crucial publics during the stress of the crisis.

Publics fall into the following categories:

Enabling publics—those people with the power and authority to make decisions. They include the board of directors, shareholders, investors, and key executives. Notifying these enabling publics should be a priority.

Functional publics—the people who actually make the organization work: employees, unions, suppliers, vendors, consumers, and volunteers in the case of nonprofit organizations.

Normative publics—those people who share values with the organization in crises: trade associations, professional organizations, and competitors.

Diffused publics—those people linked indirectly to the organization in crisis. The main diffused public is the media. Others are community groups and neighbors of the physical plant.

Notifying Publics

In order to notify publics, a system must be devised to reach each public and should be described in the plan. For internal publics, many companies use a chain procedure, such as a telephone tree, in which each person is specifically designated to call others.

The person who learns about the crisis first notifies the CEO, the head of public relations, and the head of the department that may be involved. The chain should be clear and error-free, even in the event that certain individuals are not reached.

An appropriate means of notification must be decided upon for each public. A news release, for example, is not appropriate for enabling publics.

Board members are often reached by telephone or fax. E-mail or other computerized communications are also used. The media can be told by telephone, wire services, fax, press conferences, E-mail, or news releases. Other methods used for notifying publics are telegrams, personal visits, letters, advertisements, bulletin boards, or meetings (see the sample chart, Fig. 2.2).

Identifying the Crisis Communication Team

The crisis communications team members with backups should be prese-lected. A *crisis communications manager* is usually, but not always, the head of public relations. He or she has specific responsibilities including communication with top management, making decisions, drafting or approving major statements, and notifying the rest of the crisis communications team.

YOUR COMPANY

MESSAGE: There has been an explosion in the plant. There are injured employees. We do not know, at this time, the cause of the explosion or the extent of injuries of the employees. An investigation is underway.

Methods of Communication

PUBLICS	TELEPHONE	E-MAIL	FAX	Letter By Messenger	Letter By Mail	NEWSLETTER	BULLETIN BOARD	PERSONAL VISIT	NEWS RELEASE	MEETINGS
EMPLOYEES		* J. Naas				* J. Naas	* J. Naas			
EXECUTIVES	* Nelson J.	* Nelson J.						* Nelson J. M. Yerima		* Nelson J.
CUSTOMERS					* Damian L					
BOARD OF DIRECTORS	* Nelson J.			* Damian L.					*Gina A.	
ELECTRONIC MEDIA	* K. Stone		* K. Stone						*Gina A.	
DAILY NEWSPAPERS	* Gina A.								*Gina A.	
WEEKLY NEWSPAPERS			* Gina A.	* Damian L	* Damian L					
SHARE HOLDERS		* Ann C.				* Ann C.				
COMMUNITY LEADERS			* Karen N.		* Karen N.					

* Staff member responsible for communications and followup.

FIG. 2.2. A sample chart of how a company or organization might plan to communicate with key publics during a crisis. It includes key talking points and ways of communicating. The lists of publics and types of communication can be longer, shorter, or different depending on organizational needs.

The *assistant crisis manager* assumes responsibility when the manager is unavailable (a second backup may be beneficial, if possible).

The *crisis communications control room coordinator* sets up the room with necessary furniture, equipment, supplies, and tools. An efficient secretary can be appointed for this position.

Other PR personnel have the responsibilities of preparing news releases and statements, contacting the media, and reporting all actions to the crisis communications manager. These people may notify employees or volunteers through letters or by writing telegrams to the mayor and governor, by telephoning union officials, and others.

Crisis Directory

The company should prepare a crisis directory listing each member of the crisis team as well as key managers in the company, key publics or organizations, along with titles, business and home telephone numbers, cellular phone numbers, Fax and E-mail addresses, as well as business, home, and vacation addresses.

It is also helpful to list phone numbers for friends, neighbors, and relatives who are frequently in contact with persons crucial to the crisis recovery.

The crisis team should be large enough to get the job done, but no larger. Too many people make it difficult to get tasks completed and decisions made. There is no time in a crisis for egos; each person must be a team player. It is also preferable that crisis team members be generally healthy and capable of working under stress. They should be reliable professionals, whether go-fers, interns, or secretaries.

Identifying the Media Spokesperson

The media spokesperson must be selected very carefully. To the public, this person *is* the company or organization.

Actually, sometimes several persons are spokespersons. This is an arguable point in the public relations profession. Some argue for "one spokesperson per crisis, usually the CEO." Others argue for several spokespersons, depending upon areas of expertise. Clearly, the decision is a matter of what suits the company and type of crisis best.

Even if the CEO is an effective spokesperson, he or she may not be particularly knowledgeable about a technical aspect of the crisis. For example, during an oil spill, the company CEO is not the only important spokesperson; also needed is a person qualified to talk about what will be necessary for the cleanup. Frequently, university professors are called upon for specific knowledge about technical aspects of a crisis and for credibility.

Another school of thought is that CEOs have no credibility because they have too much to lose. However, if lives are lost or in danger—including the lives of animals—most professionals agree that the company head must be the chief spokesperson.

In all cases, at least one, and preferably two or three, backup spokespersons should be preselected in case the preferred person is unavailable at the time of the crisis. Crises occur when people are on vacation, on business trips, or sick with the flu.

When the 1989 San Francisco earthquake struck, both the numbers one and two spokespersons for the Pacific Gas and Electric Company were at the World Series game at Candlestick Park. The third spokesperson on the list was called and pressed into service.

An effective crisis spokesperson must have some position in the company. It is usually not the PR head, even if the PR person is normally the company's spokesperson. The spokesperson must be articulate, powerful enough to make decisions, accessible throughout the crisis, able to talk clearly in concise sound-bites, and pleasant to the eye of a camera. Moreover, the spokesperson in a crisis must appear rational, concerned, and empathetic. He or she should be pretrained, rehearsed well in advance of the crisis, and briefed prior to the crisis. The organization's legal advisor should be consulted before statements are made.

If the public relations department is small or a one-person operation, it may be beneficial to have capable, trustworthy volunteers to perform some tasks. Public relations firms specialize in crisis planning and crisis handling and might be used. A nonprofit organization can often get PR firms to help pro bono (done or donated without charge). Many nonprofit organizations have PR practitioners on their boards of directors, anticipating the need for their assistance during a crisis.

At times, one person *may* be required to perform all communications roles. On the other hand, in large companies several people may perform each role.

List of Emergency Personnel and Local Officials

If the crisis is a disaster or emergency, various emergency personnel need to be contacted. A list should be made of contact numbers for police, fire officials, hospitals, the health department, utilities, and paramedics.

If the crisis affects large numbers of people or is a threat to the safety of people, government officials must be contacted. This list should include the mayor, governor, city council members, county officials, state legislators, and U.S. Senators and Representatives.

Sometimes union officials must be notified and therefore should be listed, as well as citizens' groups and key affected community organizations.

List of Key Media

After key executives are called, the media is the next most important public to notify of the crisis. A list of media contacts—newspapers, television, radio, wire services—should be complete and listed in order of importance. If particular editors or reporters are important to telling the story to the organization's benefit, a list of their home numbers and emergency numbers will be advantageous.

The media list should contain morning and afternoon metropolitan dailies, certain weeklies, all TV news stations, Associated Press, United Press International, Reuters, all radio news stations, and trade publications.

Crisis Control Center

The location of the crisis communications control center must be determined in case regular office space is unavailable. After disasters and emergencies, offices are often damaged, without power, or inaccessible.

Several possible sites should be listed in the CCP. Also listed should be persons instrumental in gaining access to the room. Suppose, for example, a local church has offered its conference room. Who has given the permission? Who can unlock doors of church and conference room, and what about electrical outlets, furniture? The site should include a space for the media to work.

Equipment and Supplies

Determine and list equipment, materials, and supplies needed by the crisis team, media, and visiting publics. The list could include, but is not limited to, the following:

chairs,
desks,
bulletin boards,
flip charts,
computers or typewriters (maybe manual typewriters in case power is a problem),
computer printers,
telephones,
cellular phones,
battery-powered televisions, radios,
one or two chalk boards,
maps of plant or crisis area,

flashlights or battery-powered lamps,

police radio,

walkie-talkies,

company letterhead,

pens,

pencils,

telephone directories,

contact lists,

media directories,

press kits,

CMPs and CCPs,

street and highway maps,

food and beverages,

copying machine,

first aid kits,

cameras and film,

extension cords, and

generator power packs.

Pregathered Information

Prepare and gather various documents that will possibly be needed during a crisis. Have identical sets of documents in various locales to assure availability. Information that can be gathered in advance are safety records and procedures; annual reports; photos; company backgrounder; executive biographies; map of the company; location of branch offices; quality control procedures; product manufacturing procedures; and fact sheets of company data such as numbers of employees, products manufactured, and markets served.

Skeletal news releases can be prepared as long as the PR practitioner anticipates the type of crisis and can make a statement on behalf of the company. A news release can be written with blank spaces for data such as magnitude of the crisis, dates, and names that are unique to the particular crisis (see Fig. 9.2).

Key Messages

Messages must be tailored to each public just as means of communication are selected for each public. The first statement made to each public sets the stage for the rest of the crisis. It establishes credibility or the lack of it.

The statement should be approved by top managers as well as lawyers, but should not be delayed for long periods of time.

The statement to all publics should include the nature of the crisis, emergency, or accident. As in all journalistic endeavors, it should include the 5 W's and the H (what, where, when, why, who, and how). It should include, if known, what steps the organization will take to recover. It should mention deaths or injuries and include a statement of the corporate culture, the company's heart.

In some instances, recovery actions to be taken in the early hours or days should be mentioned. Persons to notify are also an integral part of the message.

The key messages may assume responsibility on behalf of the company, but should not readily place blame on others if there is any room for speculation.

Key executives and members of the crisis communications team should review a draft of the crisis communications plan and make final changes, corrections, and additions based on their areas of expertise. They should concern themselves with what will work and what will not work.

When the final draft is completed, it should be distributed to all necessary personnel. The plan should be reviewed and updated at least once a year.

The crisis communications team should test each component of the plan. There can be practice drills and/or written or oral exams. The telephone tree can easily be practiced to check for glitches, for example. Role-playing exercises can be devised for a mock crisis with employees or actual reporters playing media roles.

Spokespersons should be drilled and trained for addressing the media. There are numerous agencies that specialize in such training. Training takes place prior to a crisis, but briefing may, and should take place even during a crisis—prior to a news conference, live one-on-one interview, or interview by an investigative journalist. The name of the game is "preparedness."

Appendix A is a generic crisis communications plan for a large multisite corporation. Appendix B is the crisis communications plan for Big Brothers/Big Sisters of America in Philadelphia, Pennsylvania. Appendix C is a crisis communications plan developed by the University of Florida. Your best plan may have elements from all of them as well as elements unique to your company or organization.

Crisis Makers

What causes a crisis? Human failure, terrorism, nature, equipment failure, any number of things can be the cause. We look at two causes here—rumor and various television phemomena: "gotcha" journalism, "checkbook" journalism, newsmongers, and the "nonexpert expert."

Although television news programs have featured investigative and consumer protection pieces for years, in the 1990s, "gotcha journalism" has become popular in talk shows that have no connection to journalism or to news departments with experienced investigative units. They are "out-to-get-you" for entertainment and ratings.

Some television shows pay handsomely for a juicy story, an interesting consumer-protection-type attack. Those deals have come to be called "checkbook journalism." Critics of the process say people will say anything if they are paid enough money.

Also in the 1990s, news programs resorted to sensationalism, also called newsmongering, in their quest for higher ratings and in the battle for viewers. The term "yellow journalism" used to be applied to such practices.

Rumor is studied because it can happen to anyone; there is often no explanation of why it happened or who started the rumor. Rumors can cause the longest and most damaging of crises. Even outrageous rumors endure or repeat, and they are difficult to battle.

RUMOR

Did you hear?

Children are being kidnapped at K-Mart stores.

Mikey, the little boy in the Life cereal commercials died after he drank a carbonated beverage containing General Mills' Pop Rocks, an "exploding" candy.

Designer Liz Claiborne, on "The Oprah Winfrey Show," told viewers that 30% of her profits go to the Church of Satan. Then the video transmission blacked out and when it was restored, Claiborne was gone.

Corona Beer has urine in it.

Procter and Gamble's man-in-the-moon and stars logo was a disguised way of demonstrating the "666" devil-worshipping sign and represented the company's alliance with Satan.

All of the rumors just mentioned are unfounded, untrue rumors. K-Mart is not a kidnapping center. The little boy who played Mikey is an adult. Liz Claiborne never made the statement and Oprah never zapped her off the air. Corona Beer is good and urine-free.

Procter and Gamble's logo, which had existed in slightly different designs for over 100 years was not, in the least, indicative of a connection with Satanists.

These rumors have spread over the United States, turned stomachs, perpetuated negative images, and cost millions of dollars in loss of revenue. Corporations have had to fight in the press, in the courts and, in the case of Procter and Gamble, in the churches to stop the rumors.

Incidentally, Procter and Gamble's woes were caused by religious fanatics. The company eventually gave up the battle and altered the logo on its products (Wilcox, 1989).

The Nature of Rumor

Crises can, and often do, begin with rumors. In fact, a crisis can actually be a negative rumor. "Deep-sixing" rumors is an important task in crisis control and crisis communications.

A rumor is information usually passed by word of mouth with no verification of fact and no credible source. Rumors can be positive or negative. They can be absolutely false or partly false. They can also be undeniably true or premature facts. There is an expression "There's a ring of truth in every rumor." Because people know and believe that expression, they tend to believe there is truth in rumors that are patenti, false and even ridiculous.

A rumor can begin as in the children's game, "Gossip," in which Child 1 whispers something to Child 2 who repeats it to Child 3, and so on. By the time, the message reaches Child 10, it is usually unrelated to the original message. This is rumor spread innocently, but rumor can also be malicious and intentional.

A victim rarely knows how a rumor started or who has heard it. This makes it difficult to curtail its spreading, which happens quickly and often with disastrous consequences.

How Rumors Start

One of the difficulties in establishing the source of a rumor is the realization that each person who passes it on may change it and thus be a contributing part of its source.

The sources cited are rarely the actual sources. Rumors themselves cite a specific person or institution that sounds credible, but is not readily available for verification. For example, the teller of the rumor will say, "I read it in last week's paper!" "What paper?" we ask. How many people will go back and look for an article in last week's newspaper, especially considering that "last week" is also a vague term.

Sometimes, the rumor teller insists, "My aunt in Chicago was there when it happened!" This sounds convincing. Who will call the aunt and get specific details? Is there really any aunt at all?

Some psychologists have started rumors in order to research them. Dr. Ralph Rosnow, Temple University, had research assistants start a rumor that students in one class were caught smoking marijuana during a final examination. Later, students were interviewed and asked if they believed the story and if they passed it on. Research revealed that the students who believed it most were more likely to pass it on. Those who did not believe it did not (Goleman, 1991).

Rumors are often started innocently. This was the case when comedian Johnny Carson on his late night show told a joke about a shortage of bathroom tissue. People heard about the shortage, but not that it was a joke. There was a run on bathroom tissue in grocery stores. Soon the shelves were empty; the stock was depleted. This rumor was merely annoying to grocery stores and customers who remained tissueless.

Some innocently started rumors, though, can cause real damage. The Cable News Network once broadcasted a news story about the Individual Retirement Account (IRA). It cited McDonalds, the home of the Big Mac, as a corporation that contributes to its employees' IRAs. The rumor, however, circulated in Great Britain that McDonalds supported the Irish Republican Army—also called the IRA. Members of parliament received numerous letters attacking McDonalds for financing attacks on British soldiers and civilians.

How Rumors Spread

Rumors spread because people believe they are news, news with some emotional relationship to their lives. The rumors somehow seem plausible. Often, the rumor refers to something causing distress or fear, and the people who spread it are hoping to relieve their fear or distress by giving a reasonable explanation or denial.

Dr. Allan J. Kimmel, Fitchburg State College, Fitchburg, Massachusetts, studied 229 college students. The students passed on rumors about AIDS because they were personally relevant and upsetting. "The more frightened people were by a rumor, the more likely they were to repeat it," he said. "In repeating something that makes you nervous you may learn some contrary fact that will calm you. On the other hand, it can escalate your fears if the person you tell believes it" (Goleman, 1991, p. C1).

Rumors are also spread because people distrust the "establishment"—organizations, governments, and big corporations. They spread because people want to be thought of as "a person who knows." Information is power. Telling rumors may give people who feel they lack power a sense that they are powerful. People, therefore, who have trouble making a success of their lives and careers are also more likely to believe and spread rumors.

Types of Rumor

There are various types of rumor.

The *intentional rumor* is started to achieve a purpose. People start rumors to help their own businesses. For example, a young, aggressive manager of a new restaurant getting off to a slow start in a campus community, started a rumor at the college that a famous rock star was related to the owner and that the rock star *might* drop in that night. Needless to say, business was booming that night with patrons hoping to see the celebrity who never showed up.

The manager, when asked if the star would show up, responded, "You never know." He offered each patron who asked a free drink. No one left angry. The manager said the ploy was a marketing technique to get people into the restaurant for the first time. He felt the food, the ambiance, and the service would get them back in the future.

The financial community thrives on intentional rumor. There are rumors to make stocks rise and rumors to make them decline.

The *premature-fact rumor* is an early version of what will eventually be true. In the workplace, frequently employees hear and pass on rumors about layoffs that eventually turn out to be fact. Denying this type of rumor can be more damaging than being silent.

The *malicious rumor* is often started to damage competitors' businesses. For example, someone tells us, "The stew in the restaurant across the street is made up of last week's leftovers." This may or may not be true. It may be true of half the restaurants in town, yet told to the right people at the right time, it spreads and causes a decline in patronage.

The *outrageous rumor* is one that is so unbelievable that people say, "It has to be true. Who would create such a story?" The Snapple Beverage

Company suffered from such a rumor that the "k" on its label, which stands for "kosher," actually stood for Ku Klux Klan.

The *nearly true rumor* is so named because it is partly true. People hear it, attach credibility to a part of the story, then draw a conclusion that the rumor must be entirely true. This could have been the case with the rumor circulated nationally that Reebok, during apartheid, was manufacturing and selling in South Africa. This was a crisis for Reebok because the company featured African American athletes in its commercials and marketed to African American consumers. It was true that Reebok once had manufacturing plants in South Africa, but they had been closed in 1986.

The *birthday rumor* is one that continues to emerge over and over again. It is as regular as birthdays.

These categories of rumors overlap. The outrageous rumor may also be malicious. The premature-fact rumor may be intentional, and so forth. One rumor that fits both the nearly true and the birthday categories is the ancient rumor that Chinese restaurants cook dogs. It is true that in China dogs are a delicacy, but that does not mean that owners of Chinese restaurants in the United States are out hunting your pets. This rumor can be traced to the 1850s in the United States and is even older in Great Britain. The same rumor has now been told of Vietnamese cuisine in Texas, Mexican cuisine in Southern California, and Native American cuisine in Wisconsin (Goleman, 1991).

Fighting Rumor

Step-by-step instruction on what to do in the case of rumors is difficult, if not impossible. Variables such as potential damage, geographic location, type of organization affected, the nature of the rumor, and what crucial publics are affected require each organization's actions to be tailor-made.

There are, however, some general suggestions for avoiding a crisis brought on by rumors, as well as suggestions for fighting rumors that are already circulating. Be mindful, nevertheless, that this is not an exact science. Some of the suggestions are conflicting because there are various schools of thought on how to handle the problem.

The following suggestions are steps organizations *may* take to minimize the chances of a crisis caused by rumor:

1. Because the victim of a rumor is often the last to hear it, you could establish a rumor center in which various employees or volunteers enlist supporters to be on the alert for rumors.

2. Have rumor workshops prior to the circulation of rumors to advise personnel what actions should be taken in the event of a damaging rumor. Consider what rumors might be most damaging to your organization or

company. Study rumors that have caused problems for companies in similar businesses.

3. Make sure your company has such strong positive relationships with its key publics that the publics would at least doubt a negative rumor, if not totally disbelieve it.

4. Keep employees informed. Employees left in the dark are fertile ground for the growth of rumors commonly spread by "the grapevine." Even if events that are bad news, such as layoffs, are a possibility in the near future, give employees real information and promise to keep them up to date. This will be more advantageous than letting rumors circulate that are likely to be more imagined and more negative than reality. Informed employees can be a company's strongest supporters and loudest defenders.

McDonalds took this advice when rumors circulated that there were worms in its hamburgers. It was a well-known rumor that had plagued Wendy's earlier. It did not matter that worms cost more than ground beef per pound; the rumor continued to circulate.

McDonalds personnel who had contact with the public denied the presence of worms on a one-to-one basis to patrons who asked. In addition, they recorded names and phone numbers of those patrons. The strategy was that when these people became knowledgeable about the company, they were less likely to spread the rumor.

The following suggestions are steps organizations may take when a negative rumor is already circulating:

1. When a rumor *seems* to be developing or circulating, disseminate to publics complete, accurate information that is contradictory to the message of the rumor. Do not mention the rumor itself. You do not want to advance its circulation. Your information should *imply strongly* that the rumor is untrue. This may reduce exposure to the rumor. Be advised, however, that fewer people are likely to see the positive news than the negative news.

2. After a rumor has circulated, analyze it. What is its probable origin? Why was it started? What is its possible impact? Will it go away? Will it mushroom? Where is it centered? Is it national or confined to one city, one area?

3. Do nothing. Sometimes a denial draws more attention than silence. Some rumors do go away. When choosing this strategy, be careful that, if the rumor persists, it will not be damaging.

Gerber Products chose to hang tough and be silent in 1986 when a grocery store charged that one of its customers had found a fragment of glass in a baby food jar. Gerber's test lab could find no traces of glass, and the store had lost the fragment supposedly found in the jar (see chap. 5, Product Tampering).

The Food and Drug Administration tested 40,000 unopened jars of Gerber baby food and concluded that no glass existed. Gerber also relied on its state-of-the-art equipment designed to filter out any foreign objects larger than four thousandths of an inch. It also x-rayed for possible breakage in the production line. There was no proof that there was glass in the jar. Gerber felt it had proved there was not.

The rumor continued to spread all over the United States, but Gerber stood tough. It refused to recall. The rumor eventually died, and Gerber recovered sales, something the company felt it could not have done had there been a recall (Seitel, 1992).

4. Deny the rumor publicly and vehemently. *Prove* it has no basis in truth. Once it is shown to be unsubstantiated, a person who passes it on might be challenged with, "That is absolutely untrue. I know because . . ."

Sometimes, if the rumor is already widespread and potentially serious, a news conference is in order. The purpose is to show how erroneous the rumor is. However, in this news conference do not repeat the rumor itself unnecessarily.

Popeyes Fried Chicken chain called a news conference when a rumor circulated in Louisiana that its founder and chairman, Al Copeland, supported former Ku Klux Klan leader David Duke in a political campaign. There were 70 Popeyes restaurants in Louisiana at the time and 900 nationwide.

At the news conference, Copeland denied vociferously that he had ties to Duke. To prove the rumor false, he proclaimed his longtime support of Duke's opponent, a point that could be easily disproved if it were not true. He also offered a $25,000 reward for information leading to the source of the rumor and posted the reward signs in his restaurants. The rumor subsided.

Remember, a denial will not easily be as interesting or as juicy as the original rumor. Just saying it's not so is boring. Rumormongers expect you to deny it. Why would you admit something so negative? You must be persuasive and convincing.

5. To be convincing, get an outside expert on the subject to discredit the rumor. The expert should be a person with strong credentials who speaks with authority—a university professor, a leading physician, or some other professional.

6. Buy ads in high-circulation publications. This is a powerful tool for reaching great numbers of people—if your message is convincing. If the message is not convincing, the ad may promote the rumor. Also, be sure the rumor is totally untrue, not premature. Ads, in that case, can cause more harm than good.

A successful use of ads to fight negative, unfounded rumor happened when the Life Saver Company encountered a rumor that spider eggs were found in Bubble Yum, a brand of bubble gum that had been breaking sales records.

The company conducted surveys showing that more than half of the children in New York had heard the rumor. The company bought ads in newspapers with headlines saying, "Somebody is telling very bad lies about a very good product." The rumors faded. Bubble Yum remained a best-seller.

Some companies use a combination of several tactics to fight damaging rumors. Reebok, in its battle against the rumor of doing business in South Africa, purchased ads in more than 200 African American publications, publicized liaisons with major human rights and anti-apartheid organizations, and distributed a brochure to college students containing statements of support from African-American leaders. Its chairman wrote op-ed articles and co-hosted the Boston visit of Nelson Mandela.

Two cases of crises resulting from rumors follow. The first case, Tropical Fantasy's crisis, deals with one of the more popular types of rumor, racism. The second, Snapps fast-food chain, was a rumor about AIDS, a popular rumor because the disease is so deadly and mysterious.

CASE 1: TROPICAL FANTASY
AND THE STERILITY RUMOR

Tropical Fantasy, a line of fruit-flavored soft drinks, went on the market in 1991 and made $12 million in its first year. It gave the big guns, Coca-Cola and Pepsi, a real contest for the consumer dollar, because a 20-ounce bottle, at the time, cost only 49 cents.

Then someone started an outrageous rumor. Leaflets began appearing in low-income neighborhoods, where sales were highest, claiming that the Brooklyn Bottling Corporation was linked to the Ku Klux Klan, and that it laced its soft drinks with a mysterious ingredient that caused sterility in Black men. The rumor went further by claiming, falsely, that the television news show "20/20" had reported the news.

The rumor is *outrageous* because if there were a substance that would cause sterility in Black men, wouldn't it also cause sterility in men who are not Black? Why would a small, independent company making $2 million every month take steps to wipe out its future customers?

The Food and Drug Administration considered the matter to be outlandish. Even the Ku Klux Klan's Imperial Wizard, James Farrands, said, "The KKK is not in the bottling business" ("A Storm Over Tropical Fantasy," 1991, p. 34). Customers, however, were buying the higher priced drinks instead.

Competitors were the suspected sources of the rumor. Coca-Cola and Pepsi management denied involvement. However, route drivers for Coca-Cola and Pepsi capitalized on the rumor and helped to spread it. One former route driver for Yoo Hoo said that when Pepsi introduced a new drink in the 1960s, "All the (Yoo Hoo) drivers would get together in the bar after work every day and compare notes. We'd go out the next day to spread the best rumor anyone came up with. . . . Nothing's changed. This is a cutthroat business" (McDermott, 1991, p. 11).

The effect was devastating to Tropical Fantasy. Sales dropped by 70%.

Ironically, the employees who stood to be hurt most by the rumor were the African Americans, Hispanics, and Asians who worked for the bottling company and would lose their jobs if the company went under.

Eric Miller, the owner of the bottling company, went to battle. He sent employees back into the neighborhoods where the leaflets were distributed. They were armed with "truth flyers" designed to dispel the rumors. The New York City Health Department declared the drinks safe. Mayor David Dinkins, a Black man, drank the drink in public.

Miller never found out who started the rumor. The countercampaign was so successful that Tropical Fantasy earned $3 million in 1992. Sales were broadened to the Midwest and California in 1992.

CASE 2: SNAPPS RESTAURANT AND THE AIDS RUMOR

Rarely does a company call a news conference to fight a rumor. There are several reasons why. Companies would ideally prefer to reach only the people who have heard the rumor—not one person more. This is a difficult to impossible task. Nevertheless, many times the rumor is limited to one specific, limited location. With a news conference the media would wind up spreading the rumor to people who had never heard it. Also, some companies reason that if the rumor is not spread by the media, it is not likely to reach the crucial public by the media either. The people who spread the rumor or believe it may not read newspapers or watch television news. The Snapps restaurant chain departed from this way of thinking in 1991 and made history by holding a news conference to fight a rumor that plagued one of its restaurants.

In Fort Pierce, Florida, in 1991, Snapps, a fast-food restaurant, confronted a rumor that one of its managers had AIDS and had contaminated hamburger meat. Snapps, an Ohio-based chain, had opened its first Florida restaurant in Fort Pierce in 1990. Fort Pierce is basically a middle-class city of 40,000 about an hour's drive north of Palm Beach.

The location of Fort Pierce was important in that Jensen Beach, Florida, is nearby, and that is where Kimberly Bergalis allegedly contracted the AIDS virus from her dentist. Because Bergalis was the first person known to have contracted AIDS from a health care professional, this incident was widely publicized.

Because of their proximity to the case, the people of Fort Pierce were probably even more attuned to AIDS than people in the rest of the United States. The incident also aroused other questions about how the virus might be spread.

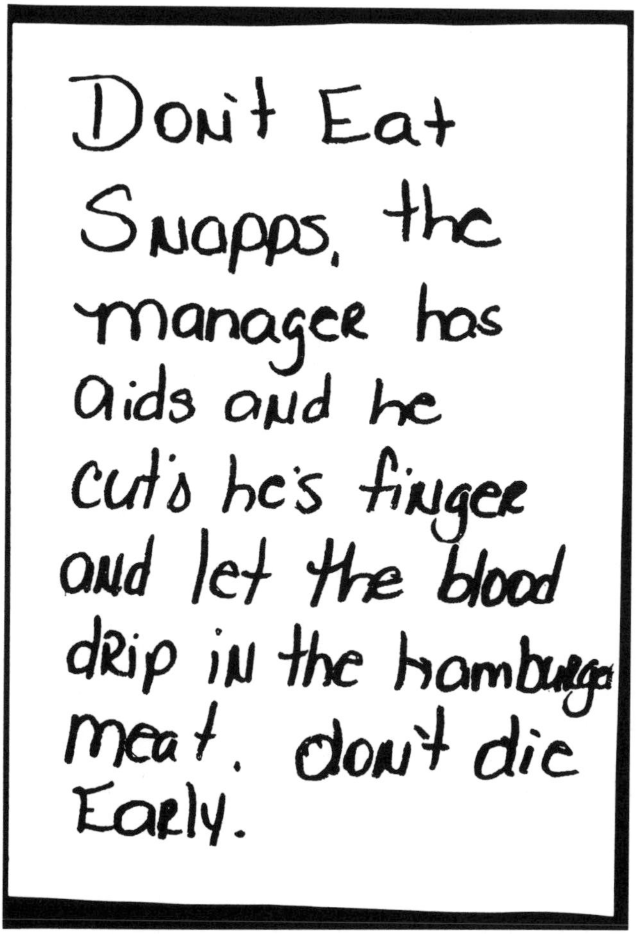
Don't Eat
Snapps. the
manager has
aids and he
cut's he's finger
and let the blood
drip in the hambarga
meat. don't die
Early.

FIG. 3.1. Handwritten flyer, circulated in Fort Pierce high schools, that helped spread the rumor that a manager at a popular restaurant was infected with the AIDS virus and that persons who dined at the restaurant might become contaminated. All managers were voluntarily tested and none of them tested positive for the virus. The health department cooperated with the restaurant's public relations efforts and during a news conference, explained that the disease could not be spread in that manner. Printed with permission of Snapps Restaurant, Inc.

The center of the rumor was a crudely handwritten flyer (see Fig. 3.1). The flyer was circulated primarily in two public high schools with student bodies that made up a large chunk of Snapps' clientele.

One of the more successful restaurants in the chain, the Fort Pierce Snapps saw its business drop to 50%. Snapps' corporate office in Columbus, Ohio, sent Regional Vice President Donald G. Gilbert to remedy the crisis.

Gilbert formed a damage control task force that included a lawyer; a private investigator; and Richard M. Gruenwald, a public relations consultant for Dick Gruenwald Associates of nearby Palm Beach Gardens. The team worked closely with Dr. Rod Cardiff, director of the HRS St. Lucie County Health Unit. Gilbert, the home office, and owners Jack and Jeff Roschman monitored and approved actions of the task force.

The first task was to find the source of the rumor. The private investigator felt certain that a student in one of the schools had written the flyer. Police procedure called for a complaint to be filed before the police could enter the case. The investigator and the lawyer were able to collect enough information to file the complaint.

The next step was to have the restaurant managers tested for AIDS. This decision brought about a necessity for checking legalities. By law, the managers would have to volunteer to be tested; the company could not make that requirement.

All seven managers did volunteer, including one who had been with the Fort Pierce restaurant, but had been transferred to another city. The law also required that the results of the tests be given to the person taking the tests and not to the employer. The procedure took a week.

After the results were in, it was discovered that all the managers, as expected, tested negative for the AIDS virus.

Meanwhile, the restaurant was continuing to lose business. Layoffs were threatened if business did not improve. "This was a double-edged sword," said Gilbert. "We had to be sure of our facts, have everything in place for the complaint filing and act quickly, as business was continuing to go down hill."

Gruenwald, the public relations counsel, and his associate, John Futch, suggested a press conference. "We all agreed that a press conference would bring everything out in the open," said Gruenwald. "The problem was there. Why hide it?"

Snapps is considered to have made public relations history by being the first fast-food chain to address an AIDS rumor by going on the offensive and holding a news conference. "We were most impressed with the way that management accepted our recommendations," said Gruenwald. (See Fig. 3.2.)

To add credibility to the occasion, the press conference was held in the health unit's offices, and the health unit's director spoke on behalf of the franchise. At the conference, an announcement was made that the chain was offering a $5,000 reward for information leading to the arrest of the person or persons who started the rumor.

The news conference was attended by company executives as well as the county health director, who announced that all Snapps managers had been tested for the virus, and no traces of it were found. He further stated that AIDS is not transmitted through food, that there was no danger in eating at Snapps.

Store's business cut 50 percent by AIDS rumor

BY PHIL LONG
HERALD STAFF WRITER

FORT PIERCE - In a highly unusual move, an Ohio-based fast food restaurant went public Wednesday to confront a rumor that one of its managers had AIDS and had contaminated hamburger met.

"The rumor is totally false," said Don Gilbert, regional vice president at Snapps, a company with 44 stores, mostly in Ohio.

"All of our managers have been tested and none has AIDS," he said.

But in a little over a month since the rumor started, business in Florida's only Snapps store has dropped almost 50 percent, Gilbert said. Five of the store's 40 positions remain unfilled, and employee hours have been cut. Layoffs are possible, he said.

The firm is promising a $5,000 reward for information leading to the arrest of the person who photocopies or circulated a crude, hand-drawn flier that accuses the manager of having AIDS and contaminating hamburger meat with his blood.

In what may have been the first press conference of its kind involving a national food chain, Gilbert met reporters in the lobby of the health department. He was flanked by the county's health director, Snapps employees, a company attorney and a police detective.

Snapps managers have been tested and they don't have any trace of the virus, said Dr. Rod Cardiff, director of the St. Lucie Public Health Unit.

"There is nothing unsafe about Snapps," he said. "AIDS is not transmitted through food. There is no danger with going to Snapps and eating there."

Fort Pierce police Lt. Irving Hamrick, who suspects that a teenager is responsible because the fliers have been circulated at the county's two public high schools, said his department is investigating.

Prosecutor Linda Craft said the person responsible for the flier could face up to a year in jail on the misdemeanor charge of criminal defamation. it is illegal to publish anything that causes "hatred, contempt, ridicule or obloquy," to an individual, Craft said.

"They are not only affecting my job, but the jobs of many other people employed by Snapps," said Anita Farley, a Snapps worker who has been with the restaurant since it opened in July.

AIDS rumors are not new. McDonald's and Burger King have faced them before. Neither have gone quite so public...

FIG. 3.2. News story of the Snapps crisis in the *Miami Herald*, May 9, 1991. Note the reporter recognized that the news conference was not a common method of fighting such rumors. (Reprinted with permission of the *Miami Herald*)

Two West Palm Beach television stations led their 6 P.M. newscasts with the story including interviews with customers. Employees talked about how their jobs were affected. Associated Press and Knight-Ridder News Service picked up the story and used it in newspapers all over Florida as well as in many newspapers out of state.

"The press was most cooperative and news coverage was excellent," Gilbert said (see Fig. 3.2).

Gruenwald, looking back, says his philosophy is that "if you cooperate with the media, they—for the most part—will cooperate with you."

The Denver Post picked up the Knight-Ridder story; its lead emphasized the unusual public relations tactic, "In a highly unusual move, an Ohio-based fast-food restaurant went public yesterday to confront a rumor that one of its managers had AIDS and had contaminated hamburger meat" (Knight-Ridder, 1991).

The article went on with the restaurant's denial, the offered reward, and a statement that AIDS is not transmitted through food. Then, it pointed out that other fast-food restaurants have been plagued by AIDS rumors, but none had fought the rumor through the news conference (Knight-Ridder, 1991).

The private investigator discovered that a 16-year-old female high school student had written and distributed the flyer, apparently after a class discussion on AIDS. "The girl admitted to writing the flyer," said Gilbert, "but we determined that the student's action came after the AIDS rumor had been circulating in the community and she didn't start the rumor."

"The student, through her parents and attorney, agreed to issue an apology," said Gilbert. "We used the apology in a press release and a full-page ad in the local newspaper."

The minor, saying she wrote the flyer because she was concerned about her friends and wanted to do them a favor, wrote the following apology:

> I apologize to the community in helping to spread a rumor about Snapps, a local fast food restaurant. As a young person who has taken a course concerning aids and having great concern for the people in the community, I took it upon myself to prepare a flyer concerning Snapps without knowing whether the information I received as a rumor was true. I now realize that I was wrong and I apologize to Snapps, its managers and employees. It was not my intent to harm their business and I am sorry that Snapps' business has suffered as a result of the rumor. I have since returned to eat at Snapps and I encourage others to do so as well.
>
> Sincerely,
> C.J., a minor

Because she was a minor, her real name was never revealed. State Attorney Bruce Colton said spreading the rumor could violate state laws that make libel a misdemeanor punishable by up to one year in jail. Prosecutor Linda Craft said the person responsible for the flyer could face up to a year in jail on the misdemeanor charge of criminal defamation (Knight-Ridder, 1991).

NEWS

**DICK
GRUENWALD
ASSOCIATES**

PUBLIC RELATIONS

4362 Northlake Boulevard, Suite 109
Palm Beach Gardens, Florida 33410
(407) 622-3200
FAX: (407) 627-6403

June 3, 1991

**SNAPPS SERVES
15,000 FREE HAMBURGERS
OVER WEEKEND**

FORT PIERCE --Snapps Restaurant celebrated its first anniversary in Fort Pierce giving away 15,000 free hamburgers Saturday and Sunday.

It was quite a turn-around for the drive-in eatery that saw its business drop dramatically with a rumor that one of its managers had AIDS.

Last week Snapps management announced that a Fort Pierce teen-ager, identified only as "C J", had apologized for writing and distributing a flier stating that a Snapps manager had AIDS. "C J was one of our customers over the weekend," regional vice president Donald Gilbert said.

Since the apology announcment, business has picked up but still has a long way to go to return to normal, Gilbert said.

The weekend event was most encouraging, Gilbert said. There were several large groups including one church with more than 100 kids and a compact car with 13 kids.

# #

For media information: Dick Gruenwald

FIG. 3.3. One of several news releases distributed by the public relation's firm hired by Ohio-based restaurant to manage the crisis. (Snapps Restaurant)

Eatery plagued by rumor fights back

STUART NEWS

FORT PIERCE - A Fort Pierce eatery gave away 15,000 hamburgers last weekend, battling recent rumors that an employee at Snapps restaurant tainted food with the AIDS virus.

Among the many people eating at the restaurant at 25th Street and Orange Avenue was a teenager known only as "C.J." The Fort Pierce Westwood High School student apologized recently for distributing a flier warning fellow students not to eat at Snapps.

Snapps Regional Vice President Donald Gilbert said the weekend promotion was a dramatic turnaround for the eatery, which saw business plummet because of the untrue rumor.

County health officials said food cannot be tainted by the AIDS virus. All the Snapps managers tested negative for the fatal virus.

FIG. 3.4. News story in the nearby *Stuart News*, June 5, 1991, about the restaurant's crisis recovery process. (Reprinted with permission of the *Stuart News*, in Stuart, Florida)

Gruenwald advised the company not to press charges against the girl. "It was never felt that the girl acted maliciously," he said. "Also, she did not start the rumor. It had been circulating before she wrote the flyer. If we had filed charges, we could win the battle, but not the war of public opinion. The public apology would bring her sympathy and perhaps a boycott to the restaurant. Then, the case might drag out, thus hurting the chances for a return to normalcy."

The media carried the story of the apology with headlines as follows:

The Palm Beach Post—"Student Apologizes for Restaurant Rumor" (Reeder, 1991).

The Stuart News (Stuart, Florida)—"Student Apologizes for AIDS Rumor About Eatery" (Cheek, 1991).

The Miami Herald—"Student Apologizes for Spreading Rumor About Restaurant" (Long, 1991).

As in most crises cases, recovery stories are not featured as prominently, nor as long, as the original stories.

Snapps management continued an aggressive effort to win back customers. Its advertising agency, Haunty & Welter of Columbus, Ohio, launched a strong radio and newspaper, and later, television campaign with a free hamburger weekend, June 1 and 2. "This was a tremendous success," said Gruenwald. "The girl who wrote the flyer, who we called CJ, attended the event." More than 15,000 free hamburgers were served. The event was promoted in ads using CJ's apology (see Fig. 3.3 and Fig. 3.4).

"If we had to do it all over, we would have followed the same crisis management and damage control program. In retrospect, this was an excellent example of crisis teamwork, everyone working together for the common good," concluded Gruenwald.

Gruenwald said the source of the rumor was never found. The restaurant changed names and managed to stay in business, although it never did quite recover its former popularity.

"GOTCHA" TELEVISION JOURNALISM

Rumor as a source of crises is as old as mankind itself and will probably exist until the end of time. "Gotcha" journalism, often not journalism at all, is a trend in the 1990s among television news shows and television talk shows as well. Although investigative teams doing consumer protection pieces have existed for years, there is a new irresponsibility, a drive to entertain the viewer more than to protect the consumer.

Americans are addicted to television and get most of their news from television, so "gotcha" journalism is a feared source of crisis, even for reputable organizations and businesses.

"60 Minutes"

In 1968, the grandfather of television news magazines, "60 Minutes," made its debut. Called "the *Time Magazine* of the Air," it was the first national news program to earn consistently high Nielsen ratings. It is still the premier news magazine show, usually in the weekly top ten, and often the highest rated show in prime time.

A popular feature of "60 Minutes," even in the early years, was its investigative "in-your-face" journalism in which Morley Safer, Dan Rather, Mike Wallace, and the other anchors would zero in on a company or organization that had taken advantage of consumers.

Safer has said that the investigative practices of the show are careful and responsible. He described a story on the American Motors jeep, which was prone to roll over. The show taped 10 test runs and gave the tape to American Motors, asking them to repeat the test themselves at the same speeds on their own track with their own driver. American Motors refused, but offered to film the tests themselves and send the tape to "60 Minutes." Safer said, "I don't know if they doctored it or if they cheated on speed, but they sent it to us. And we ran it" (Wiesendanger, 1994, p. 6).

For years, "60 Minutes" viewers took pleasure in watching the company heads sweat and stumble over explanations. As the camera zoomed in for a close-up of the terrified subject's twitching face, we were gratified and comforted to know that television was a watchdog for consumer rights and fairness.

"60 Minutes" still does occasional investigative consumer protection pieces, but somehow it is not so comforting anymore to watch people on the hot seat. Television is now more of an "attack dog" than a "watch dog." There are many programs that thrive on the destruction of individuals, organizations, and companies, and they are doing it for sheer entertainment, for high ratings. Sometimes they are ruining the lives of innocent people and the businesses of innocent companies in the process. We do not have the confidence in these shows that we had and have for the "60 Minutes" staff.

Of course, this does not mean that "60 Minutes" has never been guilty of faulty journalism. Washington apple growers will tell you about one incident in 1989 in which a "60 Minutes" investigation based on unscientific evidence cost them about $140 million dollars in loss of sales. (Seitel, 1992).

The show in this case aired an investigative piece citing a study that declared that Alar, an ingredient used in red apple production, caused children to develop cancer later in life. Needless to say, the sale of red apples nearly stopped. Schools removed them from the lunch menus. Grocers removed them from their produce departments. Parents were enraged.

The media went into its frenzy, and the issue was covered widely in newspapers, magazines, and broadcast media. In the meantime, the American Council on Health and Science said publicly that it thought the threat of cancer had been exaggerated.

Biochemists at the University of California, Berkeley, said that experts in both toxicology and epidemiology concluded that the amount of carcinogens present in Alar were too infinitesimal to be a threat. No case was ever made against Alar by the government protection agencies.

In 1994, Mike Wallace and a "60 Minutes" news producer were reprimanded by CBS for poor judgment when they secretly taped an interview with another journalist by placing cameras in draperies. Wallace apologized on camera when the segment aired.

Critics claim that "60 Minutes" has relaxed its formerly high standards, that it is getting a bit tired. "60 Minutes" claims that people watch, even though it does not resort to the sensationalism that other news magazines do. All news magazine shows, including "60 Minutes," suffered a decline in ratings during the 1993–94 television season ("Just Talk Into the Curtains," 1994).

"Gotcha journalism" exists in numerous television news magazines. As one business owner said, "The only thing worse than '60 Minutes' coming to visit is '20/20' coming to visit."

Consultants tell news producers that news programs must be dramatic and exciting to get viewer attention. Some manufacture the drama, and that is where irresponsibility, poor journalism, and sensationalism enter the picture.

"Dateline NBC," a network news magazine, was widely criticized for rigging a General Motors truck to explode in one of its consumer protection pieces. Conversely, then, "Dateline NBC" performed an admirable task in September 1994 when it criticized the news media's practices regarding President Clinton.

In May 1994, the president had been slaughtered by the media for getting a haircut from Beverly Hills hairdresser extraordinaire, Christophe. The complaints were twofold: (1) He cut the presidential hair aboard Air Force One parked on a runway at Los Angeles Airport that caused traffic delays. (2) The haircut was a frivolous expense for which taxpayers paid.

According to the "Dateline NBC" report, the *Washington Post* ran 59 stories about the president's "bad hair day." Nine of the stories were on the front page. NBC News programs mentioned the incident 20 times; other news outlets reported similarly.

The criticism in the update resulted from an investigation by a reporter for New York *Newsday.* He discovered that the president's haircut caused no flight delays, except for an unscheduled air taxi that was delayed for two minutes. Also, the haircut had cost less than $50 ("Cutting It Close," 1994).

Walter Cronkite partially blames television news magazines for the deterioration of television journalism. He calls them an inexpensive way to "give a semblance of public responsibility without bothering with the vast expense of original news gathering" (Rottenberg, 1994, p. 36).

"Checkbook" Journalism and Newsmongers

In the 1980s, the tabloid shows premiered and subsequently were blamed for changing the direction of television news programs. "Entertainment Tonight" aired first in 1981 with celebrity gossip in a newscast format. It never pretended to be anything but entertainment, but it looked like news.

Then in 1986 "A Current Affair" premiered on the Fox Network. Claiming to be a news magazine, it was a televised version of the supermarket tabloid newspaper. Not so coincidentally, Rupert Murdoch, owner of Fox, also owned the tabloid newspaper, *Star.*

"Hard Copy" and "Inside Edition" followed in 1989. All were successful. Each in 1994 reached more than 6 million viewers nightly.

All do investigative pieces. "Hard Copy" vowed to do even more in its 1994–95 season. These shows are not known for responsible journalism, but they are known for sensationalism and "checkbook journalism" in which subjects of interviews are often paid in the hundreds of thousands of dollars.

Cronkite blames tabloids for part of the whole degeneration of society. "We've always known you can gain circulation or viewers by cheapening the product, and now you're finding the bad drive out the good" (Rottenberg, 1994, p. 36).

What he refers to is television newscasts that attempt to boost ratings by adopting characteristics of tabloid shows: recreated news, sleaze, unconfirmed sources, and misleading teasers. It has become difficult to know where news ends and entertainment begins.

The "Nonexpert Expert"

In the 1990s, there are innumerable talk shows. The expression, "Everyone will be famous for 15 minutes," almost seems to be true. Most of the people who will enjoy 15 minutes of fame will enjoy it as a host or guest on a talk show.

"Meet The Press" is the "high brow" of the talk-interview shows. Then there are the "white collar talk shows" such as "Donahue" and "Larry King Live." The average viewer of these shows is probably not as informed as the average "Meet The Press" viewer, but is considerably more informed than viewers of the "blue collar talk shows" such as "Geraldo." The well-informed viewer demands more responsibility from a talk show in its investigative processes and presentation.

On these talk shows, as well as on newscasts and television magazine shows, the "nonexpert expert" has emerged. "People's opinions are often not distinguished from actual facts and evidence," said psychologist Lawrence Balter (Roan, 1994, p. L4).

Sociologist Vicki Abt, like many critics of talk shows, said that the host-stars "act as pseudoprofessional counselors without suitable credentials to do so" (Roan, 1994, p. L4).

Even more alarming, members of the studio audience in many of these shows take on the positions of the "experts" and proceed to verbally attack individuals or representatives of organizations and companies as if they had studied the issues for years.

This result takes on a particularly damaging aspect when guests on talk shows or news magazines relate experiences in which they have total belief based on little knowledge. They can be so convinced that the emotion shows in their faces and in their body language. Viewers become compassionate with the subject of such a heartwrenching scene and never question the facts of the story.

The case that follows shows how one industry dealt with a crisis brought on by a nonexpert expert on a talk show.

CASE 3: CELLULAR PHONES AND THE CANCER SCARE

The cellular telephone industry enjoyed rapid growth in the early 1990s. It was averaging approximately 10,000 new customers daily as cellular phones become a necessity rather than a frill.

On January 21, 1993, a Florida widower, David Reynard, still grieving over his wife's death six months before from brain cancer, appeared on the Cable News Network show, "Larry King Live," and told millions of television viewers that he believed his wife's fatal illness was caused by electromagnetic waves from a cellular phone.

Following is an excerpt from the transcript:

Mr. Reynard: There were several things that were quite obvious. And a second MRI basically showed she had a large (unintelligible word) type tumor located just behind and above her left ear.

Larry King: When did she die?

Mr. Reynard: May the 24th of last year.

Larry King: When did you start to think, "This has something to do with the cellular phone?"

Mr. Reynard: I think when I saw the first MRI and saw the location of the tumor. It appeared that it was in the location directly next to the antenna, and the tumor seemed to be growing inward from that direction.

The show then played a graphic videotape of the dying wife relating her deposition of the matter. To many viewers, this supporting "information" served to verify the claim, despite the fact that no scientific or medical data had been presented. In fact, data was presented to the contrary, but it could not compete with the emotionality of the man whose wife had died.

Here's another excerpt from the transcript as Dr. Eleanor Adair, a Yale University scientist, was questioned by King:

Dr. Adair: Yes, I was co-chair of the committee that spent nine years reviewing the literature and looking into all kinds of questions similar to this one—the possibility of health effects.

Larry King: And?

Dr. Adair: And the standard is set at levels well above those that are emitted by such devices as cellular telephones.

King: Could his wife have been a victim?

Dr. Adair: No, I don't believe so, no.

King: You don't see any connection at all?

Dr. Adair: None at all, because the power output from a cellular telephone is just too low. It can't do that kind of damage to tissue.

King: And they've been sufficiently tested?

Dr. Adair: They have been tested, and the frequencies at which these devices operate have been tested in laboratory experiments for many, many years.

King: To your knowledge, have there been lawsuits?

Dr. Adair: There are lawsuits pending, and one that was just concluded yesterday with respect to the police radar instruments that also had been alleged to cause cancer.

King: Do you make any relationship between the position of the antenna and the position of the tumor?

Dr. Adair: No, I don't. Cancers occur in the brain at many places. People have had cancers as long as individuals have inhabited the earth. . . .

As viewers began to call into the talk show, one claimed getting dizzy when using a cellular phone. One challenged Dr. Adair's research, although citing none to the contrary. One asked if a cordless phone was dangerous too.

Stocks began to fall. Motorola, the largest manufacturer of cellular phones, and McCaw Cellular Communications Inc., the nation's largest cellular carrier, both dropped more than 15% (Kaye, 1993).

Thus, a crisis was born for the cellular telephone industry—in both manufacturing and service companies. Cellular One, a division of McCaw Cellular Communications, Inc., in the Pacific Northwest, is one of those service companies. McCaw Cellular is the largest cellular carrier with 3.8 million subscribers, 250 locations in the U.S., and 105 markets.

Ken Woo, Cellular One

Ken Woo, the company's media relations manager, had been with the company for a year and a half when the crisis erupted.

At Cellular One, media relations reports to district public affairs, which reports to the director of sales and marketing. The director of sales and marketing reports to the vice president and general manager of the Washington and Alaska district who reports to a regional president for Cellular

One. The regional president reports to the president and chief executive officer of McCaw/AT&T Wireless Services.

Despite all the layers, Woo said he has "a dotted line relationship to Bob Ratliffe," who reports directly to the president/CEO of McCaw and also to Marilyn Laurie, the Senior Vice President of Public Relations and Employee Communications of AT&T.

Woo's department, which consists of nine staff specialists and one administrative assistant, interacts regularly with Ratliffe's division, McCaw Corporate Public Relations. "I talk to Bob regularly. Then, other district public relations people get together via conference call every two weeks, more often if there are 'hot issues' to be dealt with, like the cancer scare," said Woo.

"I heard about the Reynard case from Steve Young at CNN who was preparing a report on it," said Woo. "Then Ron Nessen, vice president of public relations for the Cellular Telephone Industry Association (CTIA) sent an industry alert to all carriers.

"My first reaction was to gather facts. I had some knowledge of the technology of cellular phones, but we needed more. We had to understand what we were being targeted for, and we had to find experts to support whatever response we would come up with."

Woo's office contacted Dr. Arthur Guy, a University of Washington professor emeritus in bioengineering, asking him to brief them on the issues. Woo also attended a biolelectromagnetics meeting in Los Angeles to round out his knowledge of the subject.

Reynard filed suit against the manufacturer of his cellular phone, NEC America, and the cellular carrier that provided the phone's service, GTE Mobilnet. Although Cellular One was not in the legal battle, the crisis affected all cellular phone manufacturers and all service companies.

Reynard continued to make appearances on television shows. He told his story on "20/20," "Nightline," "The Today Show," "Donahue," and "The Faith Daniels Show." As each show aired, more and more consumers grew fearful of cellular phones. There were phone calls by the thousands to manufacturers and carriers, including Cellular One and McCaw Cellular. One news story is Fig. 3.5.

Woo is concerned about Reynard and people like Reynard whom he calls "nonexpert experts." He said, "They are the sound bites that are popping up lately on television news regarding people expressing opinions for which they have no expertise. David Reynard was a nonexpert expert making claims unsubstantiated by his own doctors that his wife's brain tumor was the direct result of cellular phone use. His own doctors said they doubted the cause-and-effect claims."

Woo followed the pretrial testimony in the case and said, "His wife's physicians said the size of the growth seemed to indicate the tumor was there long before he claimed she began using a cellular phone."

Cellular industry waits out a scare

BY MARCIA A. LUDWIG
JOURNAL AMERICAN BUSINESS WRITER

The past two weeks have been rocky for the cellular communications industry.

News reports and talk shows spread fear that portable cellular telephones may cause brain tumors, causing stocks to fall and public-relations personnel to work overtime trying to calm the public.

But analysts say the scare eventually should blow over, leaving no visible scars on the companies or their stocks. Company spokespeople agree.

"We give (the scare) a six- to eight-week life expectancy," said Hershcel Shosteck, a cellular-market consultant and analyst with his own firm in Silver Spring, Md.

The scare first erupted Jan. 21 when CNN's Larry King hosted David Reynard, a St. Petersburg, Fla., man who claims his wife's fatal brain tumor was caused by the cellular phone he bought for her.

McCaw Cellular Communications Inc.'s stock fell $2 in the next day's trading to close at $36.25. The Kirkland-based company's stock rose the following Monday, Jan. 25, but then slid to $32.50 by the end of the week. The stock made two modest gains last week, edging up $2.75, and closed last Friday at $33.75 a share. McCaw is the nation's largest cellular carrier.

Motorola, Inc., of Schaumburg, Ill., one of the largest cellular phone and equipment manufacturers, watched its stock fall from $61.375 the day before the talk show to $53.375 a share last Friday.

"This has been a great example of how one story...got sensationalized by the talk shows. It's impacting business. Motorola lost (11) percent of the value of their company," said Bob Ratliffe, vice president of corporate affairs at McCaw.

To make matters worse, the Federal Food and Drug Administration on Friday issued a statement saying that although there is no proof at this point that portable cellular phones cause cancer, there is no definitive proof that they do not. Therefore, it advised cellular-phone users to limit the length of their calls and possibly to switch from portable phone usage to phones with remote antennas, such as car phones.

(The cellular industry is underwriting a story on portable-phone safety in response to the scare. Cellular carriers point to thousands of existing studies done on different frequencies showing no long-term health effects of cellular phone usage.)

Craig McCaw, chairman and chief executive officer of McCaw, spoke about the FDA's statement to CNN's Lou Dobbs Friday afternoon. He said he was "encouraged" by the FDA's actions so far.

"We believe in our hearts that we're right," that cellular phones are safe, he said.

Ratliffe uses his cellular phone an average of 6,000 to 7,000 minutes a month, far above the average user's call time of 170 minutes a month.

"I'm not worried at all," he said.

Analysts said although cellular-company shareholders have been nervous lately, they should adopt a similar attitude for the long term.

This scare is comparable to the video display terminal scare a few years ago, said Paul Andrews, analyst with AG Edwards & Sons Inc. in St. Louis.

People were worried about the electromagnetic fields generated by computer screens, but that scare "was in the news for six to nine months, then it went away. People are still using video display terminals," he said.

The Eastside's other cellular carrier, US West's NewVector Group in Bellevue, has been busy educating its customers about the scare and has prepared a bill insert for the next billing cycle that details information currently available, said Lisa Bowersock, spokeswoman.

Only a "couple hundred" calls from concerned customers have been received nationwide on the issue, out of roughly 10,000 calls received by U.S. West each day, she said.

US West NewVector is a subsidiary of US West Inc. of Englewood, Colo. Its price has remained stable the past two weeks and closed at $39.875 a share last Friday.

Both Bowersock and Ratliffe said they have detected no increase in sales of their cellular services or cellular phones from their dealers.

FIG. 3.5. News story in the *Journal American*, Bellevue, Washington, February 8, 1993 about the cellular telephone cancer scare. (Reprinted with permission of the *Journal American*)

The case was subsequently thrown out of court, but not before it had frightened cellular phone users and caused damage to the industry. There are apparently plans, on the part of Reynard and his lawyers, to either appeal or refile different charges.

Woo primarily blames the media. Once a journalist himself, this is a sensitive point with him. He said, "These nonexpert experts are handy for reporters on the run with no time to check out their expert credentials. It's a form of 'instant public opinion', 'instant polls.'

"In the old days when I was a journalist, we used to call them 'man on the street interviews.' It is not scientific, does not accurately measure public opinion, does not provide balanced or accurate information, but is used for instant analysis-justification or a particular point of view."

Woo said, "You are seeing more of these kinds of sound bites-quotes as deadlines shorten and writers and reporters file for more editions and broadcasts than in the past. In the O.J. Simpson case there was little public information available and 'analysts and consultants' were hired to provide commentary on the guilt or innocence of people.

"There was also the invasion of Haiti where retired military officers were called in to second guess where and when an invasion might take place and under what circumstances. Then you have the 'Buckwheat' fraud on ABC-TV's '20/20' where nonexpert witnesses 'substantiated' a bogus Buckwheat."

Even though a nonexpert expert caused this problem, it was still a very serious crisis. The only crisis that would be worse is if the charges had been substantiated.

The Cellular One staff benefited from its corporate culture, which Woo said was in a "we" mode during the crisis. "We have an entrepreneurial spirit that is fed by highly educated professionals working at being the best in their field. We value innovation, making the system work for customers, simplicity, excellence, team work, good judgment, and delivering on our promises."

Woo felt that his media relations staff has good relationships with the media. He thought that he had good relationships with the West Coast media dating from the time when he was a CBS reporter based in Los Angeles. "There's a good exchange," he said. "I hope it was because of my relationships with people that we had a strong degree of responsible reporting on this issue."

During the crisis, the workday was expectantly busy. It started with reviewing overnight sweeps and opinion polling. Then key media were checked to see what new information had been reported on the subject.

The corporate team updated the staff on what new information they had. Then Woo would share stories and situations with field communicators. They would brainstorm new ideas dealing with the issues. Next, Woo would follow up on work from the previous day and end the day by meeting with key editors and writers to talk about what was known and unknown.

During the crisis, an industry and public affairs roundtable was established that consisted of public relations executives from member companies. The roundtable planned an information program aimed at the following publics:

Wall Street analysts,
government regulators,
congressional hearings, and the
general public.

Ratliffe of McCaw's corporate public relations operation attended these sessions and reported back to Ken and the staff at Cellular One. Cellular One was concerned primarily with two publics: consumers and the media.

For consumers, the company developed a document called "Communications Guidelines for Questions About the Health Effects of Cellular Phones" for employees who had contact with customers.

These employees were instructed not to generate their own materials, but to speak from information on the document. They were also urged to conform to regular company policy and refer calls from the media to public relations personnel.

The communications guidelines had three tiers. The first tier gave the employees speaking points basically stressing that cellular phones did not cause cancer or any other health defects, that the company is concerned about customer health and safety, and that people were unnecessarily frightened.

The second tier was used if the customer caller wanted additional information. In this case, a letter was mailed to them along with a position paper about the safety of cellular phones.

The third tier was used if the caller was still unsatisfied with the response. These customers were referred to corporate personnel to be handled personally.

Woo followed a document he had written and refined over a period of years in a previous position with another company. He had input from Jim McFarland and John Renforth who were, at the time, with Ogilvy and Mather and served as public relations counsel to Woo's company.

Woo is not a great believer in news releases and says they are "the most useless justifications for killing trees." Instead, during the height of the crisis, he conducted briefings with key regional writers and editors and compiled research materials into a booklet titled "Cellular Telephones and Electromagnetic Fields" that explained the health and safety of cellular phones.

Todd Wolfenbarger, McCaw Cellular

Todd Wolfenbarger is director of communications at McCaw Cellular. Bob Ratliffe is vice president of communications and there are about a dozen people in the department. "Unlike Ken Woo," said Wolfenbarger, "we deal with industry groups, with stock prices, and with issues that affect the company as a whole.

"We have 22 field communicators nationwide, and Ken is one of those. What essentially happened in the crisis is we would develop a message with Motorola and the Cellular Telephone Industry Association (CTIA) and distribute it through our field communicators, who would take it to the media and the consumers" (see the McCaw news release in Fig. 3.6).

Wolfenbarger admits that the cellular industry made an early error in that the original Reynard lawsuit was filed months before "The Larry King Show" and was a prodrome to the crisis. "In fact," he said, "there was a CNN report that ran a week and a half before. 'The Larry King Show' gave the crisis legs, and it ran in a way beyond anything we could ever have imagined."

He said that at the time of the lawsuit, McCaw had consulted scientists who told them that the risk factor was "unmeasurable." "We couldn't get some scientists to study the stuff because they wouldn't find anything. They said, 'We don't get funding by doing studies that find nothing.' So," said Wolfenbarger, "McCaw believed science and decided it would not be a big deal."

"What was wrong," he said, "is we had a really complicated message. We had Dr. Arthur Guy from the University of Washington with 30 years of electromagnetic experience. He didn't want to oversimplify things because the functioning of the cellular phone is not a simple process. So, here's this PhD being quoted about electromagnetic fields and another guy saying simply, 'My wife is dead!' Then, the camera cuts to shots of his wife, and then we see that glint of a tear in his eye. It was public perception against science and we couldn't win."

Another incident that was a mistake, according to Wolfenbarger, was a news conference called by Motorola. He said, "Motorola had great information, a lot of research on hand, so we took a back seat to Motorola in the way the conference was run. They had their lead scientist, who is a brilliant guy, but he's not used to reporters firing questions at him. I think he took for granted that he wouldn't go into much detail so he said, 'There are a thousand studies out.' A reporter yelled, 'Can you name two or three of them?' He couldn't, even though he was right; there are many studies. So, it looked bad."

During the crisis, McCaw's communications staff met at 6 a.m. in the boardroom to discuss what had happened in the news the previous day.

NEWS FROM McCAW®CELLULAR...

FOR IMMEDIATE RELEASE

**McCaw Cellular / Cellular One Encouraged by Customer Responses
-- Congressional Briefing Re-affirms Cellular Safety --**

Kirkland, WA -- Feb. 2, 1993 -- McCaw Cellular Communications, Inc., which provides cellular phone service in more than 100 markets across the country primarily under the name Cellular One®, said Tuesday it was encouraged by the response of its more than two million customers to the recent stir caused by an alleged link of cellular to health risks.

The company's Customer Care centers reported a confident customer base with customer inquiries at normal levels. "While we understand why our customers might have been alarmed following the news stories, we are encouraged by their response," said Bob Ratliffe, McCaw's Vice President of Corporate Communications. "The scientific community has spoken to Congress and the market has started to rebound as customers get the facts that cellular is safe. I'm happy to report their actions speak louder than other peoples' words," he stated further.

In a representative California market, where McCaw has a customer base of 90,000, only 20 calls have been received about the health-related news stories. In fact, a sales promotion has resulted in a shortage of supply of portable phones.

McCaw Cellular Communications, Inc. (NASDAQ:MCAWA) operating under the name Cellular One® in most of its markets, is the largest cellular service provider in the United States and is developing and marketing a broad range of wireless communications services, including a cellular network that spans the continent, and is capable of transmitting voice and data communications.

McCaw Cellular owns a 52 percent interest in LIN Broadcasting Corp., which is engaged in cellular telephone operations, television broadcasting and specialty publishing. It also has a 32 percent stake in American Mobile Satellite Corporation, which is developing a satellite-based communications network to provide personal communications service to remote areas of North America now out of reach of terrestrial communications systems, and a 51 percent stake in Claircom, Inc., a joint venture with Hughes Network Systems, which is licensed to provide telephone service to commercial and private aircraft. McCaw Cellular is the nation's fifth largest paging service provider.

Contacts:
Bob Ratliffe, Vice President Corporate Communications
(206) 828-8685 or (206) 979-4254 Cellular

Todd Wolfenbarger, Director of Communications
(206) 828-1851 or (206) 660-5704 Cellular

# # #

McCaw Cellular Communications, Inc. • 5400 Carillon Point • Kirkland, WA 98033 • (206) 827-4500

FIG. 3.6. News release disseminated by McCaw Cellular during the cancer scare crisis. (Printed with permission of McCaw Cellular.)

There were numerous inaccuracies reported, one reporter quoting another reporter, and so on.

Wolfenbarger said, "We had one person who was dedicated to calling reporters and correcting errors—'If you write about this issue again, I just wanted to let you know this is not the case. We have some information I can send you that will explain.' This was helpful because few errors were repeated."

The communications staff also developed talking points. The talking points were put together into a customer response book, which was distributed to field organizations such as Cellular One.

"Our talking points were similar to CTIA's talking points," said Wolfenbarger. "There's a real sharp guy running their department, Ron Nessen, who used to be President Ford's press secretary. He has a good feel for dealing with government agencies and how they react."

The government agency that the industry was most concerned with was the Food and Drug Administration (FDA), which neither endorsed nor condemned the cellular phone. The FDA did advise consumers to limit their use of cellular phones. The industry took the FDA's inaction as positive.

Craig McCaw, chairman and CEO of McCaw, appeared on CNN's "Moneyline" with Lou Dobbs, and said, "We believe in our hearts that we are right." He also touched on the company's concern that it was suddenly on the wrong side of the health and safety issue. He mentioned that cellular phones reduced stress in business and that stress caused illnesses.

Wolfenbarger said, "Craig McCaw asked real specific questions of scientists. If the information had been negative and that phones were not safe, Craig, who is very health conscious, would have a problem admitting it.

"We do think of ourselves as safety enhancers. Cellular phones save lives during earthquakes and hurricanes. Half a million people, each month, call 911 from their cellular phones to report accidents."

McCaw president, James Barksdale, decided that it was best to offer consumers options. Reporters at *USA Today, The New York Times,* and *The Wall Street Journal* were told that if McCaw customers had a problem with the safety of phones, they had three options:

1. They could trade in the cellular phones for transportable phones with antennas.
2. They could suspend service for up to three months, then access it back without cost when they felt comfortable doing so.
3. They could cancel their contracts without cost.

Wolfenbarger said fewer than 50 customers canceled. Of those, about half, he believes, had severely delinquent accounts and were looking for a way to get out of their obligation.

The story competed for news time and space with other consumer crises. The Jack-in-the-Box fast-food chain had the *E. coli* crisis that was killing children who ate its hamburgers. "There was metal in tuna fish, lead in paint—all within a one-week period," said Wolfenbarger, "and I think all those crises helped ours die down. I can remember '20/20' debating whether it would do tuna fish or our story. After a while, people just sort of decided that everything is out to get you in one way or another."

He said McCaw considered comparing risks in its messages, but decided it did not want to say that anything was dangerous. "We kind of ditched that," said Wolfenbarger, "and decided to promote the facts that the phones are safe, that we had extensive research to prove it, that we are concerned about the safety of our customers, and that we are going to study this issue for a long time."

AT&T and McCaw Cellular Communications merged in 1995; Cellular One became AT&T Wireless Services.

REFERENCES

Cheek, M. (1991, May 25). Student apologizes for AIDS rumor about eatery. *The Stuart News*, p. 1.

Cutting it close. (1994, September 21). *Burrelles Transcripts* of "Dateline NBC," No. 129.

Goleman, D. (1991, June 4). Anatomy of a rumor: It flies on fear. *New York Times*, p. C1.

Just talk into the curtains. (1994, November 28). *Newsweek, CXXIV*, p. 76.

Kaye, S. D. (1993). Taking stock of cellular. *U.S. News & World Report, 114*, 85.

Knight-Ridder News Service. (1991, May 10). Chain denies AIDS rumors. *Denver Post*, p. 18A.

Long, P. (1991, May 25). Student apologizes for spreading rumor about restaurant. *The Miami Herald*, p. 1B.

McDermott, M. I. (1991, July). Vicious rumors in Brooklyn. *Food and Beverage Marketing*, pp. 10–11.

Reeder, J. (1991, May 25). Student apologizes for restaurant rumor. *The Palm Beach Post*, p. 1.

Roan, S. (1994, September 11). Are TV talk shows undermining America's collective psyche? *Seattle Times*, p. L4.

Rottenberg, D. (1994, May). And that's the way it is. *American Journalism Review*, pp. 34–37.

Seitel, F. (1992). Glass in the baby food. *The Practice of Public Relations, Fifth Edition*. New York: Macmillan, p. 468.

Wiesendanger, B. (1994, June/July). Morley Safer versus public relations. *Public Relations Journal, 50*(6), 6.

Wilcox, D. L., Ault, P. H., & Agee, W. K. (1989). Procter and Gamble fights a rumor. *Public Relations Strategies and Tactics* (p. 620). New York: HarperCollins.

Managing a Crisis

WORKING WITH THE MEDIA

There are three possible results of a crisis: (1) The organization is put out of business, ruined, possibly sued, and key executives possibly charged with crimes. (2) The organization continues to exist, but has lost some image and respect in its publics' eyes, perhaps a great deal of financial position. (3) The organization, in a hard fought battle, has won a war of public opinion and is seen as favorably as before or perhaps more favorably.

Information about a crisis reaches publics by media more than by any other means. An organization may have to work very hard to get in the media during normal times. Its public relations (PR) personnel struggle to get a news release used. However, in a crisis, the media will find them.

It is true, unfortunately, that bad news sells. This has always been true. Even Shakespeare wrote about it in *Julius Caesar* when he said, "The evil men do lives after them. The good is oft interred with their bones." A negative story is deemed more newsworthy than a positive one; the media considers your positive news "puffery." To be honest, it probably is.

It is a PR practitioner's dream that every publication, every electronic news outlet will run prominent stories saying, "Company A is the greatest. Its products and services are the greatest, and it has the best PR people imaginable."

Plan, in advance, a system whereby you are notified of erupting crises. You want to be among the first, if not the first, to know. This can be done by instructing company telephone operators to reach you 24 hours a day, leaving a voice-mail greeting on your personal line during after hours and cultivating friendly relations with key personnel in the media, the fire department, the police—people who can notify you if they learn of a crisis affecting your organization.

Prevention

Warning signs, called prodromes, are crucial, since prevention is the best cure for a crisis. Strong community relations programs that get play in the media and endear your company to its publics will help this effort. Actually, ongoing proactive public relations programs of any kind are insurance policies against crises.

A strong people-centered, rather than a profit-centered corporate culture can also be a good prevention tool. Corporate culture is the way an organization does business, its unwritten but firmly established values.

The corporate culture must be established in such a way that honest, open communication is a basic value. Problems such as the CEO not speaking to the head of public relations and ignoring complaints from consumers can be a signal of an impending crisis that can be devastating. If employees are stressed from overburdening workloads, that, too, can ignite a crisis.

Before a crisis, or at the onset of a crisis, you must anticipate what the media needs and wants. Looking at the big picture, the media wants to sell newspapers and win ratings wars. In the 1990s, the media gives the public what it wants to know rather than what it needs to know. There is a fine line between news and entertainment, and crises make for entertaining news. The public is perceived to enjoy watching, reading about, uncovering, and hanging organizations, companies, and individuals that *might* have done harm to people, or even worse, to animals.

Never say "No comment!" To the public, refusing to comment appears to be an admission of hiding information or even guilt. If you have not responded, the public does not hear your side. They conclude, "Company X refused to comment, therefore it must have done something terrible." If there is some legal reason for not revealing certain information, explain this as much as possible and promise to reveal the information at a specific time. Do all you can to have the information at that time.

Do not assume that the story will go away. The media can do their stories without you. It can build its cases against the organization, "the bad guy," through talking to disgruntled employees, volunteers, customers, and more interestingly, to disgruntled former employees, former volunteers, and former customers.

It can use computer files and call up long-forgotten problems and mistakes and, in a few seconds, regurgitate them and place them before the eyes and ears of the public. The people thus hear the negative story.

Carl Bernstein (1994), who with Bob Woodward, investigated the Watergate crisis for *The Washington Post*, said, "There are always people, if you work hard enough, who will want to tell the truth." In other words, do not wage a war with an enemy who buys ink by the barrel, paper by the ton, and controls the airwaves.

What will the media want to know?

What happened?
Were there any deaths or injuries?
What is the extent of the damage?
Is there a danger of future injuries or damage?
Why did it happen?
Who or what is responsible?
What is being done about it?
When will it be over?
Has it happened before?
Were there any warning signs of the problem?

If your organization has erred, it is usually better to reveal the mistake at once, apologize, and make amends. The story may end right away as long as the crisis itself is not continuing. Cover-ups make a crisis persist. Whether your company has erred or not, do all you can to get control of the situation as much as possible and as soon as possible. When you release your own bad news, you decrease the likelihood of rumor, supposition, half-truths, and misinformation.

If the disaster or crisis has already resulted in injuries or deaths, or if there is a threat to the safety or well-being of groups or individuals, talk to the media immediately and indicate that you are looking into the situation, that you "just found out five minutes ago." This way, the media representative, while realizing the crucial aspect of the problem, also realizes that you, the company, care about people, and you understand the media's demands. It may buy you an ally.

If the situation is not urgent (and be certain of this), it is advisable to look into the situation, to make attempts to fully understand, and to have answers prepared for the media.

If the media calls you first and you are not aware of the crisis, do not rattle on without knowing details. Ask if you can call back in a few minutes, saying frankly, "I need to find out what's going on." Get the facts. Call the reporter back at the appointed time. Communicate.

Remember the media and the public are entitled to have the facts. The idea is to help provide the media, in its coverage, with a minimum of criticism of the organization or company.

The goal is to keep or get the public trust through the media. The media needs you for information for interesting stories. Your organization needs

the media to communicate with the public en masse. If this symbiotic relationship is kept in mind, the public relations professional will be in a more
proactive position during a crisis. He or she will feel more in control of the
organization's own bad news.

The spirit of cooperation must be established. In a crisis, there are three
responses to a media request:

1. We know and here's all the information.
2. We don't know everything at this time. Here's what we know. We'll
   find out more and let you know.
3. We have no idea, but we'll find out and tell you.

Give the media access to the material it needs: backgrounders, statistics,
photos, and spokespersons.

Spokespersons

Identify the *primary* spokesperson, who in a crisis is not usually the head
of public relations. One primary spokesperson reduces the possibility of a
conflict about statements or organizational values and explanations. Speaking with one voice is more crucial in a crisis than during normal operations.

The CEO is considered by most public relations professionals to be the
spokesperson of choice during a crisis, especially if people have been injured, if there is danger of physical harm or if there are millions of dollars
in damage.

The CEO has the most credibility as a true representative of the company,
as a person who has and will make decisions and is believed to actually
speak for the company. If the company has a heart, it is the CEO's.

Alternate spokespersons should be selected if the primary spokesperson
is not available. Supportive spokespersons, people who can speak authori-
tatively on technical subjects, are frequently of value too. As an example,
if patrons of a restaurant get food poisoning, a physician might be a supportive spokesperson to tell the public about symptoms and treatments.

News Conferences

If a news conference is warranted and can be arranged swiftly, call one. Be
certain to have a prepared statement read in total and distributed to the
media. This assists you in setting the tone for the rest of the session.

Spokespersons, whether the CEO, other top executives, experts, or public
relations professionals, should have major talking points. Also called key
messages and speaking points, these talking points are one or two sentence
summaries used to remind you of messages you want to be sure to get

across to the public. They can be details of the crisis or positive information about the company.

Positive information may include the company's safety record, safety procedures, evacuation procedures, and any information that says, "We are very concerned; we care."

The Pepsi Company, as well as some of its local bottlers, during the crisis in which consumers claimed to find hypodermic syringes in cans, released to the media their canning process (see chap. 5, Case 8). After the public learned of the bottler's precise and cautious procedures, it was difficult to imagine how the syringes could have been placed in the cans during the canning process. This information is credited with shortening the acute crisis stage.

Be mindful during a crisis, however, that it is not the time to bring up unrelated community service projects no matter how many you have. If lives are in jeopardy, no one wants to hear about how much money you give annually to scholarships.

Spokespersons should rehearse their statements and talking points to be comfortable with the information, comfortable in front of cameras, and so prepared that he or she need only glance occasionally at notes. Preferably before a crisis, practice sessions should be held in which employees fire the most difficult, rude, pointed questions at the spokespersons to simulate the actual crisis news conference.

Do not prolong the crisis by calling an unnecessary news conference or engaging in other activities that can keep the crisis in the news. During a crisis, you want to get off the news pages and broadcasts.

Ten Do's for Media Interviews

When dealing with the media or when being interviewed by the media, either in a one-on-one session or in a news conference, note the following "do's":

1. Do listen to the whole question before answering.
2. Do use everyday language, not the jargon of your business or profession. Even if the reporters use the jargon, use the common vernacular unless the interview is with a professional publication.
3. Do maintain an attitude showing you are calm, courteous, responsive, direct, positive, truthful, concerned, and, if necessary, repentant and apologetic.
4. Do understand the reporter's job. Respect deadlines. Return phone calls promptly.
5. Do be accessible and pleasant.

6. Do try to treat the reporter as a partner, an ally in maintaining or restoring your good image.

7. Do tell the truth, the whole truth. Misleading and omitting facts are also forms of lying. (Some seasoned public relations practitioners disagree with this position and even insist that no organization in a crisis is ever totally open and honest with the media or anyone else from the outside. This is an arguable point in a moot debate. Even these skeptics would agree that it is important to *appear* open and honest.)

8. Do look the reporter in the eye. In your response, address each reporter by name if possible.

9. Do use your crisis communications plan.

10. Do keep employees informed of the crisis. They may be unselected spokespersons.

Ten Do Not's for Media Interviews

At the same time, there are "do not's" when dealing with the media:

1. Do not be a wimp! Being concerned and empathetic does not mean that you must shake in your boots.

2. Do not guess or speculate. Either you know or you don't.

3. Do not get overly upset about being quoted out of context. Unless a complete transcript of your interview is printed, you are almost always quoted out of context to a degree. If the quote is completely wrong or libelous, that is another matter.

   Asking an editor for a retraction or correction is permissible if a reporter has been undoubtedly biased. A friendly letter delivered immediately and followed by a phone call is generally most effective. "Demanding" a retraction should usually be a lawyer's job as is a charge of libel. Proving libel is difficult and costly.

4. Do not play favorites with the media. Always favoring one newspaper or one television station is bad business. It can haunt you later.

5. Do not pull advertising because reporters are not cooperative. The purpose of advertising is not to help the newspaper anyway.

6. Do not consider your news release "golden." It will be changed, except in small-staffed newspapers. If it is written well with real news, you have done the best you can do.

7. Do not stick to a story if it has changed just to be consistent. The media realizes that things change. Johnson & Johnson experienced this during the Tylenol crisis. It had announced there was no cyanide in its plant. Then later, they discovered that there was. Johnson &

Johnson's public relations staff told the media the truth. No publication made a big deal over it.

8. Do not be trapped into predicting the future.

9. Do not wear sunglasses or chew gum.

10. Do not smoke—unless you are in a place such as Winston-Salem, North Carolina, where the economy is based on cigarette sales and smoking is a way of life.

Trick Questions

A media critic once said, "Being interviewed is like playing Russian roulette. You never know which question will kill you." Sometimes reporters get away from the five W's. Metzler (1994) identified several types of questions that they have been known to ask. Metzler's questions as well as a few others follow:

Speculative questions begin with "if." These can be embarrassing and dangerous. For example, a reporter may ask, "If the earthquake had happened during business hours, how many people would have been killed or injured?"

Leading questions imply that the reporter already has the answer; you are merely to verify it. An example is, "You do agree that the company could have avoided this tragedy, right?"

Loaded questions are designed to cause an emotional response. Some television reporters thrive on these because responses to them make for more exciting videos. A sample might be, "Isn't it true that you knew there was asbestos in the ceiling and failed to do anything about it?" In the case of a loaded question, rephrase it and answer your own question. You could say, "Do you mean, '*Were* we aware there was asbestos?' No, we were not."

Naive questions are those showing that the reporter has not done any homework and does not know what to ask. An example is, "Tell me what does your company do?" Reporters who ask such questions are dangerous because they desperately need a story. Make sure they get the story you want them to have. Give them media materials such as press kits, backgrounders, biographies, and news releases.

False questions have inaccurate details in them. If the question is, "You fired half of your over-50 staff, right?", the public relations professional, knowing the statistic is wrong, could counter with, "No, only 40%," not realizing the reporter was aiming for that information all along. She or he never thought it was 50%; it was a figure taken out of the air.

The know-it-all question says, "We have the story. I just need a few wrap-up facts." The reporter may want the PR practitioner to merely confirm an already formed viewpoint. He or she may not have a story at all, but wants you to release only "the dirt."

Silence is actually the absence of questioning. This method is used by a reporter who wants the PR practitioner to spill his guts, to talk on and on. Many people tend to babble because there is silence. Remember, silence is the reporter's problem, not yours. Use this opportunity to reinforce positive statements.

Accusatory questions are designed to force you to blame others. Never fall for this. Maintain your innocence if that is true, but do not cast blame on others.

Multiple-part questions can be confusing to you as well as to the public. Ask which part you should answer first. Then answer each part as a separate question. Also, you can say, "I'll take the first part first." Then, restate it yourself the way you want to answer it. Do the same for subsequent parts.

Jargonistic questions are those in which technical words or professional jargon are used. In response, use everyday language. Jargon builds a barrier between you and the publics and erodes trust.

Chummy questions are those in which the reporter, pretending to be the PR practitioner's buddy, may ask, "Say, Pal, off the record, what do you think . . ." The PR practitioner should remember that nothing is off the record and should be careful about supposed friendships.

Labeling questions are efforts to make issues negative or simplistic by seeming to ask for clarity. The PR practitioner should not accept the reporter's labels unless they are fair and accurate. An example could be, "Would you call the company's work schedule 'stressful'?"

Good-bye questions, at the end of an interview, may even come after the camera or tape recorder is turned off. The reporter shakes hands and says, "By the way, . . ." Watch out for what follows. The interview is not necessarily over.

Remember—in all questioning—be positive, concerned, empathetic, and apologetic, if necessary.

Reporters

A discussion of trick questions may seem to be a warning that the reporter is some kind of sinister creature whose life goal is to harass public relations practitioners. This is usually not true.

There are jerks in every profession—including the media. If you stay in public relations long enough, you will come in contact with them. Know who the jerks and enemies are. Sometimes you can work around them by dealing with other reporters. Sometimes you should follow advice given by the late President John F. Kennedy, "Forgive your enemies, but never forget their names."

There are also those journalists who apparently make themselves feel better by labeling public relations people "flacks." There is no reason to take any of this to heart. Reporters do not hate your profession. In fact, many of them seek public relations jobs.

Newspaper and broadcast journalists in record numbers are becoming public relations practitioners. Newspapers are failing. Most on-the-air personnel in television cannot expect to have jobs in their middle age. Everyone is downsizing. Public relations is the fastest growing communications profession, largely because of crises and the forecast of crises to come.

Reporters are frequently not knowledgeable of or interested in the issue they cover. The story may have been assigned to them. Their task is to bring back an interesting story, a story that will get them a promotion, a raise, an extended contract, an Emmy, or a Peabody. They want their stories prominently displayed in the newspaper or at the top of the broadcast. They want to get this award-winning story back before the deadline. All would rather that you would assist them than be an obstacle to them. Obstacles make awards and raises difficult to obtain.

After reporters have filed stories, they are frequently finished with them. They do not write the newspaper headlines that you hate—that's the job of editors you rarely, if ever, see. Sometimes, if the story continues, other reporters will be assigned.

If you are breaking the news of a crisis or a development in a crisis, and you know of reporters who are known to be fair and accurate, you can sometimes give them your story. This does not mean that if you dislike the reporter assigned, you can call another. This works only when no other reporters are involved, and you cannot be charged with playing favorites (see Case 5, United Way of King County).

Choosing the news outlet for bad news is not an unheard of or new tactic. When death was imminent, physicians attending King George V injected lethal doses of drugs into his veins in order to hasten his death. They wanted him to die in time to make the deadlines of *The London Times,* a morning newspaper considered more responsible than what was, in 1936, considered the "inferior news organs of the afternoon."

The two cases that follow resulted from the scandal that grew from charges of overspending on behalf of the CEO of United Way of America. Both cases describe how public relations personnel handled the media during the crisis. The methods are distinctly different—one is totally reactive and the other a bit more proactive. The public relations staff, at least, managed to arrange how it would reveal information.

CASE 4: UNITED WAY OF AMERICA AND THE CEO

One day in the Washington, DC area, in late November 1991, Tony DeCristofaro, then Director of Public Relations, United Way of America (UWA), was told by the organization's Senior Vice President of Communications, Sunshine J. Overkamp, APR, that she had learned from Lisle Carter, UWA's general counsel, that *The Washington Post* was collecting information for a story on United Way.

Persuading the media to do a story on your organization and its "wonderfulness" is a real high in the public relations world. However, when you "hear" through connections and various routes that a major newspaper such as *The Washington Post* is collecting information and has not called you, it is time to worry. True, the story could still be full of praise for the organization. It is also true, and more probable, that just the opposite is the case. DeCristofaro recalls Overcamp saying at one point, "The world as we know it is changing."

It seems that Charles Shepard, a respected investigative journalist for *The Washington Post,* was digging for information for a story on William Aramony, United Way's CEO for 22 years. Shepard, while a reporter at *The Charlotte Observer* in the 1980s, had uncovered the PTL scandal and subsequently won the Pulitzer Prize for his work.

"He's a very good reporter," said DeCristofaro, drawing out the "r" in "very" in admiration of the man who made his job difficult for several months.

Neither DeCristofaro nor anyone else on the staff called Shepherd. "For two months," he said, "we got reports from many people whom he was calling regarding the subjects, types of questions, and directions he was taking." There were indications that there were problems, if not a scandal, brewing.

First, let us look at United Way and its place in the minds of Americans. United Way is perhaps the largest fund-raising organization in the United States. At the time, there were 2,100 United Ways raising more than $3 billion dollars each year for 40,000 large and small charitable organizations.

Most of United Way's money is donated by campaigns in corporations and plants, raised by American workers with hard-earned salaries—men and women on assembly lines, laborers, clerks and secretaries, and blue collar workers as well as white collar workers—all individuals who believe in the spirit of helping others, and they had helped others for years through United Way. A scandal at United Way could not only damage the organization itself, but all the charities served by United Way, all United Way's employees, and the spirit of giving itself. If you cannot trust United Way, can you trust anybody?

The internal investigation continued, and Shepard at *The Washington Post* continued his investigation too. Said DeCristofaro, "Charlie would send over 20 questions he wanted responses to. I would give the questions to the lawyers, to Sunshine, to Hill and Knowlton, and to Aramony. We would work on finding facts. I had much more intense contact with Bill than I normally had."

On February 16, Shepard's article ran in *The Washington Post.* The article, on the front page, bore the headline "Perks, Privileges and Power in a Nonprofit World." It praised Aramony's brilliance, creativity, and how he "transformed the United Way movement into the most successful and respected charity in the country" (Shepard, 1992, February 16, p. A1).

It also mentioned his $463,000 yearly salary, his hiring of friends and relatives, his using nearly half a million dollars to buy and decorate a New York apartment primarily for his use, and his chauffeured automobiles. It mentioned more than $100,000 spent for first-class air travel, sometimes on the prestigious and expensive Concorde, and sometimes first-class travel with friends to Super Bowl games (Shepard, 1992, February 16, p. A1).

Still, the extensive article was basically balanced with glowing references and criticism. The Associated Press did not immediately pick it up, neither did other newspapers.

At the same time, the nation's people were not in the mood to accept scandals or inequities of any kind. PTL, Oliver North, and John Sununu were fresh in the news; they were not even history yet. The recession had affected the public to the point that it did not accept inflated or lavish salaries, perks, or extravagances of corporate executives of large profit-making companies.

This climate made it unreasonable to expect a distrustful public to trust Mr. Aramony, considering that he worked for a nonprofit-making organization raising money for charities, and that 85% of those funds were to go to the charities with 15% to fund-raising and necessary expenses pertaining to the fund-raising.

The 14-member executive committee of United Way, headed by Dr. LaSalle Leffal, Department of Medicine, Howard University, hired Hill and Knowlton as public relations counsel in early December, 1991. Hill and Knowlton advised the organization to conduct an internal investigation. It engaged IGI, Inc. (Investigative Group International) headed by Terry Lenzner. Lenzner had been a lead investigator for the senate investigative committee for the Watergate scandal. These PR counsels and attorneys put their heads together and formed a United Way crisis team with three leaders:

1. Senior Vice President of Communications
2. Associate Counsel
3. Senior Vice President—Administration

The team helped IGI gather documents for its investigation and worked with Aramony. "It devised a plan," said DeCristofaro, "on what we were to do, what would be said, and when it would be made public." The plan was based on the organization's original crisis plan, but geared to the specific incident.

In mid-January 1992, DeCristofaro had his first direct link to *The Washington Post*. "Charlie called and we spoke about information he wanted— mostly documents—and he wanted an interview with Bill Aramony," said DeCristofaro. He complied with all requests.

In early February a preliminary report of the internal investigation showed that nothing illegal was revealed. It did find some incidents of nepotism and matters of questionable ethics and poor judgment. United Way knew it would have an image problem, but that didn't affect the attitudes of the members of the executive committee toward Mr. Aramony. After all, Aramony had worked tirelessly on behalf of the organization since he was a volunteer 40 years before. The committee gave him a vote of confidence.

DeCristofaro remembered, "When the story was mild, there was great relief. Nevertheless, I knew there was another story. It was just a matter of when the second story would come out." (Reporter Shepard expresses his point of view of United Way's public relation's reponse in Fig. 4.1.)

The public relations department at UWA had a crisis plan concerned with issues of funding controversies, employee issues, embezzlement, local issues, and salaries, including Aramony's. Staff members were aware of Aramony's salary; such information was available for the public. Many reporters already knew about it, but it had never been printed in a newspaper as widely read as *The Washington Post*. DeCristofaro said that he and other staff members, however, did not know of Aramony's lavish spending until the crisis erupted.

On Feb. 20, a second article ran in the *Post* written by Charles Babcock. The headline was "3 Large Locals Ask United Way About President's Spending" (Babcock, 1992, February 20, p. A6).

The New York Times reported what *The Washington Post* had previously reported and stressed the still incomplete investigation—at Aramony's request—as well as the unanimous vote of confidence given Aramony by the executive committee of the board. The article also indicated that some local United Ways might withhold dues, pending the outcome of the investigation (Teltsch, 1992, February 24, p. A12).

The following day, the day Shepard's second article ran, the onslaught of the media began, involving CNN, Associated Press, NBC, CBS, ABC, Jack Anderson's "Washington Merry Go Round" syndicated column, as well as other local media such as *Regardies*, a local magazine.

The employees and local United Ways were learning about the problem from the media, not from the organization. Members wanted United Way out of the media. They wanted the issue dead. "Everything we did created media attention," DeCristofaro said, "and we couldn't say the charges were not true." He said his department, although it had little information to disseminate, tried to get the facts out as soon as possible to the following publics:

1. membership,
2. employees, and the
3. general public.

DeCristofaro said, "We had to furnish the member organizations with updates on what was going on. We asked the AT&T sales department and received a cut-rate price on faxing. True, AT&T's chairperson was on our board and he may have had some influence, but it was not an automatic privilege."

From the Reporter's Point of View

BY CHARLES E. SHEPARD
WASHINGTON POST

I began researching the United Way of America/Bill Aramony story in mid-November, and we published our first article in mid-February. It was clear from the start that the allegations I was investigating posed a serious threat both to Bill Aramony's career and reputation and to the image of the organization he had run for so many years. Some of those I sought out in my reporting said they were hesitant to talk to a reporter about Aramony for fear that they might harm the United Way movement.

United Way's initial response was guarded; after arriving at the United Way of America to interview Aramony—a process I expected to take several hours—I was told I would get just half an hour. The Post was determined to press for answers to all questions, and we continued, after that truncated interview, to pose questions through United Way of America's communications staff. I was also eventually given a second session with Aramony.

Despite the curious reluctance to make Aramony available for any length of time, United Way of America showed an admirable commitment to answering my many rounds of follow-up questions. That commitment seemed to strengthen as the board grew to recognize that its problem was with Aramony and not an overzealous reporter. At first, it seemed to me, the board just didn't grasp what Aramony had done.

United Way's Tony DeCristofaro, whom I had never met before, displayed a remarkable mix of patience, intelligence, and good cheer in collecting my follow-up questions and coming back promptly with all the answers he could get. I have tremendous admiration for Tony's integrity and abilities, and we've since become good friends. I consider him a model for skilled communications work— he masters the material, makes reporters feel at ease with his friendliness, humor and candor, and comes across as someone who genuinely wants to get the answers the reporter needs.

FIG. 4.1. Charles Shepard, the reporter from *The Washington Post* whose investigative story on Aramony uncovered the crisis, speaks about the United Way's public relations response.

Still, it was difficult. The publics were upset. There still was not enough information to reveal. The internal investigation was still incomplete. The PR staff members were faxing copies of *The Washington Post* articles to United Way chapters because newspapers in other cities did not cover the situation as extensively as the *Post*. The local media were using stories from the Associated Press, and sometimes those stories were only excerpts. Editorial cartoons, as in Fig. 4.2, were plentiful.

The board members of United Way and top executives of corporations such as IBM, Sears, American Express, and J.C. Penney were not willing to

FIG. 4.2. The United Way crisis was tailor-made for editorial cartoonists, like Chris Britt, of the *News Tribune* (March 1, 1992), Tacoma, Washington.

be interviewed. The board members would say to the media, "Call the PR department."

Typically, as in any crisis, the media wanted the PR department to be a conduit—to provide them immediately with information and access to people they *wanted* to interview, people with the power to make decisions and speak for the company. However, no one with those qualifications would agree to go on "NBC Nightly News" or "Nightline." Ted Koppel had to say, "United Way would not comment." That was not a good PR move.

Aramony was certainly not talking. The chairman of the board is said to have literally ducked into the men's room to evade the media. DeCristofaro said he could only speculate about why they refused. It is logical that these people would not want to associate their companies with the scandal. However, it did not look good to have no spokesperson.

DeCristofaro felt that the board members might have quelled the journalistic fervor during the time that the public relations department was hampered. "The investigation was incomplete. We couldn't get the story out of the press. We were unable to say Aramony was gone."

On February 26, a satellite teleconference was scheduled for local agencies of United Way. On the podium was Aramony; Leffal; and Berl Bernhard, an outside general counsel. They answered questions from the audiences and basically revealed what was going on. Member agencies were assured that everything would be revealed.

On that day, Aramony tendered his resignation, but the executive board asked him to stay to maintain stability in the transition. The board accepted his resignation, which was to be effective when a successor had been named. However, he refused to apologize. According to DeCristofaro, he made a watered-down statement that was entirely too qualified. He dodged the apology and left the public to draw its own conclusions. "Public perception is all we get," said DeCristofaro.

Public perception is the total problem. Not very many years ago, the expression "rank has its privileges" was accepted by those with or without rank or privileges. That is not so in the 1990s. The public is extremely critical of any excesses. The people who make United Way function, the contributors who helped to pay for Aramony's extravagances have never, and perhaps never will, have the experience of riding first-class in an airplane.

In a country with few wimps, some outspoken individual or group can be expected to object vociferously if any organization supported by public funds is suspected of spending those funds unwisely. Moreover, if the public fails to speak out, the media of the 1990s, in anticipation of the public's interests and concerns, rarely misses making the case known to the masses.

The public and the member agencies of United Way were furious that Aramony was still there after the story appeared in *The Washington Post*. The investigation continued. DeCristofaro said that all through the crisis they saw Aramony in the office daily. He reportedly said, "It's you PR people who are making this a crisis."

The day after the teleconference, Aramony left, and his longtime friend and deputy, Alan S. Cooper, became acting president. After Aramony's departure, the newspaper articles and editorials continued urging United Way of America to regain the public trust. An editorial in *The Christian Science Monitor*, read, "The task before the United Way will be to establish good business principles and restore confidence in the integrity of charities" (*The Christian Science Monitor*, 1992, March 3, p. 20).

Ken Dam took over as temporary head of the organization. Cooper stayed on in his regular position as senior vice president and then retired in June.

Six weeks passed after the first article came out, and the investigation was complete on April 2. The report was ready on April 3. The United Way public relations department made a deal with Federal Express similar to the one it had with AT&T and sent the report to all its member organizations. There were complaints after two classes of publics developed—those who received documents overnight and those who received it later. DeCristofaro said, "It was a matter of budget and numbers. We sent overnight mail to 1,000 cities, and the rest got it in two days." Naturally, the "rest" felt like unappreciated stepchildren.

The report, according to a DeCristofaro news release, contained "a series of recommendations concerning personnel practices, executive compensations and benefits, corporate governance, and affiliated organizations."

On June 25, the board was restructured. On August 26, former Peace Corps Director, Elaine Chao, was named CEO. "Once the leadership changed, things looked up," said DeCristofaro.

Before the crisis, 2,100 member organizations, such as United Way of King County, took their own actions. Some withheld dues. Others quit. Some stayed on. Income dropped by 80%. With income so seriously down, a third of the staff at headquarters was cut in June, 1992. Some left voluntarily when offered a severance program.

In April, 1995, a federal jury found Aramony guilty of 25 counts of fraud, conspiracy, and money laundering. Recovery progressed although the budget was considerably decreased. Chao and United Way set out to win back the member organizations that resigned to win back the public trust. A plan was put into place to restructure programs and staff to begin what Chao called "a new era of strength." She wanted to make the national organization strong by making the local chapters stronger and more effective.

The acute stage of the crisis lasted about six months. The anniversary stories were written. The ashes continued to smolder.

During the crisis, DeCristofaro's annual review came up, and he was promoted to Vice-President, Communications. He resigned from United Way in May, 1993, and he became Vice-President, Media, Hill and Knowlton, in Washington, DC. Overcamp also resigned.

In September 1994, Aramony was charged by an Alexandria, Virginia, federal grand jury with defrauding the United Way of America of more than a million dollars, including personal gifts to his girlfriend and personal vacations.

CASE 5: UNITED WAY OF KING COUNTY AND THE CEO

There are over 2,200 local United Way organizations in the United States. Each is autonomous with its own governing body and board of trustees. The money raised by each local organization remains in the community it serves to support charitable organizations.

Most local United Way organizations pay optional dues to national headquarters, United Way of America, based in Washington, DC. In return for dues, organizations receive information resources, research on giving, marketing and advertising materials, and volunteer training.

At the time of the crisis, the dues formula was .5% of money raised in campaigns. Organizations that choose not to pay dues still benefit from operating under the long-respected United Way name. Thanks to William

Aramony's relationships with corporations such as J. C. Penney and IBM, local United Ways receive monetary donations as well as equipment and supplies.

Diane Turner was director of public relations for United Way of King County, Washington, during the crisis. She reported to Clydean Zuckerman, vice president of marketing and community resources, who reported to chief professional officer (CPO) Roberta Van der Voort. Turner, explaining the United Way headquarters said, "It's like the headquarters of a trade union. Each local is separate, and headquarters is a unifying element."

Turner learned about the brewing problem in December, 1991. "We heard a rumbling," she said, "of an investigative reporter from *The Washington Post* looking into the internal workings of United Way of America. At that time, we speculated that it resulted from the actions of a disgruntled employee or group of employees. Bill Aramony had done so much good work over so many years that this will go away. So, let's keep quiet and watch and see."

In the late 1980s, the Washington State United Way had weathered a crisis when member agency Planned Parenthood began offering abortion services against the wishes of the Roman Catholic Church and against United Way's rules of not contributing to agencies that perform medical services. Planned Parenthood subsequently resigned from United Way.

Also, in the late 1980s, another crisis occurred when Roberta van der Voort was hired as chief professional officer (CPO) at a salary of $139,000. Critics felt the salary was too high. The United Way board disagreed. It felt she deserved every dime, that no respected or self-respecting chief executive would work for less. Therefore, during her first year in the position, various corporations chipped in to get her the salary from sources other than the United Way budget.

The Washington Post Article

The Washington Post article began the crisis for United Way of America, but the King County agency did not yet feel the sting of it. "Even when the article came out (on February 16), we felt it was still possible that it might go away. We knew about Aramony's salary (it was public record), but the extravagance was news to us," said Turner.

United Way of King County decided to withhold dues paid to United way of America until the investigation was completed. This was communicated to the publics, including the media (see Fig. 4.3 and Fig. 4.4).

On March 1, Diane Turner was scheduled for surgery, and Lynnann Marcellus, who had recently worked as an account executive for Hill & Knowlton, was hired as public information manager. "I found out when I came out of the anesthesia that the rumors about the investigation and Aramony were persisting," said Turner.

GENERAL TALKING POINTS
REGARDING UNITED WAY OF AMERICA
APRIL 2, 1992

United Way of King County is continuing to maintain its
position to delay the decision on paying dues until our
Board of Directors has an opportunity to review the report
in its entirety.

We are sensitive to the financial situation at United Way of
America, but at the same time, have **a responsibility to the**
citizens here in King County.

Our concerns regarding United Way of America revolve around
tighter financial management, greater accountability, and
increased responsiveness to local United Ways.

It's important to remember that **United Way of King County**
is separate from United Way of America. Our volunteer Board
of Directors sets local policy **and** makes decisions based on
what we feel is in the best interests of the citizens of
King County.

Regardless of the outcome of this report, the residents of
King County can feel good about the fact that **roughly 90**
cents out of every dollar they give stay here, and directly
serves this community.

FIG. 4.3. Talking points spokespersons for United Way of King County used
when being questioned by publics about the Aramony crisis. (Printed with
permission of United Way of King County.)

When she returned to work in late March, Hill & Knowlton, their pro
bono public relations counsel, was already working with the PR staff. "When
you are in a crisis situation, you frequently need an outside perspective,
someone who can calmly see the bigger picture of where the crisis can lead
and how to contain it," said Turner. Much of Hill & Knowlton's work was
consultation and advice, not the day to day tasks of a public relations department. It was up to the regular public relations staff to communicate with
volunteers, media, and staff.

United Way of King County made an early strategic decision that pervaded
the entire crisis. Said Turner, "Our first strategy was that we decided to
separate ourselves from United Way of America, to communicate to our
publics that we are autonomous, not a chapter of a larger organization.

United Way units withhold dues in 'high living' probe

BY DEBERA CARLTON HARRELL
P-I REPORTER

Less than a week after reported allegations that United Way of America officials indulge in high living, local United Way officials say they will withhold dues until an investigation is complete.

United Way groups statewide said this week they are deeply concerned about public perceptions that United Way of America President William Aramony is paid too much and lives in luxury off public donations while supposedly working for the needy.

"We operate in the public trust, and any issue like this that could potentially impact the level of human services in King County is something that concerns us very much," said Lynann Marcellis, manager of public information for United Way of King County.

According to a recent report in the Washington Post, United Way of America paid $20,000 in one year for chauffeur services in New York for Aramony, who earns $463,000 a year. Aramony also flew on the Concorde jet to speed up his schedule, the Post said.

The Post and syndicated columnist Jack Anderson also reported last week that, under Aramony, United Way has created several spin-off companies—one of them run by Aramony's son, Robert—that have engaged in questionable business activities.

One of the companies, reportedly given $900,000 by United Way, used about $430,000 to buy and decorate a New York City condominium for the senior Aramony's use, it was reported.

The King County chapter, like most other agencies throughout the state, will delay paying quarterly dues to United Way of America—usually less than 1 percent of total money raised—until local boards have a chance to review the outcome of the nationally ordered investigation.

An independent first will conduct the investigation, which is expected to take about a month.

Ron Gibbs, executive director of United Ways of Washington State, said the state's 26 United Way charities raised $80.5 million last year.

Marcellis said last year's quarterly dues from the King County chapter to United Way of America were $417,000, generated by 1990 donations of $42.4 million. Last year, the local agency raised $45.5 million in donations and pledges. The dues go for services such as training, staff support, education, governmental lobbying and advertising, chapter officials said.

Bill Dodge, executive director of United Way of Chelan and Douglas Counties in Wenatchee, said his chapter will also defer dues payments "until we get some kind of good news."

He added, "We're very concerned he [Aramony] has access to a condominium and a chauffeur when—my God—we're trying to get money from great-aunt Martha who's willing to give us $25 and is on Social Security."

Warren Dobbs, executive director of United Way of Spokane County, said his group, too, will defer dues payments, until the investigation is complete.

Chapter directors throughout the state, while wary of defending Aramony outright, credited him with improving the level of training and education services, raising advertising revenues and unifying agencies across the nation.

They cite, for example, Aramony's recent coup in negotiating with the National Football League for $45 million in free public service advertising for United Way.

Chapter directors stressed that local United Way organizations, while paying dues, operate independently of the national group, which does no fund raising.

"They're just allegations at this point," Marcellis said. "People locally should understand that when they donate funds to United Way locally, 90 percent of every dollar goes back into the community to people who need health and human services right here."

FIG. 4.4. This February 21, 1992 article by Debera Carlton Harrell, a reporter for the *Seattle Post-Intelligencer*, was one of several she had written that convinced the United Way public relations department that she be "selected" to be the reporter who was first given the United Way announcement of cutting dues to United Way of America. Other media received the story by PR Newswire. The public relations department counted on the likelihood that Harrell's story would be complete and accurate and that other reporters would read her article in the morning newspaper and garner much of the information they needed from it. This eliminated a media frenzy over the announcement. (Reprinted courtesy of the *Seattle Post-Intelligencer*)

"It was a matter of 'It's them, not us!' "

United Way Publics

The organization had four external publics and five internal publics with which to communicate. Each public had a different interest in the crisis.

1. *National media*—seeking a sidebar to the controversy, wanted to know how the crisis affected nonprofit organizations in King County, Washington, serviced by United Way as compared to how nonprofits in other cities were affected.
2. *Contributors*—wanted to know how their monies were being spent or whether they should donate elsewhere.
3. *Charitable agencies*—wanted to know if they could count on United Way donations.
4. *Local media*—wanted the same kind of information as the national media, but focused on the local angle; they wanted to know where United Way of King County stood on the issue, what it planned to do.
5. *Volunteers*—needed to know where they stood, whether their work was worthwhile, whether the organization was corrupt throughout.
6. *Employees*—needed to know about their jobs. If donations were decreased, jobs would certainly be lost.
7. *Board of trustees*—needed to know what its position was in order to guide the organization to normalcy.
8. *Other United Way organizations*—wanted to know how other cities were coping with the crisis.
9. *United Way of America staff members at headquarters*—wanted to know about actions of local United Ways to determine how their actions would impact them.

National Media

"Our second strategy," said Turner, "was to tell our own bad news. We wanted to establish openness and honesty." They set up editorial boards with their board chair, the CPO, PR personnel, and editors from key media in the city.

United Way of King County, which includes Seattle, raises more money per capita than agencies in other cities of comparable size, according to Turner. Also, she said, the organization had earned national notice in the fund-raising community with its unique and successful Donor Choice Program in which people have the ability to choose which charitable institutions will receive their contributions.

It is likely that this reputation and the publicity surrounding previous United Way crises were the reasons the King County organization was called on by the national media. "Nightline" and "Prime Time Live" on ABC-TV, *Newsweek*, and *The New York Times* all began to telephone, requesting information and on-camera interviews.

The national press did not call about the investigation as it did to De-Cristofaro. It called to ask how the controversy would affect the local United Ways, whether donations would decrease, or whether charities benefited by United Way would suffer. At first, some attempt was made to respond to these requests, but eventually the decision was made to decline participation in the national response in order to focus on the local issue.

Turner said, "What was the advantage to respond to an issue for which we were not responsible?" Ultimately, the organization felt that the local publics would decide the fate of United Way of King County; therefore, time and energy should be spent on communicating with these publics.

Contributors and Charities

"We were concerned," said Turner, "about the charities and the people in the community who need help from United Way. If contributions drop, our assistance to 147 member and affiliated organizations would also drop. Through this entire process we stressed 'separate' and 'autonomous.' At one point in March, all we did was take calls from the press and the angry public."

Turner and Marcellus took most of the calls. Many were contributors through company employee plans who wanted to withdraw their funds. Some were people associated with member agencies that benefit from United Way funds. Others were merely concerned citizens.

"Our position," she said, "was to listen to callers and agree with their anger and concern. We used phrases like 'We are equally horrified,' and 'We feel the same as you.' Then we would go on to say that we are separate; we will continue to serve the public as usual. We made it clear that we were victims, not villains" (see Fig. 4.3).

Local Media

The local media was especially important because it would get the messages out to all the other publics, including future contributors and irate contributors who do not complain, but just cancel their donations.

The local media wanted to know how funds were spent. United Way opened its doors and accounting books, giving explanations for every ex-

penditure. If necessary, the finance manager answered questions. No room
was left for misinterpretation.

During the crisis, strategic statements, as well as questions and answers,
were prepared in advance. It was determined that van der Voort, the CPO,
would not be the spokesperson because she had worked for United Way
of America, and that connection might be construed to cause questions and
further problems. Amazingly, no reporters made the connection on their
own.

The first vice chairperson of the volunteer board, Karl Guelich, was named
spokesperson. The Hill & Knowlton counsels, all the vice presidents, the
chairman of the board, the CPO, and the PR staff trained Guelich to talk to
the media. He was given the prepared list of questions and answers, speaking
points, background information, and the latest news articles.

Two four-hour sessions were held in which every question or situation
imaginable was thrown at the spokesperson for practice in responding in
interviews for television, radio, and newspapers.

The local media was extremely interested in the controversy. One newspaper had four or more reporters calling about the story. Turner said, "It
became overwhelming to tell the same information to various people at the
same newspaper who didn't seem to know about each other. None of them
had background information, so we had to tell them the entire story. So,
finally, we telephoned the assignment editor and asked for one reporter."

Internal Publics

The crisis communications team, in late April, developed a Rapid Communications Plan. Its purpose was to communicate pertinent information to the
most important constituents. In addition to Turner, the CPO and each vice
president participated in the determination of what publics would get what
information, how they would get it, and who would be responsible for the
communication. Board members and executive directors were either faxed
or phoned. Volunteers received communications by mail.

In May, after the investigation of headquarters was released, the board
discussed whether to sever the connection to United Way of America completely and finally, or make a less drastic decision.

Going public with a decision of such importance would usually warrant
a news conference, but Wiley Brooks, president of the Wiley Brooks public
relations firm specializing in damage control, suggested to Turner that a
news conference would be a circus and that they should try announcing
through one reporter.

"We are familiar with the local reporters," said Turner. "We know their
investigative style, their interests, how they write, their reputations." Turner
spoke of one reporter at the *Seattle Times* as being the type who would

have insisted upon bringing up past crises and problems with the local United Way.

The decision to use a reporter at the other Seattle metropolitan daily was based on the fact that United Way wanted the story to break in the morning. The board meeting was expected to culminate in the evening so the story could be given to *The Seattle Post-Intelligencer* (called "the PI"), a morning newspaper.

"We selected Debera Carleton Harrell, a reporter at the PI whom we knew to be accurate and fair. She had covered a story about us before and nothing, such as a quote, was taken out of context."

Harrell came into the office around 11 a.m. and interviewed Zuckerman to get background information, a chronology of events, and other pertinent facts. Then she agreed to wait until after the board meeting to get final details. For hours the board hashed over the decision. The meeting ended around 7 p.m., and a news release was immediately prepared.

The board determined that the alliance of United Way of King County with United Way of America was of value in dollars and cents. Its collaborations with corporations (ironically brought about by Aramony) were crucial, as were its research information and its training of volunteers.

Nevertheless, the board did decide to cut the dues it paid to the national organization by half. The balance of the funds would be used to fund summer youth programs in the city of Seattle and in King County. This decision was spurred by the Los Angeles riots. The board wanted to do its part to avoid a similar disturbance in the Seattle area.

Harrell returned about 8 p.m. after the board made its decision, and a news release was drafted for all the media. In addition to receiving the news release, she interviewed Guelich, the vice chairperson of the board and the spokesperson. Then she returned to her office to write the story for the morning edition of the newspaper (see Figs. 4.4 and 4.5).

In the meantime, the PR staff distributed the news release to PR Newswire and to all the publics (see Fig. 4.6). It was timed so that by the time the media got the wire, the office was closed for the evening. "What we knew," said Turner, "was that all the media writes from the morning paper, the *Post-Intelligencer,* and the rest of the media had to get that first information from Debera's story, the story we knew would be accurate. It was a matter of timing and a way of organizing, not controlling, our own news."

The next morning there were numerous media calls, but all of the reporters had Harrell's story in the *Seattle Post-Intelligencer* as a foundation. All of the background was in it, so there was no need to ask United Way spokespersons for that information.

The story stirred another round of calls from the national media. The public relations staff stuck to their guns. The disseminated message was,

From the Reporter's Point of View

BY DEBERA CARLTON HERRELL
SEATTLE POST-INTELLIGENCER

I don't recall all the particulars of the story, but I do remember that I was trying to track United Way's decision closely after we ran the national stories about the Aramony brouhaha. So I kept in touch with the United Way locally, and knew when they were planning to make a decision on whether or not to withhold dues.

I wasn't aware they "selected" me. I do recall pestering them so a decision did not slip through the cracks of my multi-story-juggling schedule. I think they valued the fact that I was informed about social services in the community, since I had covered such services extensively, and that I knew how important it was not to misrepresent United Way's role locally. Important, not in an image sense (although I'm sure that was part of their criteria), but with respect to potential community impacts because of the broad range of services United Way funds.

They set their own meeting schedule; I hope it's very clear that the time of their meeting wasn't negotiated in any way. No deals were cut, although it was to our advantage that United Way chose to have a night meeting, because we're a morning paper (although it could have worked against us if the meeting had gone too late, since our first edition copy deadline is 8:30 p.m.). Since it wasn't a public meeting, I had no choice but to wait until the meeting had ended and the decision made before turning in the story.

If I recall correctly, and this would make sense given other similar scenarios, United Way suggested and I agreed to come in earlier in the day to interview Board members for background. This worked well for me because it meant I would have time to digest the information and even pre-write some of the story (it's called "A-matter" and we do this, whenever possible, for election coverage and other late-breaking stories) then top it up with the final decision on deadline.

I might emphasize that we were not interested in making United Way look good or bad. Our interest was in the news itself–how the local organization would respond to a crisis at the national level. It was important to us to make readers clear about what the relationship was–and wasn't–between the local United Way and the United Way of America. And because even United Way of King County had taken some past "hits" in media accounts (executive salary and Planned Parenthood controversies), we considered it in the public interest for readers to know about agency accountability and where their donations were going given the current state of affairs.

FIG. 4.5. Debera Carlton Harrell, the *Seattle Post-Intelligencer* reporter who was "invited" to be the first reporter to receive the United Way announcement about dues paid United Way of America, speaks about her role in the crisis.

News Release

United Way
of King County

107 Cherry St.
Seattle, WA 98104-2223
Phone (206) 461-3700

For Immediate Release

MAY 5, 1992

Contact: Diane Turner
(office) 461-3867
(home) 838-6914

King County United Way and United Way of America

King County United Way Votes to Continue Some Financial Support for
National Association

SEATTLE — The King County United Way board of directors voted today to allocate half
the amount it would normally have contributed to the national United Way association
for 1992, and affirmed its support for the need for a national association. The remainder
of the money will be used to provide needed services in the local community.

"The board's decision today reflects concern over the apparent excess and
mismanagement that have occurred at the national association, but the national board of
governors has demonstrated a desire and an ability to put the organization back on
course and to provide its very valuable services," said King County United Way Board
Chair-Elect Karl Guelich. "It is our belief that the new national association will operate
more economically, but that it needs time and resources to work toward that end. We
hope that this funding level will provide the encouragement it needs to make necessary
changes, keeping it in business long enough for it to do so."

The board will allocate $214,000 to the national association and also authorized
spending an additional $65,000 to purchase services from national. Another $149,000
that would have been paid as dues will be used for employment programs for at-risk
youth, working in collaboration with its affiliated agencies, the business community, the
City of Seattle and other municipalities.

Guelich said the local organization has spent the past three months re-evaluating its
relationship with the national office. "While the recent revelations have caused us to take
a critical eye to our relationship, the intense re-assessment also has renewed our
appreciation for some of the benefits that we get from the national association," he said.

Guelich, managing partner of the Seattle office of Ernst & Young CPAs, also credited the
national board of governors with taking "swift, significant and appropriate action" by
publicly sharing and approving the recommendations of a special independent
investigative report. "The national board of governors has been taking the kind of
positive steps needed to restore confidence in the national office."

continued on back

 S-823

FIG. 4.6. News release distributed by Diane Turner about the decision of
United Way of King County to cut its dues to United Way of America. (Printed
with permission of United Way of King County.)

King County United Way and United Way of America

PAGE 2

The national board immediately removed United Way of America President William Aramony from the payroll and named Kenneth W. Dam, an IBM vice president and former Deputy Secretary of State, interim president and chief executive officer. A search committee, which includes local United Way volunteers and staff, was established to find a new chief executive. King County United Way President Roberta van der Voort serves on that committee.

The local United Way had withheld its 1992 dues pending today's decision. Responses from other United Way local organizations throughout the country have varied dramatically, from providing no support to the national association to paying national dues in full.

Local United Way organizations, such as King County United Way, are entirely independent from the national organization. However, they traditionally pay dues to the national association and in return receive a number of services and other benefits, including national advertising, staff and volunteer training and national fundraising support.

Guelich pointed out some of the specific steps taken by the national office since the controversy erupted:

- It apologized to local United Ways for the problems created by the Aramony administration.

- It approved implementation of all 45 recommendations made by the investigating team, including that local United Ways will be represented on the national board of governors, which wasn't previously the case.

- It opened regular communication with local United Ways to help determine how the national association can be made more accountable.

King County United Way is a local, autonomous organization run by a volunteer board of 48 directors with representatives from private companies, government, banks, the media, law, medicine, education and churches. For more than 70 years, the King County United Way has raised money for local health and human services agencies. In 1991, the local United Way organization raised $45.6 million, which was distributed to 761 agencies. Those agencies helped one in three people living in King County. Apart from state and federal governments, King County United Way is the largest financial supporter of health and social services in the county.

"More and more people need help today, and there are fewer dollars to go around," said Guelich. "We hope that the thousands of people who have given so devotedly to King County United Way in the past will recognize that we are run independently from national and that 89 cents of every dollar they give goes directly to help those in need in our community.

"We sincerely hope that our action today reveals to our many donors that we are continuing to be accountable for their contributions. Too many people in our county depend on the United Way and they would suffer if the public lost confidence in us and reduced their contributions. That would be tragic."

FIG. 4.6.   (*Continued*)

said Turner, "Our job is to raise money locally and to help organizations in our community. The investigation did not change that."

Turner reported, "At no point was there a headline that accused United Way of King County of anything. There were no negative stories about United Way of King County. We had successfully separated ourselves from the controversy plaguing the national office. Our campaign the September following Aramony's resignation was one of the top 10 most successful United Way campaigns in the United States, though we raised less than the previous year." Turner resigned from United Way of King County in December, 1992.

When Aramony was indicted in 1994, Beau Fong, who had been named communications manager of United Way of King County after the crisis, said that the organization was prepared to answer questions from the media. "We had position papers if needed, but we were not called," she said. "We still get calls from contributors asking about our connection to the United Way of America. It gives us the opportunity to tell them how the local organization operates. The money raised here, stays here."

CASE 6: AMERICAN RED CROSS AND THE RAPID RESPONSE TEAM

Fires, earthquakes, floods, hurricanes, explosions: The American Red Cross exists because there are and will be major disasters and crises. Whenever a major disaster strikes, the Red Cross is there—and so is the news media.

There are more than 2,000 Red Cross chapters in the United States and few have public affairs staffs. Other personnel, such as directors or other officers, learn to do double duty in performing public relations tasks. Some have backgrounds in public relations-public affairs; others learn by doing.

When disaster strikes in any location, members of the nearest Red Cross chapter, including members or volunteers performing public affairs chores, rush to the scene. There is also a pool of persons specially trained in public affairs, many of them volunteers, who may be dispatched by Red Cross Disaster Services Human Resources to sites of disasters to handle the media.

Frequently, there are so many reporters and camera crews—both local and national—trying to get individual interviews and special sound bites, that a one- or two-person Red Cross staff at a disaster site would be hard-pressed to accommodate everybody.

"There's a very small window of opportunity to connect with the national media," said Giselle McAuliffe, team coordinator of the Red Cross' recently developed Rapid Response Team. "The attention span of the media, and apparently the public, is shorter than it used to be. The Red Cross feels it must let people all over the nation know it is on the job helping people. When people see us on the scene, they realize a situation is critical and they are more likely to make donations to help the victims."

The national media provides the most effective way of getting that message to the vast American public, who, according to McAuliffe, are generous and caring people when they see others victimized by diasters.

The Rapid Response Team, not to be confused with the other groups of public affairs specialists dispatched to disaster sites by headquarters, consists of 12 leading public affairs experts. Their mission is to rush to the site of the disaster, locate the members of the *national* news media, provide them with information about help being given to victims (by the Red Cross as well as others), and assist them with interviews and footage of the scene.

The 12 members of the team and their manager are the following:

Giselle McAuliffe: team manager, External Communication, National Headquarters.

Doug Allen; International Services, National headquarters.

Dave Giroux; Public Relations, Dane County chapter, Madison, Wisconsin.

George Chitty; Orange County Chapter, Santa Ana, California.

Beth Heinrich; Public Affairs, Oregon Trail chapter, Portland, Oregon.

Don Madsen; Public Affairs, McCaw Cellular, Bellevue, Washington.

Lisa Matchette; Public Relations, Microsoft Corporation.

Margaret McCarthy; formerly with Media Relations, national headquarters and the International Federation of Red Cross and Red Crescent Societies, Geneva.

Rod McWilliams; Communications, Greater Milwaukee chapter.

Felix Perez; Media Relations, National headquarters.

Hope Tuttle; Communications, Seattle-King County chapter.

Cara Wade; Public Relations, Baptist Medical Systems.

Claudia Ward; Communications, Central Arizona chapter, Phoenix.

Cara Wade is a former Red Cross employee. Don Madsen and Lisa Matchette are former television news reporters whose current employers, in partnership with the Red Cross, promise to release employees for so many hours (or days) each year.

When a Rapid Response Team member handles the national media, the local public affairs person or expert dispatched from headquarters is free to more effectively handle local media demands.

Hope Tuttle, who helped design the program and is also a member of the team, said, "I know my local media. I know the needs of Channel 5 News. I don't have to look it up to know what channels have 11 o'clock news and what channels have 10 o'clock news. We don't have to sit down and gather this information.

"So, even though I have experience with national and international news crews, it makes sense that in my area, I will handle local media, and the team member from another city will handle the national media."

Each of the 12 team members is on call for two separate months each year. When called to a disaster, each serves up to 10 days. If there is still a need after 10 days, another team member—also on-call that month—is rushed to the site.

When a disaster occurs, or sometimes prior to an expected disaster (like a hurricane), the Operations Center at headquarters makes an assessment of whether assistance is needed. If so, Rapid Response Team manager Giselle McAuliffe notifies the team member on call, who should always have a bag packed and ready to go.

"I was alerted at 8 a.m. and my flight was at noon," said Tuttle who went to Houston on October 16, 1994, when floods devastated sections of Texas. In her bag, already in the trunk of her car, she had packed essential clothing, a portable radio, a flashlight, paper, pens, a backpack filled with office supplies, maps, and Red Cross signs.

The Red Cross also furnished shirts, warm sweatshirts, and jackets with the easily identifiable Red Cross patches prominently displayed on the backs and left fronts. The team members bought beige pants to make a complete uniform that was easy for persons to recognize at the site and to spot on television footage.

A national agreement with AT&T and McCaw Cellular arranged for cellular phones, air time, and mobile phone stations at shelters for free calls.

Tuttle was not the first to be dispatched. When heavy rains from Tropical Storm Alberto caused widespread disaster in Georgia, Rapid Response Team member Claudia Ward was on the scene for eight days. Beth Henrich, flown in to replace her, was there five days. Then Tuttle, accompanied by Madsen who was in training, stayed in Houston for 6 days.

Following are their day-by-day summaries of this innovative public relations program:

Ward

Tuesday, July 5

"I received my 'Go Kit' from headquarters. The Red Cross patches were not sewn on the shirts."

Wednesday, July 6

"I got the call at 9:30 a.m. to fly to Georgia. A volunteer took the shirts home, and within one hour she returned with the job completed. At 2:30 p.m., I took a flight out of Phoenix, arrived in Atlanta, and checked into my hotel at 10:30 p.m."

Thursday, July 7

"After being briefed by Metropolitan Atlanta chapter personnel and conferring with Giselle, I drove to Macon and found no national media crews there, so I continued on to Albany where the Flint River was flooding. Radio stations warned motorists to get off the roads. There were no hotel rooms, so I sought a Red Cross shelter.

"Radio stations were announcing where the shelters were, but I didn't know my way around town and roadblocks made travel challenging. I flagged down a sheriff's officer, who directed me to the shelter. I was greeted by 200 shelterees, all of whom were wide awake at 11 p.m. I had a 5:10 a.m. live interview scheduled with ABC radio. I was set up in a room with volunteers from the Marines so that when my alarm went off at 4:30 a.m., I wouldn't disturb everyone. Needless to say, I only got two hours of sleep because the Marines were hauling in cots and assembling them."

Friday, July 8

"After several attempts due to sporadic communications, I connected with ABC radio and went live from my car using the cell(ular) phone in darkness. My next challenge was to get to the other side of the river where the major media were. I was told that roads were closed and it was impossible, but some local folks directed me to some backroads, and I accomplished my mission. Next, I went on the lookout for media crews and the Red Cross operations center. A local volunteer arranged for me to stay in a room with another volunteer."

Saturday, July 9

"I learned that some national crews were in town and that others would be arriving over the weekend. I realized that another one or two RRT members could have been used on the scene. The perfect scenario would have been for one of us to make calls and another to scout the media.

"I attended a briefing at 3 p.m. with officials and the media. Throughout the weekend, I worked with the field producer of 'Good Morning America,' convincing her that Debbie Blanton, executive director of the local Red Cross chapter and a victim of the flood, was *the* person to be interviewed." (Debbie lost her house in the flood.)

Sunday, July 10

"I arranged for the field producer to go with Debbie's husband by boat to see what was left of their home. That sold the field producer on the shoot, and the field producer persuaded her producer in New York. A live shot was scheduled for Monday at 8:09 a.m. in front of the Red Cross shelter. At 7:30 p.m., NBC "Today" expressed interest in interviewing a victim at 7:09 a.m., Monday. At 10:30 p.m., Debbie agreed to that interview, too."

Monday, July 11

"Both live shots went off as planned. The ABC crew had some technical difficulties up until 30 seconds prior to the live interview. Debbie was also interviewed by *USA Today* (see Fig. 4.7) and CBS radio, and she did an excellent job of conveying the Red Cross story given her own circumstances.

"Media attention was gravitating to Bainbridge, southwest of Albany. At 5 p.m. it was decided that I was to go there. The Civil Air Patrol made

---

'Never been anything like this'

BY TOM WATSON
AND MARIA PUENTE
USA TODAY

ALBANY, Ga. – The flood of '94 struck with devastating swiftness, bringing scenes of horror: Towns suddenly divided by raging waters. Babies trapped in a car, swept to their deaths. Open coffins floating in the streets. A historic college completely under water.

It's not over yet. The waters that have flooded central-western Georgia for the past six days – killing at least 28 people – are headed down river fast toward southwest Georgia's towns.

And steady rain was still coming down on the misery here Sunday night.

"This is getting progressively worse, says the Rev. Carey Robertson at Albany's Redeemer First Assembly of God Church, where 315 people are sleeping on cots.

Stunned Georgians have never seen anything like this. In fact, devastating flooding is so rare here, most people don't have flood insurance because they can't get it.

Says Georgia Emergency Management Agency spokesman Ken Davis: "There's never been anything like this on record to date. It's eligible for a 1-in-500-year category."

"They say we don't live in a flood zone," says Debbie Blanton, head of the Albany Red Cross, who lost her home and cars when the waters rose. "You think you're prepared – but we didn't ever anticipate such a disaster."

FIG. 4.7. Excerpt of a lengthy news story in *USA Today* (July 12, 1994) about the Georgia floods. Note the results of the PR practitioner's suggestion that reporters interview an American Red Cross employee.

special arrangements to fly me there. The flight was beneficial because I was able to give more colorful descriptions of the damage in subsequent interviews. A Red Cross volunteer picked me up at the airport. This time, I was surprised to get a hotel room. I got a ride with a volunteer who went out of his way to take me to the hotel 20 miles from the shelter. It was 11:30 p.m."

Tuesday, July 12

"I completed a 7 a.m. interview with *America's Talking Network* and then hitched a ride back to town with Red Cross workers. I hung Red Cross signs throughout the shelter as media arrived for interviews. A public affairs representative from a Florida chapter arrived, and I was grateful. Difficulty in connecting my cellular phone and a lack of phones at the shelter forced me to use a local volunteer's office phone. While I was making calls, a local volunteer rushed in and told me a TV station wanted to do an interview with a Red Cross spokesperson in 15 minutes. I rushed to the Flint River to do the live interview with the NBC affiliate from Albany, New York.

"I needed to get back to Albany, Georgia, where my rental car was, that evening, then back to Atlanta on Wednesday to fly to Phoenix. The Civil Air Patrol had said it couldn't get me there because the President of the United States was flying in, but they called back and told me they could pick me up at 7:30 p.m."

Wednesday, July 13

"I met with a reporter for the *U.S. News and World Report* at the Albany airport before driving back to Atlanta and the flight home. I briefed Beth Heinrich by phone. We never saw each other."

Heinrich

Tuesday, July 12

"I received a page to go to Bainbridge, Georgia, at 2 p.m. made travel arrangements, and attempted to contact Claudia Ward on the scene."

Wednesday, July 13

"I arrived in Bainbridge at 10 a.m. and located the Red Cross shelter. "Good Morning America" was already there. I began working with the crew to increase Red Cross coverage in the story and to highlight the need for financial support. I then talked to the Red Cross staff to get an idea of what national media had been in the area and where they had been filming. Many of the crews had gone to Albany to cover the President's visit. I began calling the media on the national list. I provided updates on Red Cross relief operations to radio networks and tried to get mobile numbers for the TV crews and print reporters. I also followed up on media requests left by Claudia, provided update information, and coordinated interviews. I pitched angles and provided information for a *Washington Post* reporter who came to the shelter, then had dinner with her, at which time I provided additional background information."

Thursday, July 14

"I started calling down the national media list early in the morning with the updated numbers. Headquarters notified me that CNN coverage was a priority, so I identified and located CNN crews and pitched ideas.

"National media returned to the area and were concentrated at the marina. At the marina, I assisted with standups. A CNN crew arrived, and I provided a tour and residents to interview, and I was interviewed. An ABC crew came by and interviewed for feeds to affiliates and for the evening news."

Friday, July 15

"I talked to assignment desks. Headquarters decided that the major national media interest had passed. I made a final call down the media list, provided updated statistics, and made travel arrangements for the following day."

Saturday, July 16

"I returned home."

Tuttle

Tuesday, Oct. 18

"I got the call at 8:30 a.m. and made plane reservations for Dave Madsen and myself. I tried six rental car places before I could get a car in Houston, then flew out of Seattle at 1 p.m. and met Houston personnel for a briefing at 10 p.m. I handled two media calls immediately. We opted to stay in Houston because of its convenient proximity."

Wednesday, October 19

"We attended the job morning meeting to get overview of Red Cross activity and gap areas. We visited two shelters where Governor Richards was supposed to be. She was at the second one, so was Secretary Cisneros.

"There was only local media there, so we drove around the flooded areas and had a successful UPI-radio interview, giving them scenes as we were driving.

"We left contact numbers with ABC-TV and CNN."

Thursday, October 20

"We met CNN at the site of a highway under water, taped an interview for later use, and stayed a hour or more so that we could do a live shot for the noon news. The oil fires in the river were a big story. New shelters and new evacuations were the action. We met FX Cable at the shelter and worked with them for two hours for a live broadcast the next morning on their *Breakfast Time* show. The program is very MTVish and needed visuals and movement, yet they were tied to one spot with the satellite truck. We checked and found that all national television crews had left, but radio still had high interest, especially NPR, Mutual, and Standard News."

Friday, October 21

"FX wanted devastation shots, but also wanted a positive angle of people doing something. This was a challenge for the Red Cross at 6 a.m. because people were sleeping in the shelters, and the service centers hadn't opened yet.

"For three cut-ins to regular programs, we were able to interview a home-owner whose house had been under water, talk about the Red Cross helping victims with physical and mental recovery (a big issue), and see a high school service group shoveling out the house. In the shot, as I talked to the talent, the Red Cross patch on my back was very visible.

"We contacted all network news desks to let them know that we were available. Don was released."

Saturday, October 22

"We announced that shelters were closing except in Beaumont where the flood had not crested, and returned home on a 6 p.m. flight.

"Tuttle said that having Madsen present was essential to the success in Texas and recommended that two public affairs people be sent each time. Red Cross competed with the upcoming elections for coverage. 'The governor's race between Bush and Richards was understandable, but not to our best interests. They would come to shelters and do the kissing babies and shaking hands thing,' said Tuttle."

" 'It was a very exciting experience,' continued Tuttle who had been with the Red Cross for more than 15 years, 5 as a volunteer and more than 10 as an employee. He said, 'I really believe in what the Red Cross does, so no matter how demanding my job is, I find it exciting. I don't know if I could show the same enthusiasm if I were doing public relations for floor wax.' "

WORKING WITH LAWYERS

Legal counsel suggests that a client in a crisis should remain silent. "No comment" is the preferred response. "Anything you say can be used against you in a court of law."

Public relations counsel suggests that a client be open and honest. "No comment" is perceived by the public as an admission of guilt. "Anything you do not say can be used against you in the court of public opinion."

Courts of law proclaim that a person is innocent until proven guilty, whereas the court of public opinion often declares a person guilty until proven innocent. When you lose in the court of public opinion, you lose your reputation, your good name, and your positive image—the very qualities that make for success.

The public believes that an innocent man can answer a policeman's questions without having a lawyer present. After all, what does he have to hide? The public also believes that this innocent man can go on the stand and plead his innocence, showing all his emotion in the process.

The lawyer frequently advises clients to refrain from all these actions and reactions. Some lawyers think public relations is publicity, getting somebody's name in the newspaper. Others know what public relations really is, but choose to ignore it.

Sometimes lawyers may be cautious at a time when public relations professionals feel that open communication with publics is crucial to the positive conclusions of a crisis. The lawyer's job, after all, is to protect the company, organization, or individual. Sometimes public relations counsel may not anticipate threats to their own clients.

Lawyers know that any person with knowledge of the organization in trouble can be called into court for depositions against his or her client. Sometimes communication with publics can put the organization in a perilous situation.

A case of law versus public relations occurred in 1985 when a Delta Airlines plane crashed. After the crash, high-ranking Delta employees showed great concern for survivors and families of victims. They sent flowers. They visited. They attended funerals. The company's public relations effort was so impressive that many lawsuits were avoided.

Nevertheless, some lawsuits were filed. In court, the lawyers for Delta were said to be vicious. They accused one plaintiff of being a cocaine addict and of having a child that was not her husband's. They inferred that another victim, a homosexual, might have died soon of AIDS.

There were irate news stories calling the company a "monster." At least one newspaper wrote prominently of the airline's "Jekyll–Hyde" behavior.

Delta was upset over the negative publicity, but its lawyers insisted that they had to introduce relevant information, acquired legitimately, to fight money-hungry personal-injury lawyers (Thompson & Hess, 1986). A solution to such a dilemma is a bond of mutual understanding, a marriage of the two fields, a careful balance.

The legal profession is much much older than recognized public relations (although, in effect, public relations has been practiced for centuries). As a profession, public relations is moving towards a day when professionals will have to pass a kind of "bar exam." The Accreditation in Public Relations (APR) credentialing offered by the Public Relations Society of America is a step towards this certification.

Lawyers are becoming more adept at public relations. The American Bar Association provides media training for its primary officers. They realize that a defendant can win a battle in a court of law and lose it in the court of public opinion.

In Chapter 3, Case 2, a crisis team consisting of public relations and legal representation for Snapps restaurant in Florida made a decision not to prosecute or sue a teenager who had helped spread a rumor that caused a drastic loss of business. The members of the team decided that although they might win a victory in court, it would be a case of winning the battle and losing the war.

The teenager had apologized publicly and had behaved properly repentant. The public might have boycotted the restaurant had further action been taken against her. It would have been a matter of the powerful restaurant ruining the life of a well-meaning child who made a mistake in judgment.

Conversely, a defendant can lose in court and win in the battle of public opinion. Sometimes the latter offers a brighter future.

This was the case with Mayor Marion Barry of Washington, DC. He was convicted of a drug charge, served his time in prison, then returned to the nation's capital to resume his political career. Although few voters doubted that Barry was a drug-user, there was resounding resentment of the way he was "set up" for the arrest. Anger at those responsible for the "set-up" also translated into support in the court of public opinion for Barry, who was reelected mayor again in 1994.

More and more, lawyers are influencing public opinion outside the courtroom. We have seen the results of this when a lawyer representing a prisoner convicted of a serious crime has persuaded "60 Minutes" or "20/20" to tell a story of the innocence of the client. The lawyer may have exhausted all legal channels or his client may have been unable to afford the legal battle. An effective letter to the television news magazine changed everything.

The public is often not aware of how the news magazine series got the story; true public relations professionals (or lawyers performing public relations acts) are more concerned about their client's needs than they are about promoting their own visibility.

The televised account of a poor, innocent man imprisoned for years for a crime he did not commit is a public relations tool that appeals to the court of public opinion. In many cases, on the basis of the convincing television profile, viewers appeal to courts for new trials, or judges grant new trials in anticipation of public reaction. Sometimes the prisoner is subsequently freed.

Public relations was used in the trials of Leona Helmsley and William Kennedy Smith. In a similar way the White House, under former President Bush, conducted a successful public relations campaign to get public approval and, therefore, congressional approval of the nomination of Clarence Thomas to the Supreme Court.

Lawyers on both sides of the O.J. Simpson murder trial began to influence public opinion as soon as he was arrested. Nearly everyone in America had an opinion about whether he was innocent or guilty before the trial even started. That opinion was swayed considerably by lawyers on both sides, as well as by the media using the case to sell newspapers and win broadcast ratings.

The necessity of merging law and public relations leads to an even greater need for precrisis planning by representatives in both fields.

Effective crisis planning sets up scenarios for each type of crisis likely to affect the organization. Different strategies and tactics should be outlined for each kind of crisis. Examples are reflected in such statements as these: "If there is a loss of life, we will . . ."; "If there is no loss of life, we will . . ."; "If the media is unaware of the story, we will . . ."; "If the media is pressing, we will . . . ."

Lawyers who have not adapted to public relations procedures should be advised that some key stakeholders can be dealt with personally; others get their impression through the media.

Refusing to talk to reporters will not make the story go away. Reporters will get the story—and it may not be the story you want to be told.

The board of directors of the United Way of America were not aware of this when its CEO, William Aramony, was accused of excessive spending (see chap. 4, Case 4). No one on the board would talk to the media. The story started as a brief section in a long, basically flattering article about Aramony in one newspaper. Editors of other newspapers read the article, focused only on the negative aspects, and soon public perceptions of misuse were nationwide.

The media is a conduit to the public. The public rarely has any real evidence, at least not as much as juries in courtrooms do. Even though the public is well aware that reporters err, people still tend to believe what they see and read. They make decisions on sound bites and column inches selected and written by reporters.

The court of law and the court of public opinion will remain crucial institutions deciding the fate of individuals, groups, organizations, and corporations. Both the public relations professional and the lawyer must learn to put clients in the best light in both courts to gain the best possible outcome from a crisis.

Discussion of Cases

During the United Way of America crisis, the local Seattle agency, when making an important announcement about its position in the case, selected a newspaper and a reporter to get the story. The reporter finished gathering information and interviewing the spokesperson in the late evening for the next morning's edition. At that point, the agency distributed a news release with the basic information to all other media and closed shop for the night.

That release was received by media outlets that night. However, further questioning of United Way could not occur until morning.

By morning, the selected reporter's accurate, fair story was on the stands. As a matter of routine, all media personnel read the morning newspaper.

Other media outlets got details and a thorough understanding of the issue from the newspaper story. This tactic resulted in fewer calls and fewer questions to the agency, thus eliminating the frenzy sometimes associated with coverage of crisis developments. It also set the tone for the story, which was covered well and accurately by the other media outlets. The afternoon newspaper and the electronic media had their story as soon as possible, considering that the information was not ready until the evening prior.

As media trends, technology, procedures, and techniques change, organizations must adapt to the change as the American Red Cross has with its Rapid Response Team.

The team was developed because "the window of opportunity" for getting national news coverage is shorter than it was in previous years. Where the media can arrange to be present at the site of a news-making event in a short period of time, public relations professionals, if they find it necessary to get their messages across, will have to adjust to travel demands also.

REFERENCES

Babcock, C. R. (1992, February 20). *The Washington Post,* p. A6.
Bernstein, C. (1994, August 9). Interview on CBS "This Morning."
Metzler, K. (1994, March). Shooting it out with the media. *Hemispheres Magazine,* pp. 51–53.
Shepard, C. (1992, February 16). Perks, privileges and power in a nonprofit world. *The Washington Post,* p. A1.
Teltsch, K. (1992, February 24). United Way awaits inquiry on its president's practices. *New York Times,* p. A7, A12.
Thompson, T., & Hess, J. (1986, November 15). Delta accused of Jekyl–Hyde behavior in wake of crash. *Atlanta Constitution,* pp. 1, 10.

Product Tampering Crises

Often the first step in overcoming a crisis is determining what the crisis is. When manufacturers face crises resulting from claims made against their products, they must determine whether the crisis is a result of product failure or of product tampering.

Perrier, trusted and respected for its pure, fresh, sparkling water from a French spring, learned in 1990 that its scare was actually a problem with its product. There were traces of a cancer-causing substance called benzene found in a bottle of Perrier. It turned out to be not a case of malicious tampering; a faulty filter was to blame.

The company recalled 70 million bottles, suffered a loss of sales amounting to $40 million, and paid an additional $25 million (in advertising, public relations, etc.) to recover from the crisis (Barton, 1993).

Pillsbury in 1984 found ethylene dibromide (EDB), also a carcinogen, in several of its products made from grains. It pulled the products. The move cost millions of dollars in lost sales and staff hours of employees, not to mention embarrassment (Baskin & Aronoff, 1993).

Beech-Nut was also caught in an embarrassing situation when the federal government charged that it defrauded and misled consumers by saying it made 100% apple juice when actually the juice contained various other products, but very little apple juice.

Beech-Nut paid a $2 million fine and $140,000 in investigative costs to the Food and Drug Administration. Beech-Nut's president pleaded guilty to ten counts of violating the Food, Drug, and Cosmetic Act and was given a $100,000 fine as well as a period of probation (Seitel, 1992).

The Beech-Nut, Pillsbury, and Perrier cases turned out to be "product failure" crises. Such crises can be quite different from "product tampering" crises as we shall see from two cases: Johnson & Johnson and the Tylenol Murders (1982), and Diet Pepsi and Syringes-in-the-Can (1993).

CASE 7: JOHNSON & JOHNSON
AND THE TYLENOL MURDERS

Before September 30, 1982, manufacturers felt that if they made a good product and dealt fairly with consumers, retailers, employees, and other publics, they could maintain a positive image and be considered consumer-friendly, a good company with which to do business.

Johnson & Johnson was one of those companies. It was an old and trusted company. With 165 companies in 53 countries throughout the world, it made baby products: baby powder, lotions, shampoos, cotton swabs, adhesive bandages, surgical instruments, Reach toothbrushes, Ortho-Novum birth control pills, and pharmaceuticals in the World Health Organization list of essential drugs. Johnson & Johnson was a household name.

The corporation also had a positive image among its employees. It was listed as one of the 100 best places to work.

There was a company credo written by the son of the company's founder in the 1940s. The credo said that the company had four responsibilities in the following order of priority: (1) to the consumer, (2) to employees, (3) to the communities, and (4) to stockholders.

The company also had continually good relationships with the media. Little did it realize just how crucial those relationships would be.

September 30 began like any other workday at the headquarters in New Brunswick, New Jersey. Then a fateful telephone call came in that turned the workday into one of many from hell for the executives.

A reporter from the *Chicago Sun-Times* telephoned a public relations staff member asking questions such as, "How long has Tylenol been on the market?" and "What is Tylenol's share of the market?"

The reporter did not know why he was asked to prepare background information on Tylenol. The Johnson & Johnson staffer, who then alerted most of the department, thought the call was a bit strange and reported it to Public Relations Director, Robert Kniffin. Kniffin called Arthur Quilty, an Executive Committee member who had responsibility for McNeil Consumer Products Corporation, a subsidiary. Quilty alerted James Burke, CEO. The reporter later called back and explained there had been reported deaths from the intake of Extra-Strength Tylenol.

Corporate Vice President, Lawrence Foster, who was on vacation, called in, as was his daily practice, and when he learned what had happened, immediately returned to the office and took charge of the public relations activities.

The corporation had no specific crisis communications plan—few companies did at the time. It did have an emergency plan and call list for such incidents as plant fires. The first step was to notify the chain of command.

There was an immediate meeting in Burke's office with top executives, including Lawrence Foster, Head of Public Relations; David Clare, President and Chairman of Johnson & Johnson's executive committee; Joseph Chiesea, President of McNeil Consumer Products Company; and David Collins, Chairman of McNeil.

In that meeting, Foster dispatched Kniffin to McNeil's headquarters in nearby Fort Washington. Collins, who had been president of McNeil Pharmaceuticals and knew the subsidiary well, was sent to McNeil by Burke. This would actually have been the next step in a crisis communications plan—had there been such a plan.

The executives all say that it was a period of great fear. There were no warnings, no prodromes. Nothing like this had ever happened to them or any other company that provides products for human consumption. What was going on? Was there a psychopathic murderer in the plant?

When the story ran in the media, the public also was afraid. The very idea that you could take a capsule for a headache and die was terrorizing. People were saying, "I have a terrible headache, but I'm alive." Even consumers outside the Chicago area were afraid of Tylenol capsules, if not afraid of all over-the-counter pain medication.

Collins immediately set up a seven-member crisis team. The team's first task was to find out what sickness they were actually facing. Then they would determine how to go about the healing process.

The crisis team handled decisions in the area of communications and was in charge of all strategies and tactics. With Burke's approval, it decided to recall all Tylenol capsules from stores in the Chicago area.

The recalled batch was tested and two additional cyanide-laced capsules were discovered. Still, the team and company were uncertain of how the cyanide got into the capsules. It indeed hoped that the criminality was not in the company, but there was no certainty.

Johnson & Johnson had one over-riding priority:

"Warn the public."

The company did just that by being completely open and cooperative with the media in getting the news out.

Foster said he believes that three points marked the reason why Johnson & Johnson was successful in coping with the crisis:

1. It was open to the media.

2. It was willing to recall the product no matter what it meant to the company.
3. It appealed to the American sense of fair play and asked the public to trust the company.

Foster was responsible for the communications aspect of the crisis team's work. The team was concerned with aiding police and the FBI in finding the responsible party and in dealing with the Food and Drug Administration (FDA).

First, the crisis team identified its key publics:

1. consumers (through the media),
2. the medical profession,
3. employees and other internal groups, and
4. the Food and Drug Administration.

All were notified initially, and the team kept in touch with them throughout the crisis.

The first story was in the morning edition of the *Chicago Sun-Times* on October 1. The *Chicago Tribune* ran a story that same afternoon under a banner headline:

5 Deaths Tied to Pills
Fear Killer Put Cyanide in Tylenol

A study of the *Tribune*'s coverage reveals that the newspaper was as supportive of Johnson & Johnson as it could be in the telling of the bad news, especially considering the usual "in-your-face" coverage of crises in the 1990s. Two *Tribune* stories are shown in Figs. 5.1 and 5.2. The company's executives, the police, the FBI, and the newspapers knew from the start that the tampering could possibly have happened at the plant. Nevertheless, there was no insinuation of this in the *Tribune*.

The name Johnson & Johnson was not mentioned on page 1. In the continuation of the story on page 2, nearly buried in the middle of 12 column inches of copy was the following statement:

A spokesman for Johnson & Johnson, parent firm of the company that makes Tylenol, said Thursday evening his firm "launched an investigation this morning to track down the capsules."

The spokesman, Robert Andrews, and two other Johnson & Johnson officials met for an hour and a half with Elk Grove Village detectives and evidence technicians.

He said his firm is "collectively shocked." (Houston & Griffin, 1982, p. 2)

Other remedy may be safe,
but customers don't buy it

CHICAGO TRIBUNE

Dust is collecting on some drugstore shelves in the Chicago area, and people apparently are learning to live with headaches in the wake of last week's tragedy involving Extra Strength Tylenol laced with cyanide.

An informal survey of drugstores throughout the Chicago area showed that sales of most acetaminophen products have dropped while sales of aspirin have increased slightly. Acetaminophen is the nonaspirin substance used in Tylenol and other pain relievers.

"In general acetominophen products are not selling. Point blank. Done in. Dead. Aspirin products are picking up a bit, but the scare seems to have spread through the shelves," said pharmacist Paul Bablak of the Hinsdale Medical Center Pharmacy. "We're collecting a lot of dust on our shelves. People are scared, and you really can't blame them."

If the fear of cyanide poisoning can be measured by the still-packed medication shelves at drugstores, then the fever is spreading through the metropolitan area, several other pharmacists said.

"I think everybody's walking around with headaches," said Jerry Denny, a pharmacist at Family Pharmacy in west suburban La Grange. "All the acetaminophen products are just sitting on the shelves. Even generic acetaminophen is moving slowly."

The slow sales were found not only in smaller, private drugstores but also in chain stores. Jane Armstrong, director of consumer affairs for the Jewel Foods Co., which operates almost 200 Jewel grocery stores and Osco drugstores in the Chicago area, said, "It's too early to tell what's happening to other acetaminophen products. We have noticed an increase in aspirin sales, although it's not a groundswell at this point."

The results have been the same for major drug wholesalers in the area. Drug buyers from several large wholesalers said they expect orders to increase for aspirin and the substitute acetaminophen products once fear subsides, but they added that it is too soon to accurately measure the effect of the tragedy on drug sales.

FIG. 5.1. One of four news stories in the *Chicago Tribune* on October 1, 1982, the first day of news coverage of the crisis. Note that the story never mentions Johnson & Johnson. (Copyrighted Chicago Tribune Company. All rights reserved. Used with permission.)

Stores around nation pull Tylenol capsules

BY BARBARA MAHANEY
CHICAGO TRIBUNE

Stores nationwide quickly ordered personnel Thursday to strip their shelves of Extra-Strength Tylenol capsules and hospital spokesmen reported rashes of phone calls after cyanide-tainted capsules were linked in three deaths and possibly two others in suburban Chicago.

The nation's largest grocery chain, Safeway, in Oakland, Calif., ordered all stores to remove bottles of the over-the-counter pain killer in the 96,000-bottle lot-- MC 3000--which was recalled by McNeil Consumer Products Co., of Fort Washington, PA.

All 1,000 Revco Discount Drug Centers and 400 CVS pharmacies in New England pulled every bottle of Extra-Strength Tylenol. "We have pulled it off our shelves completely," said Bernie Thomas of Perry Drug Stores, Inc., which operated 124 stores in five states, including 98 in Michigan.

Meanwhile, poison centers and hospitals were reported swamped with thousands of calls from worried consumers, many of whom said they took Tylenol capsules from the recalled lot, but apparently suffered no ill effects.

"We've had questions ranging from 'Do you know anything about Tylenol being contaminated' to 'Oh my God, I just took Extra-Strength Tylenol, am I going to die?'" said Cathy Piccillo of the Indiana Poison Center, which received 50 phone calls.

FIG. 5.2. Another of the four stories in the *Chicago Tribune* on the first day of coverage of the Tylenol murders. Again, there is no mention of Johnson & Johnson. (Copyrighted Chicago Tribune Company. All rights reserved. Used with permission.)

There were four stories about the crisis in that one issue. Other than this quoted passage, all other mentions of the company were of McNeil Consumer Products Company, not as familiar a name to consumers as Johnson & Johnson.

The captions for the related photographs on pages 1 and 2 did not mention the company. The caption on the second page indicated that medical examiners believed "the capsules were tampered with after leaving the manufacturer's plant in Pennsylvania" (*Chicago Tribune*, October 1, 1982, p. 2).

On Saturday, October 2, the headline in the *Chicago Tribune* was "Stewardess is 7th Capsule Poison Victim." The page 1 headline was not the dominant headline on the page. A bomb explosion that killed hundreds of people in Tehran, Iran, took that honor. There were two other stories: (1) about the efforts to track the source of the poison, and (2) about funeral services for the victims.

On Sunday, October 3, the banner headline on page 1 was "Shoplifter Is Sought in Poisoning Probe" and centered on a man who had been arrested a couple of months before for stealing Tylenol. The continued story on page 4 had excerpts referring to the Johnson & Johnson plants.

The first excerpt read as follows:

. . . Consumers nationwide were urged to stop using Extra Strength Tylenol capsules. Johnson & Johnson, parent company of the painkiller's manufacturer, announced it is recalling all Extra Strength Tylenol in the Chicago area . . . (Shanker & Grady, 1982, p. 4).

The second excerpt took the following form:

. . . Investigators have been unable to determine how and where the cyanide capsules were placed in any of the suspect containers—whether the killer infiltrated the drug company's sophisticated manufacturing and distribution system at some point between plants in Pennsylvania and Texas and warehouses elsewhere or whether the killer removed and replaced containers once they had been placed on the shelves of local stores.

Stein said he could not rule out 'factory error' because of the reported disclosure by Lawrence Foster, a spokesman for Johnson & Johnson.

Foster said potassium cyanide is used in chemical tests at some of McNeil's laboratories, but not in the manufacturing process. The labs are remote from the manufacturing areas and cyanide would be detected even if someone tried to introduce it during manufacturing, he said . . . (Shanker & Grady, 1982, p. 4).

There was a second front-page story about a 12-year-old who had died from the poison 4 days before.

Thirty-three telephones were installed to communicate with the publics. Pretaped statements were placed on certain toll-free telephone lines to expedite news gathering. The messages were regularly updated.

A full-page ad was placed in major Chicago newspapers offering consumers an exchange of Tylenol capsules for Tylenol tablets.

During the first week of the crisis, Kniffin handled the media from McNeil, whereas Foster was in charge at headquarters. Approximately 180,000 news stories ran in newspapers nationally. The story was at the top of television and radio newscasts.

Two thousand telephone calls were taken from the media. Thirty thousand calls from consumers came in during the first months following the deaths.

Still there were glitches.

During the first three days, as the *Chicago Tribune* article showed, Foster issued a statement to reporters that there was no cyanide actually in the manufacturing plants. A few days later, the Associated Press heard that there was cyanide in the plants and called Foster to confirm the report.

Lo and behold there was! After checking again, Foster discovered that indeed a small amount of cyanide was used in the manufacturing plant for quality assurance testing of some kind. However, it was kept in a completely separate facility from the production line. Also, none of it was missing. There was no way that it could have gotten into the capsules accidentally. Even if it had, it would have been so dispersed as to be harmless.

Foster called the Associated Press and told them the truth. He had a reputation for being honest, fair, and ethical. He could not afford a cover-up. When he told the wire service that there was no way the cyanide could have gotten into the capsules, the reporters believed him and agreed not to run the story—unless some other news outlet got the information too.

Sure enough, the Newark *Star-Ledger* got word of the information, called for confirmation, and again Foster asked, "Trust me." Again, the reporter agreed.

Keeping his promise to the Associated Press, Foster called and told them that the Newark *Star-Ledger* had the information but had also agreed not to run it. The Associated Press agreed once more not to run the story unless still another newspaper or TV station got the information. After all, the *Star-Ledger* was basically a neighbor to the company.

Then *The New York Times* got the information. Foster decided to give up. He called both the Associated Press and the *Star-Ledger* and asked them to use discretion in running the story.

The resulting stories had very little impact. They were run in insignificant places in the Sunday newspapers. The facts were not blown out of proportion as has happened with other crises. The newspapers merely reported the information as Foster had revealed it.

Foster realized then that his positive dealings with the media over the years had paid off. The story could have made front-page headlines everywhere, but it did not because the media trusted the public relations professional from past dealings.

The FBI and the FDA never found any evidence of tampering at the two Johnson & Johnson plants. They found that the contaminated capsules had come from both plants—one in Texas, the other in Pennsylvania.

There, for the first time, was basic proof that the tampering was not an inside job. The finger now pointed to some external, malicious psychopath who bought the Tylenol, laced it with cyanide, and placed it back in the containers and on the shelves of stores.

After the crisis team discovered what had transpired, its members were relieved to be assured that the contamination could not have occurred in the plants.

The task of the team now turned to saving Tylenol and restoring sales. They were not worried that the company would go under: They are very diversified in their products. Sales were not down for other Johnson & Johnson products. There was no boycott against the company, just a fear of Tylenol capsules. The future of Tylenol was at stake.

To reach the employees who had been on pins and needles while the company battled the crisis, Chief Executive Burke spoke to an assembly at McNeil and promised that Extra-Strength Tylenol was coming back. Employees wore "We're Coming Back" buttons.

Those employees who had been manufacturing Tylenol were given other temporary jobs. Videotaped reports of activities were shown to employees explaining what was going on with the crisis.

To reach retailers, distributors, and the medical profession, approximately half a million electronic mail packages were distributed.

On October 2, an extortion note was received demanding a million dollars for the end of the tampering. Up to this point, there was a debate over total recall. The FBI and the FDA had not wanted a recall because it would be a signal of giving in to terrorists.

The decision not to recall would have flown if it had not been for a copycat crime that took place in Northern California on October 5. The company decided then that removing the product from all stores was the only way to show the public that it was concerned about the welfare of its customers. On October 5, all Tylenol products were removed from stores nationwide.

Later, there were approximately 250 copycat reports, and all were found to be groundless.

During the recovery period, a decision was made to repackage the product. A 60-second television commercial featuring the medical director at

Our Credo

We believe our first responsibility is to the doctors, nurses and patients,
to mothers and fathers and all others who use our products and services.
In meeting their needs everything we do must be of high quality.
We must constantly strive to reduce our costs
in order to maintain reasonable prices.
Customers' orders must be serviced promptly and accurately.
Our suppliers and distributors must have an opportunity
to make a fair profit.

We are responsible to our employees,
the men and women who work with us throughout the world.
Everyone must be considered as an individual.
We must respect their dignity and recognize their merit.
They must have a sense of security in their jobs.
Compensation must be fair and adequate,
and working conditions clean, orderly and safe.
We must be mindful of ways to help our employees fulfill
their family responsibilities.
Employees must feel free to make suggestions and complaints.
There must be equal opportunity for employment, development
and advancement for those qualified.
We must provide competent management,
and their actions must be just and ethical.

We are responsible to the communities in which we live and work
and to the world community as well.
We must be good citizens — support good works and charities
and bear our fair share of taxes.
We must encourage civic improvements and better health and education.
We must maintain in good order
the property we are privileged to use,
protecting the environment and natural resources.

Our final responsibility is to our stockholders.
Business must make a sound profit.
We must experiment with new ideas.
Research must be carried on, innovative programs developed
and mistakes paid for.
New equipment must be purchased, new facilities provided
and new products launched.
Reserves must be created to provide for adverse times.
When we operate according to these principles,
the stockholders should realize a fair return.

Johnson & Johnson

FIG. 5.3. The Johnson & Johnson credo, the document that guided the
Johnson & Johnson crisis team through the ordeal of saving the company's
image, while news reports the company's products were killing consumers.
(Printed with permission from Johnson & Johnson.)

McNeil notifying consumers of the upcoming return of Tylenol aired in October and November to an estimated 85% of all television households.

A triple-seal safety package was devised, then introduced at a November 11 news conference transmitted by satellite to 29 different sites where reporters were gathered.

Chairperson Burke announced that free coupons were available that could be used toward the purchase of any Tylenol product. He also announced a special 800 telephone number through which consumers could learn about the special promotion. More than 200,000 calls came in to the 800 number.

The company's executives did interviews with network television shows "Donahue," "60 Minutes," and "Nightline," as well as with major magazines and newspapers such as *The Wall Street Journal* and *Fortune*.

As a result of the crisis, all Tylenol capsules were discontinued as were capsules of other brand names. Tamper-proof, triple-sealed safety containers were swiftly placed on the shelves of retailers 10 weeks after the withdrawal. Other manufacturers followed suit.

The crisis cost the company more than 100 million dollars. Tylenol has regained 100% of the market share it had before the crisis.

Seven people died. Other lives were saved by the company's decision to recall all the capsules in the Chicago area. The murderer was never found.

Public relations history credits Johnson & Johnson's corporate culture, including its "open and honest" policy with the media, for the successful handling of the Tylenol crisis. A current Johnson & Johnson executive apparently concurred when he said, anonymously, "More important than a crisis plan, the Johnson & Johnson public relations department has always had immediate access to the CEO and other senior management." The company also has a new expanded credo (see Fig. 5.3).

CASE 8: ALPAC CORPORATION AND THE ORIGINAL SYRINGE-IN-THE-CAN

Steve Bryant is Vice-President and Deputy General Manager of EvansGroup Public Relations in Seattle, Washington. Like many public relations firms, the EvansGroup handles many crisis management problems for its clients. The agency has handled more food-related crises than other type, but the 1993 crisis of hypodermic syringes reported in Diet Pepsi cans was, as Bryant reflects, "the most spectacular crisis in which we've been involved."

The Alpac Bottling Company, based in Seattle, was the principal Northwest bottler of Pepsi-Cola products. It was, at the time, a family-owned business, but has since been acquired by the Pepsi-Cola Company. EvansGroup had handled advertising for Alpac on an ongoing basis for many years and its public relations on a project basis.

The Problem and Strategies

On Thursday, June 10, at about noon, the corporate attorney for Alpac telephoned the EvansGroup, indicating that KSTW-TV News in Tacoma, Washington had called about a report from another attorney charging that his clients had found a syringe in a can of Diet Pepsi. The station wanted a spokesperson to be interviewed by reporter, Steve Williams, on camera in about 2 hours.

John Eastham, then president of EvansGroup, and Bryant, as well as personnel from Alpac, assembled and prepared a response for the Alpac spokespersons. The crisis communications team consisted of Bryant; Eastham; Susan Hebert, then Alpac's director of public affairs; Al Call, Alpac's CEO; and Paul Elliot, director of operations who directed production and was the initial spokesperson.

Doug Hoffman, an attorney from a local firm, who represented Alpac's insurance company, was also an integral part of the team. Carl Behnke, president of Alpac, was out of town, but communicated by car telephone.

In the early stages, Pepsi's New York-based national public relations team, led by Rebecca Madeira, served in an advisory capacity. Anne Ward from that team kept in contact with the Alpac team. Pepsi eventually took the helm.

The team reviewed the situation, decided that Al Call would be the spokesperson for the first interview, and established principles that would be stressed in interviews. The team prepared Call with a list of media interview tips, posed sample questions to him, and critiqued his responses.

Earl and Mary Triplett related their finding what appeared to be a used hypodermic syringe in a Diet Pepsi can after drinking its contents. They were afraid that the needle might have been contaminated and believed that it was important to warn the public that "somebody" might be intentionally placing syringes into the soft drink cans. The can that the Tripletts possessed was bottled at Alpac on April 7.

"Visible top management is essential. This was a key part of our strategy," said Bryant. "When something serious like this is reported, people don't want to hear from the PR practitioner. They want to hear from the people who are ultimately responsible."

Al Call, the Alpac spokesperson, indicated that his company was investigating the situation, that Alpac was concerned about consumer safety, and that it would take all the appropriate steps to clear the matter. It was primarily a question of showing concern and compassion for consumers in general, and the Tripletts in particular. This is an essential early position on the part of any company in a crisis resulting from product tampering or product failure.

There were two very serious aspects to this crisis:

1. The Tripletts, in their 80s and said to be a very devout Christian couple, were especially credible. Neighbors, friends, and the media compared them with the Pledge of Allegiance, the Boy Scout Oath, and the Pope.

2. In his first televised interview, Earl Triplett said the presence of the syringe in the can made him worry about AIDS. Although the charge was not made, the underlying fear among consumers was Acquired Immune Deficiency (AIDS). Used hypodermic syringes *can* cause this terminal disease. As consumers learned about the incident, the obvious question would be, "Were the syringes contaminated with the mysterious AIDS virus?"

There was such a fear of the virus anyway, that the very remote possibility could plant doubts in the minds of consumers and seriously affect, if not virtually halt, the sales of Pepsi products. This kind of hysteria is common in such cases, although health officials maintained and made clear, early on, that the acid in soft drinks would kill the AIDS virus.

Credible or not, Alpac felt very strongly that the tampering did not take place in its plant. The company reviewed its quality control procedures and found no problems. It allowed television cameras to capture the canning process. Pepsi-Cola's public relations department issued B-roll (video footage to be used with a newscaster's voice-over) demonstrating the bottling procedure.

The cans pass under a mirror where workers check for foreign objects. Next, they are taken up a conveyer belt upside down, then spun and washed and placed directly into the machine that fills and caps them. Finally, they are set upside down and weighed precisely to check for leaks. An Alpac official indicated that the discovery of dust was the worst that has ever happened in the process. Even that is rare.

"The coverage of the canning process proved very helpful in the course of events," said Bryant. "It showed how unlikely a contamination of this sort would be. It also, in a very real way, established what a high quality manufacturing process was used to can soft drinks. And it bolstered consumer confidence in the long run."

Bryant said that his team also shared messages with the consumer about Alpac's excellent safety record and the limited number of consumer complaints previously received.

"We also knew very early on, through laboratory analysis, that the syringe was not contaminated," said Bryant. "The risk was limited to a chance of being stuck in the lip with a syringe, admittedly not a pleasant possibility, but not a health risk. The FDA supported this position."

Bryant said calls from other media came within an hour of their notification of the problem. "It was not a national issue at first," he said. "We did our very best to contain it to the area, and we probably would have done so had it not been for the copycat cases. This eventually made it a national issue, but for about 4 days it was a local issue."

The issue became regional when the Food and Drug Administration (FDA) issued its advisory to all Alpac distribution areas. Consumers had to be notified. Specific messages had to be tailored for certain states. For example, all Pepsi products distributed in Hawaii are also canned there, so even if there had been contamination in Seattle, Hawaiians would not have been affected.

Handling the crisis meant being responsive not only to the needs of Alpac, but also to the FDA and to the legal counsel for Alpac's insurance company. As mentioned, Pepsi was the imminent owner of the company and had an enormous stake in its future. Even though Alpac would ultimately have been responsible, soft drink consumers, especially nationwide, knew very little of Alpac.

The incident happened in June when soft drink sales begin to soar for the summer months. If the scare succeeded in causing consumers to curtail the consumption of Pepsi products, Pepsi would suffer.

"The FDA," said Bryant, "has a responsibility to investigate matters of this sort. We worked very closely with it from day one. It would have been a mistake on our part to take an adversarial stance with the government agency which, frankly, can be a mighty bear. We worked with them in developing communications. We reviewed all news releases with them before they were issued. We established sort of a common point of view. The FDA maintained the weight of its authority in the matter and at the same time became our communications ally."

Because of the pending change of ownership, Alpac's attorney was scheduled to go on vacation the day after the crisis presented itself and then leave the company. The crisis team coordinated its work with Doug Hoffman, the attorney for Alpac's liability insurance company.

"He was great," recalled Bryant. "He had a wonderful understanding of PR issues and public affairs and was very sensitive to the need to communicate. He understood that communicating effectively would help maintain the company's value and limit its liability. You can run into lawyers who want to guide the entire process by solely focusing on limiting the company's liability. That can be a disaster."

The acute stage of the crisis lasted about nine days in which the Alpac team worked 15 to 20 hours each day. Hebert and Bryant fielded as many as 200 media calls a day. Locally, it was the top news story for a week.

"Susan received calls even in the middle of the night," said Bryant. "We were constantly making decisions whenever we received new information. Fatigue became a serious factor."

An intern from the University of Washington, Erica Stone, scanned the media and wire services with help from PR Newswire and BusinessWire. "She fed us stories constantly," said Bryant. "Of course, we all tuned into broadcast news. That was easy to follow because it was always the first story."

Thursday, June 10

Alpac's crisis communications team was assembled. The FDA was informed. The team prepared a limited number of high-ranking spokespersons to respond to the media. A brief practice session was held in which questions were anticipated and fired at Spokeperson Al Call.

Suggestions were made for truthful, convincing, substantial responses to questions, keeping certain guiding principles in mind:

1. Treat the crisis seriously.
2. Apprise and support the FDA.
3. Demonstrate concern for the customer.
4. Communicate quickly and openly with a limited number of spokespersons.
5. Share company's quality assurance facts.
6. Communicate lack of health risk (this was established after it was determined there was no health risk).

Calls from the media begin to come in about an hour after the Tripletts' attorney faxed a notice to Alpac. Alpac executives had not yet read the fax, so the media informed the company of the problem. Interviews were held with KING-TV, the NBC affiliate; KIRO-TV, then a CBS affiliate; and Tacoma station KSTW Channel 11, the station that made the initial call. All newscasts contained the Alpac messages outlined by the team. Media tours of the plant were allowed that first day.

Friday, June 11

Alpac employees were advised by a bulletin board notice not to speak to the media. This was done to comply with the FDA's position of not revealing any information until the investigation was completed (for a look at the public advisory, see Fig. 5.4).

A second report of a syringe in a can was reported to Alpac directly (see Fig. 5.5). The charges came from a person who indicated that he or she (it was never revealed which) did not want to involve an attorney or the media, but merely wanted to inform Alpac.

Bryant said a decision was made to notify the FDA in a spirit of honesty. The Alpac team said the decision was made because of its determination to be cooperative with the FDA and honest no matter what.

. Of course, if the person making the charge later decided to go public, Alpac would have been accused of a cover-up. The FDA conducted overnight tests that revealed no contamination of the needle.

ALPAC CORPORATION

News Releas

FOR IMMEDIATE RELEASE

MEDIA CONTACT
Susan Hebert, Director of Public Affairs, (206) 326-7471

PUBLIC ADVISORY

LOCAL PEPSI BOTTLER AND FDA INVESTIGATING PRODUCT
CONTAMINATION REPORTS

Reasonable precautions are advised

SEATTLE (June 12, 1993) -- Alpac Corporation, a regional Pepsi bottler, is working with the FDA to investigate two separate reports of consumers finding a syringe in a can of Diet Pepsi. The second report was received during the course of investigating the first report, according to Alpac President Carl G. Behnke.

The second report came from a resident of Federal Way, Wash. Alpac received the can yesterday afternoon and provided it to investigators from the U.S. Food and Drug Administration. Preliminary FDA laboratory tests conducted overnight revealed no chemical contamination. Additional tests are underway.

After initial testing of the second can, the FDA has told Alpac that drinking the liquid contents would not appear to present a health risk to the general public or to the consumers that reported the syringes.

Alpac and the FDA urge consumers, as a precaution, to inspect soft drink containers carefully before opening and consuming them. Consumers should gently rotate the can and listen for any non-liquid sound. As an additional precaution, consumers might prefer pouring soft drinks into a second container until this incident is resolved.

Behnke said the company's first priority is consumer safety and that he and the company are doing everything possible to assist federal investigators.

On Thursday, a couple in Tacoma, Wash. made the first report of a syringe in a Diet Pepsi can. The FDA is investigating the two complaints as separate, isolated incidents.

The FDA has not advised ALPAC that a recall is warranted at this time.

Consumers with questions should contact Pepsi's consumer hotline at 1-800-433-COLA.

FIG. 5.4. A public advisory issued by Alpac acknowledging the crisis and its plans to investigate. (Printed with permission of the Pepsi-Cola Company.)

Additional television news interviews were held with spokespersons. KOMO-TV, the ABC affiliate, joined the coverage. The newspapers were basically watching to see what developed.

Bryant said, "Substantially, it was a TV news story; there was something about the visual image of a Pepsi can and a syringe that compelled news directors."

Syringe Found in 2nd Cola Can
FDA investigates tampering

BY JERRY BERGSMAN
SEATTLE TIMES STAFF REPORTER

A syringe has been found in a second can of Diet Pepsi, this time by a Federal Way resident.

Alpac Corp., the regional Pepsi bottler, learned of the second syringe Friday night when it was called by a consumer who asked not to be identified, Carl Behnke, president of the South Seattle firm, said yesterday.

Alpac and the federal Food and Drug Administration are conducting an investigation into the apparent product tampering, a felony under federal law.

"It has to be some sort of sabotage because there is no way that type of a foreign object could enter our product in the normal course of events," Behnke said.

Preliminary testing indicated no health risk from either can, said Roger Lowell, FDA district director. Tests were made in the agency's local laboratory. Samples will go to its forensic laboratory in Cincinnati for more extensive testing.

A Fircrest, Pierce County, couple Thursday found a syringe in a can of Diet Pepsi they bought in Tacoma. No objects were found in samples of Diet Pepsi collected from stores where the cans were bought.

The Diet Pepsi was part of a case of 24 bought by Earl and Mary Triplet, 82 and 79, respectively. The rest of the case was regular Pepsi.

In the latest incident, the contaminated can was part of a 12-pack. An Alpac spokesman said the can opened Friday had been sealed six months before the first one.

Alpac produces 1.3 million beverage cans a day for King, Pierce and Snohomish counties and Alaska. It has 300 employees, including 45 on the production line.

FIG. 5.5. News story in the *Seattle Times*, June 13, 1993, about the syringe-in-the-can crisis. (Reprinted with permission of the *Seattle Times*.)

Saturday, June 12

The FDA started visits to the plant. Its representatives talked to nearly all of the employees involved in production. Employees rallied on behalf of the company. The plant was inspected thoroughly. Records of quality assurance and customer complaints were reviewed.

Alpac's president, Carl Behnke, decided to issue an advisory to consumers urging them to pour soft drinks into a second container before drinking and to inspect containers before opening them and consuming their contents.

The FDA said a public advisory should be issued, and the crisis communications team asked that Alpac be allowed to make the announcement. It wanted to take a leadership position and offer its own precautions. The suggestion from the FDA did not suggest guilt by Alpac, but concern for the public should the complaints prove legitimate. The advisory also included a consumer hot-line number for the answering of questions (see Fig. 5.4).

KIRO-TV News, with a 30-minute notice, called to do a live remote to lead in its 6 p.m. newscast. The team prepared President Behnke for the experience, something he had never done. KIRO did the interview.

The rest of the media also concentrated on the advisory and the second case. CNN picked up that evening's news report from KING-TV, bringing it to national attention. The Associated Press also issued a story placing it in print nationally.

Advertising was pulled in the Seattle-Tacoma market for Pepsi products that day. Said Bryant, "We wanted to avoid having people see Diet Pepsi ads and thinking 'syringe.' Also, we wanted to avoid the appearance of being callous in continuing to promote a product that some people feared might be injurious."

Sunday, June 13

The FDA decided to issue its own advisory. This broadened awareness of the crisis to all areas served by Alpac. Local Alpac managers were coached to take calls. Advisories were customized for specific markets.

There was an explosion of media calls—local, national, and international. This was the day when the number of calls peaked at 200. Among the callers were network news operations and *The New York Times.*

Another "victim," the first of several copycats, turned up in New Orleans. These copycat cases caused a national media feeding frenzy, although some of the claims were incredible and extreme.

There was talk about a possible recall. Two Seattle television stations polled consumers asking whether they felt the company should recall Diet Pepsi. Most participants in the poll felt that the company should not recall, although reactions were mixed.

Monday, June 14

Pepsi took the lead in the national public relations effort as the crisis spread nationally (see Case 9: Pepsi and the National Syringe-in-the-Can Scare).

The FDA issued a warning against false reports of tampering and assured the public that there was no serious health risk.

At Alpac, meetings were held to advise employees of the situation. They were given a letter to distribute to retail customers, preparing them for consumer questions. The effort was successful because none of the retailers in Seattle pulled the product. Alpac employees were reminded not to speak to the media. This was done to comply with the FDA's position of not revealing any information until the investigation was completed. Following the meetings, the letters went to the retailers.

A copycat case came up in Alaska at Carr's Supermarket. A man bought a soft drink, took it to his car, ostensibly for his daughter, and returned it to the store creating a big emotional scene. "My daughter's been stabbed in the lip with a syringe!" the man shouted.

Store personnel called the local Alpac general manager, who telephoned the crisis team who, in turn, called the FDA. The FDA asked the crisis team not to report the incident, that it was suspicious. It was later discovered that the man also bought insulin syringes at the same store.

The retailer and Alpac were afraid of later being accused of a cover-up, but all concerned complied so as not to imperil the crucial relationship with the FDA. The man was eventually charged with fraud.

As the media coverage intensified, so did the fake reports.

Tuesday, June 15

Reporters started to dig deeper for what they wanted to be the story of the year. "They wanted intricate details about the production process. This is risky in that they would try to construct a scenario of how this *could* have happened," said Bryant. "They asked the size of the filtering screen, how many seconds between this point and that point, who was in charge of this operation and that."

Although the team wanted to be open, they discouraged these reporters because they were not willing to deal with "Colombos" who were trying to make a case.

"We offered information," said Bryant, "that would provide a general understanding of the bottling process, but did not provide technical details. To have done so would have required us to interrupt production managers who were busy assisting the FDA and trying to rule out production problems."

Wednesday, June 16

Sixty-five tampering reports had been made. As hoaxes were uncovered, consumers, who said they thought the false charges were a mean-spirited thing to do, got angry and began to call Alpac and Pepsi expressing support. This provided the crisis team with an opportunity for pitching a positive story to the media.

The third Washington State report, in Mukilteo, was made. Local news reports focused on it. "Then, we had a godsend," said Bryant. "A former Washington bottling inspector came to our aid unsolicited. He said, 'I've inspected this type of plant machinery for years, and I know it just couldn't happen. It's a hoax!' We couldn't have bought that kind of third party credibility, and it helped put another nail in the coffin of the crisis."

Thursday, June 19

The Mukilteo case proved by the next morning to be a hoax. More hoaxes were being uncovered than there were new cases being reported.

The hoax that topped them all was actually seen on a security camera as a woman stuffed a syringe into her can and then remarked to the checker, "Look, a syringe in my can!" Pepsi linked it to a news satellite so that news programs nationwide and worldwide could download it for their newscasts.

Behnke, scheduled for final visits of the plants, was phased out as a crisis spokesperson when necessity dictated that a spokesperson who would remain with the company should take the post.

The first editorial cartoons appeared. Bryant's favorite is one of a Pepsi delivery man wheeling in a case of Pepsi saying to a physician, "Doctor, the syringes you ordered are here." Said Bryant, "The fact that people could laugh about the crisis suggested it was no longer a serious concern and that public confidence in the reports was failing" (see Fig. 5.6).

FIG. 5.6. Editorial cartoon about the syringe-in-the-can scare by Chris Britt in the *News Tribune,* Tacoma Washington. (Reprinted with permission of Chris Britt, *News Tribune,* Tacoma, Washington).

"I recall all of us cheering when the CBS Evening News announced the dismissal of the initial case," said Bryant. "Then the next day we discovered it was a false report. The FDA apologized to the Tripletts. To this day, there has been no proven explanation of how the syringe got into their can."

Bryant and the members of the crisis communications team considered the local media coverage to be balanced and believed that their determination to be open secured that balance. Cooperation with the FDA, they feel, was essential.

Alpac had a history of a corporate culture that valued employees, so employees were cooperative during the crisis. They played a vital role in the campaign and felt a sense of being a part of both the crisis and the recovery. "Support of retailers and consumers," Bryant says, "results from a long history of positive community relations on the part of Alpac and excellent customer relations. The Behnke family had been known in the area for its philanthrophy. There was a reservoir of goodwill so that people gave Pepsi and Alpac credit for telling the truth" (note positive news story in Fig. 5.7).

Alpac had a recall manual that had elements of a crisis management plan, but not an actual crisis management or crisis communications plan. Alpac was known by the Seattle media and the public as "the local Pepsi bottler," so it shared Pepsi's reputation and image. Bryant agrees that the effective handling of the crisis further improved Pepsi's already positive image both locally and nationally.

CASE 9: PEPSI AND THE NATIONAL SYRINGE-IN-THE-CAN SCARE

When Pepsi's worldwide headquarters in Somers, New York took command of the crisis, the claims of syringes in cans of Diet Pepsi were lead stories in broadcasts and banner headlines in newspapers all over the United States (see Fig. 5.8).

Following is a chronological report of Pepsi's strategies, tactics, and results from Monday, July 14, through the end of the crisis:

Monday, June 14

On this day Craig Weatherup, president and CEO of Pepsi, had his first contact with Dr. David Kessler, commissioner of the Food and Drug Administration (FDA). It was important to Pepsi for the head of its company to communicate with the head of the FDA in a kind of merging of efforts to investigate the problem.

Weatherup also functioned as spokesperson and head of the crisis team, which also included the following:

Pepsi gets high marks for response
Consultants call actions a model of damage control

By Leah Harrison
Seattle Times business reporter

Pepsi-Cola Co.'s public-relations machinery is doing a good job handling reports of syringes and other objects found in soda cans, say professionals who work with companies facing crises.

In fact, professionals say Pepsi's handling of the situation so far is a model for minimizing damages when companies face crises—from bad earnings reports to strikes to incidents or disasters that may damage or threaten people or property.

David Marriott, a senior vice president at Elgin Syferd, a Seattle-based advertising and public-relations firm, praised Pepsi officials for seeking the advice of the Food and Drug Administration. "I don't think people will say they acted irresponsibly," he said.

"They have stressed, rightfully, that this looks more like a panic than anything else," said Larry Newman, president of The Newman Partnership, Ltd., a consulting firm in Columbia, S.C. that specializes in advising businesses in crisis.

Pepsi officials "are explaining how things really work" and showing how difficult it would be to plant syringes into cans at the company's high-speed bottling plants, Newman said.

He said statements by the FDA and local law enforcement officials amount to "third-party endorsement" that Pepsi is most likely not at fault.

Marriott, who conducts seminars on how companies should plan for possible crises, said every firm should develop a crisis-management plan.

He said the planning should include a series of "What if..." questions, such as, "What would we do if someone drove in here with a truck of explosives?"

A formal crisis-management plan should identify a team of people to handle an incident and identify each person's responsibilities. Managers should also identify "key audiences" such as employees, shareholders and the public to make sure they can reach those groups, Marriott said.

FIG. 5.7. News story in the *Seattle Times*, June 17, 1993, praising the crisis communications team's work in the Pepsi syringe-in-the-can crisis. (Reprinted with permission of the *Seattle Times*.)

Consumers shun companies in crisis

BY DENNIS CHASE
ADVERTISING AGE

PepsiCo appears to have escaped damage, but consumers say they are less likely to buy products from companies that have been involved in a public crisis over a breach in ethics or safety.

In a survey of more than 1,000 adult consumers conducted in June, just before the Pepsi scare, 80% said problems at Sears, Roebuck and Co. and 79% said problems at Food Lion made it likely they would shun those companies.

Last year, Sears was charged with making unnecessary repairs at some of its auto repair facilities, and earlier this year, Food Lion was hit with charges that it used unsanitary food safety procedures. Other companies such as Exxon Corp. and Dow Corning Corp. were also cited in the survey.

The survey, to be released by the end of the month by Omnicom Group's Porter/Novelli public relations agency, found that even crises involving simple business decisions, like layoffs, affected attitudes. About 23% said General Motors Corp.'s layoffs and plant closings would affect their purchases, and 19% said the same thing about IBM Corp.

"Companies start out in the hole," said Bob Druckenmiller, Porter/Novelli president. "People don't believe companies tell the truth."

However, PepsiCo, by responding quickly to questions about syringes allegedly found in soft-drink cans, helped itself.

"One lesson is you have to respond quickly, even if you don't have all the facts," Mr. Druckenmiller said.

The survey also found that 76% of consumes polled are most angry when companies refuse to accept blame for problems, 71% are most angry when they provide incomplete or inaccurate information, and 71% are upset when they put profits ahead of public interest.

The mail survey was done by National Family Opinion using a random sample reflecting the U.S. population. Margin of error was 3 percentage points.

FIG. 5.8. Article in *Advertising Age* about how consumers feel about purchasing products from companies in crisis. (Reprinted with permission of *Advertising Age*.)

1. *Crisis Coordinator,* Rebecca Madeira, Vice President of the Public Affairs department, was instrumental in making sure the company spoke in one voice and directed the actions of the team.

2. The *Public Affairs department* had three subteams. The *press* subteam managed media contact. A *production* subteam wrote, designed, and developed news releases (both print and video), audiotapes, charts, and photographs. The *government affairs* subteam communicated information to 400 Pepsi bottlers.

3. *Consumer Relations specialists* responded to many thousands of telephone calls, 24 hours a day (see Fig. 5.9).

4. *Scientific and Regulatory affairs* worked with the FDA in following up on each charge of a syringe in a Pepsi can.

5. Employees in *Sales and Marketing* relayed information to the management of restaurants, stores, and other retailers to assist them in keeping businesses operable.

6. *Manufacturing experts* also worked with the FDA, providing it with explanations of the production processes to be disseminated to the media and consumers.

7. The *Legal Department* briefed members of the crisis team on communications issues.

All information was disseminated both externally and internally through a communications clearinghouse.

The company's and crisis team's overall goal was to avert damage to the Pepsi name. In order to do that, the team had to consider three publics:

1. Thousands of Pepsi customers who were reached by letters and telephone calls from the sales staff. They used talking points, as in Fig. 5.9.

2. Pepsi headquarters employees who received daily news summaries.

3. Pepsi bottlers and field employees who received twice a day advisories (*Anatomy of a Crisis,* 1993).

Phase 1: Understanding the Problem

Before the team could communicate with any publics, it had to determine what the problem was. Could there be a malicious person or persons in a plant placing syringes in cans?

Madeira said, "We had to be absolutely sure that this could not possibly have happened in our plants. We needed to develop a responsible way of talking about the situation before going public" (*The Pepsi Hoax,* 1993, p. 5).

CONSUMER TALKING POINTS
Product Tampering Inquiries
(For Internal Use Only - 6/15/93)

• Yes, we've received other calls regarding alleged product tampering,   and we are working with Federal authorities to verify those reports. The calls   come on the heels of a much-publicized incident of an alleged tampering incident in the Seattle-Tacoma and New Orleans areas, and already we are discovering that certain of the reported incidents are hoaxes, or people reacting to perceived rather than actual problems.

• In fact, the FDA Criminal Investigation Unit has already made an arrest of an individual in Central Pennsylvania who allegedly falsely reported he found a syringe in our product. The penalty for this type of crime is a $250,000 fine and a maximum of five years in prison.

• Our first concern is consumer safety. For that reason, the President of Pepsi-Cola and the head of the FDA have been in constant communication to insure that everything humanly possible to assure consumer safety is first and foremost in our actions.

• First of all cans, as you might imagine, are the most difficult of all consumer packages to tamper with, and because our production processes are performed at such high speeds it's virtually an impossiblity to introduce a foreign object.

• Canned products are produced in 140 separate and distinct locations -- we produce between 20 and 30 millions cans per day. The cans themselves originate from different suppliers, and are filled at different times. It's implausible to think that these events could occur simultaneously. In fact, news reports have highlighted the safety and integrity of our manufacturing process -- it's been reported that the canning process we use is probably the most tamper-   proof of all manufacturing processes.

• *The FDA has not recommended a product recall.* They *have issued* a statement that our products are safe, and as a precaution, are encouraging consumers to pour the contents of all packages into a cup before drinking. We ask that people use their own good judgement and common sense on this matter.

• There have been no injuries, nor have our investigations found any foreign objects in any unopened cans.

• This is a criminal investigation; product tampering and false reports of tampering are criminal offenses. Therefore, in cooperation with the FDA's Criminal Investigation Unit we're unable to comment any further.

• If you see anything unusual - please don't hesitate to call us back. That's what we're here for.

FIG. 5.9. Talking points for employees responding to calls from consumers about the syringes in cans. (Printed with permission of the Pepsi Cola Company.)

Phase 2: Cooperation with the FDA

The FDA inspected the manufacturing process in meticulous detail. Pepsi's Vice President of Product Safety said, "Each and every canning line at the production plants in question was studied very carefully to see if there was any way to infiltrate the line. Employee records were checked. Shipping and customer inventories were reviewed. Consumer complainants were interviewed" (*The Pepsi Hoax*, 1993, p. 5).

It had already been determined that the cans involved in the complaints were filled and sealed at various plants and at various times. Weatherup said, "Some six months ago, some six weeks ago, some six days ago" (*The Pepsi Hoax*, 1993, p. 5).

The FDA agreed that, considering the high speed and integrity of the production line as well as the constant observation of the process, it was virtually impossible for a syringe to be placed in a can either accidentally or maliciously.

Considering that the cans came from different plants, it was obvious that the syringes were placed in the cans after they were opened. Also, no syringes were ever found in unopened cans.

No injuries had been reported. The great fear was transmission of the AIDS virus through syringes. Health officials announced that there was no risk to consumers' health from syringes in the can. Because there was no health risk and no culpability on the part of the Pepsi process, there was no need to recall the product.

Madeira said, "We were committed to putting consumer safety first, but a recall would not end the crisis or restore consumer confidence. The only thing that would stop this was to discourage—in the strongest possible terms—tampering with an opened can."

Phase 3: Developing and Implementing Strategy

Armed with research that vindicated the company, the crisis team set out to begin an extensive media battle.

Tuesday, June 15

The production subteam produced a video. It was to be a video so visually persuasive that it could eliminate in viewers' minds the possibility of malicious tampering in the plants.

Weatherup and the FDA could make announcements, but consumers were more likely to believe what they could see rather than what they were told by a company head who could conceivably lie for economic gain. Because there was no way to take all consumers to the plants, Pepsi did the next best thing and took the plants to the consumers through videotapes of the plants in operation.

The footage showed the canning process. It showed cans being inverted, cleaned, inverted again, filled, and sealed—all under careful inspection, and all in nine-tenths of a second.

This footage was transmitted via satellite to television news programs all over the United States. Three other videotapes followed over the next three days showing more scenes of Pepsi's commitment to consumer safety (see Fig. 5.10).

"A can is the most tamperproof packaging in the food supply," said Weatherup. "We are 99.99% certain that this didn't happen in Pepsi plants" (*The Pepsi Hoax*, 1993, p. 6).

Madeira said, "Our strategy was to reassure the public that this was not a manufacturing crisis. What was happening with syringes was not occurring in our plants" (*The Pepsi Hoax*, 1993, p. 7).

In addition to the videotapes, Weatherup's interviews were aired on all the television networks on Tuesday evening. Public Affairs took hundreds of calls from local print and broadcast media across the country. Kessler and Weatherup both appeared on ABC's "Nightline."

Their message was that the crisis was a series of hoaxes brought about by people trying to make easy money. Kessler mentioned that the first arrest had been made in Pennsylvania and that others would follow (*Anatomy of a Crisis*, 1993).

FIG. 5.10. Still photos and video footage of the rapid Pepsi manufacturing process convinced consumers that it would be extremely unlikely for syringes to be placed in cans, either accidentally or intentionally. (Printed with permission of the Pepsi Cola Company.)

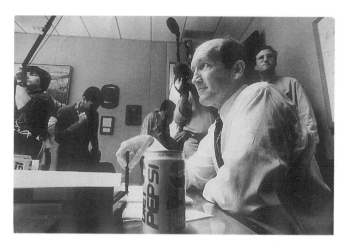

FIG. 5.11. Pepsi CEO Craig Weatherup meets the media at a news conference. (Printed with permission of the Pepsi Cola Company.)

The consumer relations section of the crisis team talked to 2,000 consumers. News releases were distributed announcing the FDA's intention to prosecute persons who filed false claims of product tampering.

Wednesday, June 16

The day began with Weatherup's appearances on CBS's "This Morning," NBC's "The Today Show," and ABC's "Good Morning America." The coverage originated from the offices in Somers, and crews were setting up as early as 4 a.m. (see Fig. 5.11).

That evening, Weatherup appeared on PBS's "The MacNeil/Lehrer News-Hour" and, that night, on CNN's "Larry King Live." Viewers who telephoned during the King show primarily emphasized their support for the company.

Madeira said, "Wednesday was pivotal. The media understood our production integrity, and we were gaining support as the day went on. We were hopeful that the FDA would announce more arrests as reports of hoaxes and recantations poured in from police across the country" (*The Pepsi Hoax,* 1993, p. 8).

As far as hoaxes were concerned, on Wednesday, the crisis team had *the* hoax to end hoaxes. A surveillance camera in a Colorado convenience store had captured a woman placing a syringe in a can as she approached the check stand.

The team prepared to broadcast the tape, but held it back after the FDA requested that it wait until an arrest had been made.

In the meantime, tampering claims were made in four additional states. Persons who had already made claims began to confess, hoping to avoid prosecution.

Thursday, June 17

The FDA held a news conference on Thursday when Commissioner Kessler was expected to announce arrests, but the Pepsi crisis team was elated when he also stated, in unequivocal terms, that Pepsi was completely exonerated, that it was a victim of the hoaxes. "The notion that there has been nationwide tampering of Diet Pepsi is unfounded," he said via satellite (*The Pepsi Hoax,* 1993, p. 9).

At this point, Pepsi released the Colorado surveillance tape, which team members called "the smoking gun." Weatherup made comments to go along with the silent video footage. The tape showed how simple and how fast it was to place a syringe in an open can. Pepsi couldn't have asked for a stronger tool to convince consumers of the hoaxes.

Friday, June 18

On Friday, Pepsi considered the crisis over. To certify the ending, it created an ad to run on Monday, June 21. The ad's headline was "Pepsi Is Pleased To Announce . . . Nothing" (see Fig. 5.12). The copy stated that the claims were hoaxes and, in effect, told people that Pepsi is still the refreshing drink consumers have enjoyed, and urged consumers to participate in special offers beginning the July 4th weekend.

At headquarters, 1,200 employees attended a meeting which was basically a celebration of their victory over the crisis. They viewed the videotapes that helped end the crisis and witnessed firsthand the ad that would appear in newspapers on Monday. The videotapes and ad were also sent to the 400 Pepsi facilities so that those employees could view them.

The company had suffered a $30 million loss in sales. It was time to rebuild its market share. In a personal letter to employees, Weatherup said, "It's time now for us to move quickly and decisively to restore . . . our business" (*The Pepsi Hoax,* 1993, p. 10).

With hot summer days approaching, Pepsi's marketing department created a "Thanks America" program. A one-dollar-off coupon appeared in newspaper ads. "Thanks America" buttons were worn by Pepsi employees, who also distributed the one-dollar-off coupons to their friends and neighbors (see Fig. 5.11).

A week after the first hoax was uncovered, consumers bought 800,000 more cases of Pepsi products than the week before the crisis. Sales began to rebound, and they bounced back completely during the summer. The week of July 4th was Pepsi's strongest week of 1993.

The Pepsi-Cola Company won the prestigious Silver Anvil Award for businesses—bestowed by the Public Relations Society of America—for its campaign against "The Great Pepsi Hoax." It was praised for showing to customers, media, regulatory officials, shareholders and other publics that

Pepsi is pleased to announce...

...nothing.

As America now knows, those stories about Diet Pepsi were a hoax. Plain and simple, not true. Hundreds of investigators have found no evidence to support a single claim.

As for the many, many thousands of people who work at Pepsi-Cola, we feel great that it's over. And we're ready to get on with making and bringing you what we believe is the best-tasting diet cola in America.

There's not much more we can say. Except that most importantly, we won't let this hoax change our exciting plans for this summer.

We've set up special offers so you can enjoy our great quality products at prices that will save you money all summer long. It all starts on July 4th weekend and we hope you'll stock up with a little extra, just to make up for what you might have missed last week.

That's it. Just one last word of thanks to the millions of you who have stood with us.

Drink All The Diet Pepsi You Want. Uh Huh.

FIG. 5.12. Ad Pepsi bought in newspapers nationwide to declare the end of the crisis. (Printed with permission of the Pepsi Cola Company.)

the company's manufacturing process is safe and that widespread tampering could not occur.

The Pepsi crisis team concurred that it succeeded because it was honest and open, and had looked at the problem through the eyes of the public (*Anatomy of a Crisis,* 1993).

CASE 10: PEPSI/SEVEN-UP BEVERAGE GROUP OF LOUISIANA AND THE SYRINGE HOAXES

The State of Louisiana is a leader in the production of natural gas, salt, sulfur, petroleum, sweet potatoes, rice, sugar cane, pecans, soybeans, corn, cotton, and muskrat fur. The state also has the dubious distinction of having more "syringe-in-the-Pepsi-can hoaxes" than any other state.

On Monday morning, June 14, 1993, Bryan Quarls, director of marketing and brand development for Pepsi/Seven-Up Beverage Group of Louisiana, walked into his New Orleans office to find reporters waiting for him. Quarls is responsible for marketing, pricing, public relations, advertising, promotions, and communications. A local man claimed to have found a hypodermic syringe in a can of Diet Pepsi.

"The first thing I did was call New York (Pepsi's headquarters is in Somers, New York) and yell, "Help!" If someone wanted to invent a story that would cause panic, create havoc, and fear, they could not have come up with a better scenario than to put in a syringe in a beverage can.

"I was totally caught off guard. I hadn't yet heard what happened in Seattle and New York; they were just beginning to write their news releases and put their strategy together."

The New York staff told him about the Seattle incident. "I said, 'That's true for Seattle, but I have a problem down here.' My biggest concern was that they wanted everything to happen in New York. Headquarters wanted to take control of the media frenzy. Doing so, they could choose their words carefully and make sure there weren't a lot of loose cannons in the field."

Quarls debated the issue with headquarters personnel. "I understood their perspective, but Pepsi is a conglomeration of companies. I didn't think it would be in our company's best interest to just defray all of the Louisiana media to New York."

Quarls wanted to remain the local spokesperson, to direct field media questions, and be a familiar face to the local community. "The local media knows me," he said. "I think their attitude was, 'He lives here. He works here. He's got some integrity in the community. We'll listen to him versus some blue coat sitting in an ivory tower a thousand miles away!' "

After the initial claim in Louisiana on Sunday, June 13, there were two additional claims on Monday and a fourth on Wednesday. In all, there were a total of 22 claims in Louisiana. Four claims, according to Quarls, "made prime time news." Of the 18 others, some made reports directly to Pepsi, some went to the news media. Many telephoned from their attorneys' offices and flatly said that they would go away if they received a check from Pepsi.

Quarls used the same dialogue with each claim: "No, Sir! If you want to give me your name and address, and if you've got the product sample available, I'll have the FDA contact you, and they will be glad to come out and interview you. Then we will followup from that standpoint." He said most of the callers disappeared. He later tried to telephone some of them and learned that they had "moved out of town" or "no longer lived at this address."

One complainant, who was still trying to get a court date in late 1994, registered this story. He said that he bought a six-pack of Pepsi from a local store and then proceeded to a blood bank to donate blood. After he donated the blood, he opened one of the cans, and lo and behold, there was a syringe in it. Was it ironic that this event happened in a blood bank where there are so many syringes?

Another person claimed to take a sip from a can and have something prick him on the lip. He then took a second sip and was cut on the lip. Why would he take a second sip after being pricked?

The Louisiana plant began employee communications on the day the staff learned of the first claim. Plant officials did not want employees to hear about the crisis from news reports. The company serves about 90% of Louisiana.

"We pulled everyone together on Monday afternoon, not just the front line sales group, but everyone from our fleet people to administrators to human resources, every employee," said Quarls. "We told them what the facts were, what we thought the issues were, that we would keep them informed of the situation. We explained that we were still in an information-gathering mode."

The officials continued to meet with frontline sales people every morning during the crisis. They responded to questions from the salespeople, who themselves have contact with about 30 industry people daily—all of whom might ask questions. Store managers, for example, wanted to know what to tell customers. They also asked, "Should the product be pulled off shelves?"

If reporters approached salespeople, they were referred to Quarls, who kept abreast of reports from around the country and was in constant contact with the New York headquarters as well as the local FDA.

Quarls admits that everyone felt the claims were hoaxes from the start. "We had to walk the fence as if they were not, but we knew early in the game that it was not physically possible. Further, each can has code dates, and there was a disparity as wide as five months on the claim cans in question. At the same time, we couldn't just go out and say these people were lying. We had to treat each claim as a potential product-tampering event."

The Criminal Investigation Unit of the FDA looked at each claim and made reports.

Quarls' first effort was to open up the local production facility for a media tour. "Our national Pepsi PR team in New York distributed a video tape featuring a canning facility from a company plant just to show the canning process," he said. "This was great for the national networks, but our local news media wanted to see our plant, the plant that distributes their Pepsi products throughout Louisiana."

Quarls not only had to convince the headquarters staff that he should open the plant; he had to convince his own management as well. Management was concerned that when the media was admitted to the plant, something might go wrong, something counterproductive to the story that Quarls wanted the reporters to write. Maybe the production line, which rarely shuts down, would encounter a problem and be the impetus to a conjecture that perhaps something unusual, like syringes, could happen.

Ultimately, Quarls convinced his plant managers and the New York staff. The plant wanted to persuade Louisiana consumers that public safety was its primary concern and that product "quality" was an imperative. Visual documentation that the Pepsi cans are virtually tamperproof was Quarls' strategy.

Quarls said that the very nature of the Pepsi plant made the claims unbelievable. "We're not like a pharmaceutical company where one plant can produce product for the entire country," he said. "Pepsi has hundreds of separate plants. Of the 27 states where people reported finding syringes in their cans, I think there are over 55 production facilities involved, all buying their own cans, all buying their own concentrate, all mixing the product on site. The odds are infinitesimal. One person couldn't have dropped 27 syringes in cans all over the country. Such an action would be a monumental undertaking that would have to require years to plan. And why?"

Reporters witnessed the production process and interviewed the plant manager who was "at their complete disposal." The media was not permitted access to the other Pepsi plant employees. Quarls and the plant managers felt that it was unfair to subject hourly employees to such pressure. "We didn't think it would be fair to go up and talk to a $7.50 an hour operator and put a camera in his face."

After the media covered the production process, television crews did followup man-on-the-street interviews in parking lots and shopping centers asking people if they felt the syringe scare was real or a hoax. The interviews were positive and indicated that public opinion was turning and Pepsi was winning, although sales had dropped as a result of the initial stories.

Consumers called with comments such as, "I don't understand what's going on, and I just want you to know I'm supporting Pepsi even though I don't normally buy your products." Quarls said, "Little old ladies called us and said 'I've been drinking Pepsi for 50 years and I'm not changing.' " He followed up each inquiry by sending a letter and a discount coupon for Pepsi.

Pepsi officials in Louisiana feel that FDA Commissioner Kessler was instrumental in helping their cause. Quarls said, "Dr. Kessler got in front early and said there was no risk to public health. That was one of the critical statements that we were able to use early in the crisis to help defray public concern and anxiety about our products."

Locally, the FDA inspected the Louisiana plant, perused personnel records, witnessed quality control procedures, and reported that it would be highly unlikely that a product-tampering event could happen in the local manufacturing process. This message, too, was relayed through the Louisiana media.

CEO Craig Weatherup's television appearances on network news shows were also effective, according to Quarls. "His impact on the national news and mine on the local news worked real well together. Our message or presentation was not as corporate as the national stuff," said Quarls, referring to his image as one of the local guys helping his company out of a tight spot.

His local connections paid off during the crisis. On one occasion, the news editor of a television station called to let him know that he was running an additional report. The station said a woman had telephoned and reported that she had poured a Pepsi for her child and that a syringe had come out of the can. Her quote was that she "just wanted the TV station to know in case anybody wants to come out and tape it."

Quarls said that he told the editor, "Step back a minute out of your role as a newsman. Look at this and tell me whether you really think it's newsworthy. You know the facts now. That lady is giving you her side of the story only, and when you get there, you'll see an open can of Pepsi and a syringe. She'll repeat that story and you'll tape it and put it on the 10 o'clock news. Quite frankly, I don't think it's news. I think it's bad journalism."

Continuing, Quarls said, "I can line them (claimants) up at your door if you want, because they're not all calling you. Aren't you a little bit curious about the ones that are calling you before they call me or the Pepsi hotline? The ones who want you to be sure to bring your cameras?"

He said the news editors all backed away from the story once they started seeing that all the reports were hoaxes, but it was a tough battle.

Quarls appeared on morning news shows, sunrise shows, everything that would give him more than a 10-second edit to explain the process and the issues. "The media began to realize that they too had been burned by bad information and didn't want to look foolish," said Quarls.

Briefly, the hoaxers were local media celebrities. They showed their infamous cans to anyone who wanted to see them. However, after the hoaxers were arrested, and public opinion had changed, most would not go in front of the camera or talk any further. Their only statements were, "Contact my attorney."

Quarls was disappointed that more hoaxers were not prosecuted. The FDA went after the most visible ones, but the others were dropped because of burdening case loads.

Another challenge after the crisis subsided was convincing the media to resolve the crisis. "When it became a nonissue," Quarls said, "stations didn't want to cover it anymore. I told them that they couldn't spend a week putting me in front of the camera and talking about tampering at Pepsi and then just ignore the resulting crisis. I told them that closing the crisis was just as important a responsibility as opening it."

Pepsi wanted the media to spend equal time making sure consumers understood what had happened and what the real issues were. "The local media," Quarls said, "agreed for the most part." Note the change in coverage in Fig. 5.13.

Also, as a part of completing the process, the plant sent letters to each of its 7,000 sales accounts, thanking them for sticking with the company through the crisis (see Fig. 5.14). Full-page ads were purchased in local newspapers to further resolve the issue (see Fig. 5.11).

Said Quarls, "Looking back, I think we made the right decision in handling the crisis locally. The combination of the national campaign and our being personable and reachable made a big difference."

Discussion of Chapter 5

The Tylenol and Diet Pepsi crises are similar in that both crises hit successful companies with respected, trusted reputations among consumers. Both companies suffered from outside tampering, although it took several days to prove it.

However, the differences are many and include the following:

1. Johnson & Johnson had no prodromes. Pepsi had Tylenol as a prodrome.

2. Deaths resulted from the cyanide-tainted Tylenol capsules. No deaths and no illnesses resulted from the Diet Pepsi tampering. Most of the syringe hoaxes were reported to the media, not to police or the Food and Drug Administration. The so-called Pepsi "victims" were obviously more concerned about financial gain and recognition than for their health.

3. In the beginning of the crisis, Johnson & Johnson was *hopeful* that the Tylenol capsules were poisoned by an outside murderer, but this was not certain until it was discovered that the tainted capsules were manufac-

Tuesday, June 15, 1993
2 in N.O. area find
syringes in Pepsi

Antoine Lewis was thirsty. He popped the lid of the cold Pepsi he bought in his building's vending machine and brought it to his mouth, expecting refreshment and relief.

He didn't expect to find a needle and a syringe...

Thursday, June 17
Pepsi cases may be hoaxes

Aluminum soft drink cans are about as tamper-proof as food containers get. Yet people in more than 20 states claim they've found needles in cans, making some consumers uneasy...

Reserve Pepsi Plant Gets Support

Pepsi officials at the soft drink's Reserve bottling plant, which supplies most of Louisiana, say increased claims of product tampering are turning the tide of public concern in their favor because people are beginning to suspect the reports are hoaxes...

Saturday, June 19
Arrests mounting for Pepsi reports

More arrests were made Friday of people who had claimed they found foreign objects in cans of Pepsi, and investigators said more charges are expected...

Wednesday, June 16
Fourth syringe found in Pepsi;
FBI on case

As the Food and Drug Administration brought in the FBI to Investigate a rash of Pepsi tampering claims, a fourth claim surfaced in New Orleans Tuesday...

Friday, June 18
FDA: No Pepsi tampering found

No reports of tampering with Pepsi-Cola cans have been confirmed, the Food and Drug Administration said Thursday, dismissing the idea of any nationwide meddling with soda cans...

Sunday, June 20,
Tamper sleuths pop top on crime

The lot of a Pepsi detective is hardly glamorous.

Investigators with the U.S. Food and Drug Administration normally spend months tracking rat droppings or insect parts in food. They hunt through factories and convenience stores, squint at food labels searching out meaning in production code numbers...

FIG. 5.13. Headlines and leads of news stories in the *New Orleans Times-Picayune* one week into the crisis facing Pepsi manufacturers in Louisiana. Notice how the primary message changes daily and becomes more supportive of Pepsi as a victim of the crisis.

June 22, 1993

Dear Pepsi-Cola Customer:

As you know by now, the "tampering" crisis is over. Not one claim has been proven, the hoaxes have been exposed, and the individual cases are being processed. It's time to begin again and do what we've done together so successfully throughout our history--build our business.

But before we move forward, let me take just a moment to say something that must be said. Thank you. Thank you for your support, for taking time to express it to me and so many of our people. Most of all, thanks for demonstrating your faith in us and our products in the most significant way possible--by keeping us front and center in your stores.

During a difficult week, you and your colleagues have been more than a bright spot. You've been a beacon. Thanks for being there. And for keeping us there with you.

Sincerely,

Bryan Quarls
Director of Marketing
and Brand Development

BQ/jh

333 EDWARDS AVENUE • NEW ORLEANS, LOUISIANA 70123 • (504)733-6630 • FAX: (504)733-8280

FIG. 5.14. Letter sent to owners and managers of stores and restaurants who sell Pepsi products. (Printed with permission of Pepsi/Seven-Up Beverage Group of Louisiana.)

tured in different plants in different states. Pepsi felt *certain* all along that the syringes were not placed in its cans during the manufacturing process.

4. Johnson & Johnson recalled all Extra Strength Tylenol capsules. The company is so diverse that it had numerous other products to keep it financially in the black. If Pepsi had recalled Diet Pepsi, consumers would have been suspicious that all their other soft drinks, canned identically, had syringes in them. Consequently, Pepsi would have had to recall all of their canned soft drinks. The move would have drastically affected the company financially.

5. When consumers purchase Diet Pepsi, both the brand name and company name are Pepsi. Not so with Tylenol. If consumers read the fine print, they see the company name Johnson & Johnson, but the brand name is not the company name.

Even the early coverage of the murders in the *Chicago Tribune* has very few mentions of "Johnson & Johnson." "Tylenol" was mentioned constantly, as was the company subsidiary that makes Tylenol, McNeil Consumer Products Co. If the cases were reversed and Diet Pepsi had been used as a murder weapon, the company name would have been in the headlines.

6. Persons guilty of the Diet Pepsi hoaxes were prosecuted. The criminal who poisoned the Tylenol was never discovered.

Gerber

Another case of product tampering occurred three days after the 1986 Tylenol tampering crisis. This time the company in crisis was Gerber, like Johnson & Johnson, a trusted name among parents of small children. Both crises took place in New York.

A woman claimed that while feeding her baby, she found bits of glass in a jar of strained peaches. Coming on the heels of the Tylenol case, another "hoax" was an early possibility.

The Food and Drug Administration checked 50,000 unopened jars of Gerber baby food produced at the same time as the complainant's jars and found no glass.

Complaints of glass in the Gerber jars turned up in 40 states and some foreign countries. As in the Diet Pepsi crisis, the complainants called the media, not law enforcement nor health officials, nor even Gerber. No glass was ever found in a jar not previously opened.

There were other similarities to the Diet Pepsi crisis such as the following:

1. Gerber did not recall. It would have had to recall all baby food in jars and suffer a severe financial loss.
2. Gerber's name is on its containers. Gerber is the brand name.

3. Several persons who attempted the hoaxes were prosecuted.
4. Each company had Tylenol as a prodrome.

Gerber's crisis communications strategy consisted of trying to prevent coverage of the complaints. In order to do this, three prestigious news outlets—*The New York Times, The Wall Street Journal,* and the Associated Press—were invited to tour Gerber plants, interview the CEO, and talk to anyone in the plant. (Pepsi had also arranged media tours.) The strategy was that stories in these chosen media would serve to impact, and thereby set the tone for, the rest of the media.

At the same time, Gerber issued news releases, based on findings of the FDA and health officials, to the news media and to retailers. Most retailers expressed their trust of Gerber and pledged support.

A direct mailing was sent to 2.6 million United States households. Each mailing consisted of a letter from Gerber's president, tips on serving baby food, and a question card. The consumer could write a question on the card and mail it to the company. In return, the consumer would receive free coupons and a response to the question.

The direct mailing was a way of evaluating consumer attitudes towards Gerber. The company received 250,000 replies, 75% were favorable.

To reach the employee-public, a special edition of the company newsletter was issued, and employees previewed television commercials airing clips about the crisis.

Company executives communicated with investors. Consequently, stock never declined.

A year after the crisis began, Gerber sales had recovered. Consumers expressing concern in surveys dropped from 81.1% during the crisis to 27.9% (Lovejoy, 1993).

Coors

Perhaps the most ridiculous tampering crisis was the one Coors suffered in 1988. A Jacksonville, Florida man claimed that he had found a mouse in his Coors beer can.

Coors offered the man $1,500 for the can containing the mouse, but the man tried to barter for $50,000. Coors refused, so he went to the media and succeeded in getting a piece on the WTLV-TV evening news. All of Jacksonville could see the mouse fall out of the can and imagine drinking a can of beer with a mouse in it. Consequently, a quarter of a million dollars was lost in sales, but fortunately for Coors, the incident did not become a national crisis.

Coors ordered laboratory tests on the mouse and learned that the mouse had been dead only a week, whereas the can it was in was sealed three months before. Also, the mouse did not drown; it was killed by being stuffed into the can's pop top opening (Seitel, 1992).

Even though the case was obviously a tampering case, and even though the man was prosecuted, the film news footage aired 72 times in the Jacksonville area. A long time passed before many beer drinkers could pick up a can of Coors.

REFERENCES

Anatomy of a crisis: The Diet Pepsi tampering hoax. (1993). A videotape produced by the Pepsi-Cola Company.

Barton, L. (1993). *Crisis in organizations: Managing and communicating in the heat of chaos.* Cincinnati: South-Western Publishing Co.

Baskin, O., & Aronoff, C. (1993). *Public relations: The profession and the practice.* Dubuque, IA: William C. Brown Publishers.

Houston, J., & Griffin, L. J. (1982, October 1). 5 deaths tied to pills: Fear killer put cyanide in Tylenol. *Chicago Tribune,* pp. 1–2.

Lovejoy, L. J. (1993). Villains and victims of product tampering. In J. A. Gottschalk (Ed.), *Crisis response* (pp. 175–184). Detroit: Visible Ink Press.

The Pepsi hoax: What went right? (1993). Somers, NY: Public Affairs, Pepsi-Cola Co.

Seitel, F. P. (1992). *The practice of public relations.* New York: Macmillan Publishing Company.

Shanker, T., & Grady, B. (1982, October 3). Shoplifter is sought in poisoning probe: Reportedly stole Tylenol. *Chicago Tribune,* pp. 1–3.

Environmental Crises

Protection of the environment is, perhaps, the foremost concern of the American people. It is certainly the issue that has increased most in concern over the past two decades.

Early in the 1970s, scientists began to worry that increases in technology and industry, along with limited natural resources and the natural wastefulness of Americans, would lead to "ecocatastrophes." Gradually, people joined the scientists in this concern.

Americans are concerned with the depletion of the atmosphere's ozone layer caused by aerosol cans, jets, and air conditioners. We are concerned about overpopulation, the urbanization of tropical forests, the "greenhouse effect" that results from excessive heat generated by industrial production, pollution of natural waterways and the air we breathe, and numerous other challenges to the ecosystem.

Rachel Carson's book *Silent Spring* (1962) warned of several environmental calamities that could befall mankind. Many of them were averted by environmental reforms put into effect following the publication of her book.

Among these heeded warnings were those predicting the extinction of the bald eagle and 40 other species of birds due to the use of pesticides. Due to the banning of DDT, the bald eagle and most of these other birds are no longer endangered. Other results from Carson's work include the passage of the Endangered Species Act ("Averting a Death Foretold," 1994) and laws regulating conservation, chemical safety, forest preservation, and air and water control.

Phillips Petroleum

In the 1970s several crises aroused fear in the ecology-minded. Notable among them is 1977 crisis in which a Phillips Petroleum production oil well blew out in the North Sea off the coast of Norway.

A constant tower of oil 200 feet high was falling into the sea, making an oil slick that eventually was 15 miles long and 12 miles wide. Bad weather and technical problems prevented the capping of the well for 8 days.

As in the Exxon crisis, described later, the spill threatened fisheries. There was a media onslaught, however, but little news was available for reporters to relay to the public. Consequently, reporters were restless.

Public relations experts rushed to the scene and were open, frank, and responsive to the media. When they had no news, they said they had none and explained, as much as possible, the delay, much of it due to Phillips' efforts to bring experts to cap the well.

History credits Phillips with responding to the crisis in a timely, competent manner.

Three Mile Island

In 1979, a nuclear accident called a "meltdown" took place at the Three Mile Island nuclear generating plant near Harrisburg, Pennsylvania. No one is reported to have died, and the degree of this accident has since been overshadowed by the nuclear accident at Chernobyl, Ukraine, in 1986. The estimate of deaths from Chernobyl may be close to 300,000, although the Soviet government reported only 7,000 (*What Chernobyl Did,* 1991, April 27).

Three Mile Island stands as the American nuclear accident that most aroused fear of radiation. There were radiation leaks resulting from the accident, but the degree was not known for some time. This mystery troubled the public as well as the media. It was eventually revealed that radiation levels of 30 to 35 millirem per hour were monitored outside the plant gate, only slightly more than from a dental x-ray with usual radiation levels of 25 millirem.

Mishaps occurred when the media naturally converged on the site. There was no spokesperson present. The public relations office of Metropolitan Edison was 60 miles away at headquarters in Reading, Pennsylvania. Remember, this crisis occurred before the cellular phone became a common business tool.

In Reading, public relations staff members were unaware of details at Three Mile Island. The small staff not only had to deal with the media, but also with employees, customers, residents and businesses in the area, local and national government officials, and even President Jimmy Carter.

Reporters had no scientific knowledge of nuclear power production, so their stories were likely to result in sensationalism. The public relations people were charged with educating the journalists. (This was also a problem during the Exxon Valdez oil spill.)

Both the PR staff and the media were dealing with risk communications—placing risks in proper perspective and providing information about the comparative risks and dangers of alternatives to nuclear power.

Eventually information centers were set up at the Three Mile Island site, as well as in Reading and in Hershey, Pennsylvania, where reporters had also gathered.

Instead of harming persons, the Three Mile Island incident wrecked public confidence in the nuclear power industry and caused greater numbers of people to join in the movement to save the environment.

In the 1980s and 1990s, some companies anticipated the public's concerns about the environment and made changes in their operations, thus avoiding crises. McDonalds, for example, switched to using all biodegradable containers.

Other companies were shocked at the degree of the consumer public's concern. In the cases that follow, we see the lessons learned by companies who were forced to respond to consumer fears of ecocatastrophes.

CASE 11: THE EXXON COMPANY
AND THE VALDEZ OIL SPILL

In the late 1980s, Exxon was one of the five largest companies in the United States with its sales of $80 billion. The CEO was Lawrence G. Rawl, who had been employed at Exxon for 37 years before getting the top job in 1986. He was considered a strong leader who disliked publicity and the media.

The crisis started shortly after midnight on Friday, March 24, 1989. The Exxon Valdez, a 987-foot oil tanker was headed for Long Beach, California, from Prince William Sound off the coast of Alaska.

A reporter later said, "The ship, longer than three football fields, was loaded to the top with enough oil to fill the Rose Bowl almost halfway to the top" (*Turning Point,* 1994, June 15).

The weather was calm. The water was beautiful. During daylight hours, you could see an abundance of sea life. It was the time of the migration that brings to the area the largest concentration of migratory fowl in the entire world. Sea otters, seals, whales, salmon, herring, and halibut inhabit the Sound.

Just before midnight, the local pilot who had guided the tanker out of the harbor went off duty. Captain Joseph Hazelwood, in command, put the supertanker on auto pilot and headed straight for Bligh Reef, one of the well-known hazards in the Sound.

Hazelwood had sailed the route more than 100 times. Some say he could do it nearly blindfolded. He had been with Exxon for 21 years, 10 of them as a captain.

On this night, Hazelwood left his post at the bridge and put Third Mate Gregory Cousins in charge, telling him to keep the tanker on course for three minutes, then turn right, thus avoiding the reef. Cousins, although qualified to take command, was not—according to government investigators—qualified to take command at that critical period when the ship had to be steered in a very precise maneuver.

Cousins waited too long before ordering the turn, and the Exxon Valdez headed for the submerged rocks. He told Captain Hazelwood, "I think we're in serious trouble." Hazelwood radioed the Coast Guard with the message, "We've fetched up hard aground. . . . Evidently, we're leaking some oil" (Smith, 1992, p. 84). Cousins and Hazelwood had just made the two understatements of 1989.

The tanker had run aground on the rocks of Bligh Reef, and a hole in the hull nearly as long as the ship was ripped open. Over the next hours and days, 11 million gallons of crude oil poured out and spilled into the Sound. It spread relentlessly. Some say the oil slick was 10 feet wide and four miles long—the worst oil spill ever in American waters.

Obviously, the beautiful waters were no longer beautiful, but more importantly, sea life perished. Estimates say that 1 million migratory fowl and one third of the sea otter population, about 2,500, died. Also, seals and sea lions fell victim to the slick. Some sources reveal that 2 million animals died as a result of the oil. This does not include halibut, pink salmon, herring, clams, and worms that remained uncounted. Some scientists claim that wildlife in the Sound may still be poisoned by the oil. Others say the Sound has totally recovered from the spill.

The weekend news reports came from local media and through the three major television networks. By Monday, media from all over the world began to pour into Valdez. The media frenzy had begun. Examples of the news coverage are included in Fig. 6.1.

In addition, hundreds of environmentalists also arrived to save the animals, the beaches, the water, and the world! Concern was rampant.

Don Cornet, now Exxon's public relations manager, was Alaska Coordinator for Exxon at that time; he reported to the head of public affairs and rushed to the scene as soon as he got word of the accident. The company's immediate strategy was to focus on the cleanup effort, on what was being done. The theory was that the initial spill was regrettable, but that after it had occurred, the most crucial task was to clean up as swiftly as possible and restore normalcy.

Frank Iarossi, president of Exxon Shipping (the grounded tanker came from its shipyards), was Exxon's main representative at the site. CEO Rawl

Excerpts from front page news story in *Anchorage Daily News,*
March 25, 1989

Crude oil fouls Sound
Oil officials react slowly to disaster

BY LARRY CAMPBELL
DAILY NEWS REPORTER

VALDEZ - As the largest oil spill in the history of the United States entered its second day, only a feeble containment effort has been mounted and a crowd of state, federal and oil company officials remained undecided about how to clean up the mess.

A 32-square-mile, multi-hued sheen continued to float and spread atop the waters of Prince William Sound. The Sound is surrounded by land on three sides. Two large islands, Hinchinbrook and Montague, lie across its open, southern end. That means that unless the spilled oil can be dealt with, it is a near-certainty that it will wash ashore somewhere in the Sound.

Valdez residents grew increasingly critical Friday of what seemed to be sluggish movement by Alyeska Pipeline Service Co., which operates the oil terminal here, and Exxon Shipping Co. in dealing with the spill. Nearly 24 hours after the Exxon Valdez ran aground on Bligh Reef about 25 miles southwest of here, officials had done little to contain the spill or clean up what was beyond containment.

Oil keeps spreading in Sound
State says Alyeska's cleanup effort inadequate, slow

BY LARRY CAMPBELL
DAILY NEWS REPORTER

VALDEZ - State, federal and oil company officials ended Saturday as they had begun it, no closer to a solution to the problems posed by more than 11 million gallons of North Slope crude oil washing around the fish-and-wildlife-rich, enclosed waters of Prince William Sound.

But while the oil of the nation's largest spill was left mostly unmolested, the chief of the state Department of Environmental Conservation assailed the Alyeska Pipeline Service Co. for its failure to respond quickly to the disaster.

FIG. 6.1. Headlines and leads in the *Anchorage Daily News* on March 25, 1989, the day after the oil spill from the Exxon Valdez.

was nowhere to be found. Iarossi dealt with the logistics of the spill response. Early on, he pointed a finger at Captain Hazelwood. There is still some confusion over whether Hazelwood had been drinking that night, but it is a fact that his driver's license had been revoked for drunken driving and that he had once been hospitalized for alcohol treatment. At any rate, Hazelwood was fired. Third Mate Cousins blamed the crisis on "poor seamanship" (*The Big Spill*, 1990).

Some Exxon employees placed the blame on Exxon's corporate culture. They said that in order to save money, the company had cut crews. The short-staffed crews had worked longer hours and had gotten little sleep. They felt that human fatigue was responsible. Moving the oil was a cardinal rule, and if an employee did not work fast enough and long enough, someone else would have his job.

Smith (1992) said that in 1986, the Exxon Valdez was designed for a crew of 33. Yet on the fateful night of the spill, the crew numbered only 19.

According to requirements of the State of Alaska, the Alyeska Pipeline Service Company, a consortium of several companies working on Alaska's North Slope, was responsible for the initial response in the event of a spill. Exxon, Atlantic Richfield (ARCO), British Petroleum (BP) and five other companies participated. At any rate, Exxon soon took over the cleanup efforts from the other companies.

At the start of the crisis, Cornet set up a media center in Valdez, a remote town with limited facilities, equipment, and accommodations. Some critics charged that the media center should have been set up in New York or Chicago, cities which could accommodate such a large gathering of media. Others insist that it had to be at the site, regardless of the difficulties. Modern media are so visual that photographs and videos of the spill, citizens of Alaska, and government officials were all necessary to the stories communicated to the public.

Contradictory statements were issued from various news sources. One statement said the damage was minimal. Another said damage was substantial.

Four days after the spill, local fishermen in the village of Cordova grew angry because cleanup efforts had not worked. They and the media were not happy about the response.

Iarossi held a press conference without first being briefed by public relations personnel; he was verbally slaughtered. Brian Dunphy, another spokesperson for Exxon Shipping, said that he would not verify the extent of the damage or what was being done about it, a statement that was not well-received.

CEO Rawl still declined to go to the site. He said that he felt "technologically obsolete." The media, the fishermen, the environmentalists, and the public were irate. Customers began to cancel credit cards. The media continued to attack more vociferously. Exxon had not anticipated the intensity of the public's concern about environmental problems. Neither had it anticipated such a large spill or the difficulties in cleanup and communications.

Alaska public relations expert, George Mason, expressed it like this: "The public had been growing more 'green,' but the spill caused a rapid and identifiable leap I call the 'greening of America.' "

Rawl eventually issued a statement via television telling the public what chemicals would be used to clean up the spill. He made no apologies to the fishermen whose livelihoods had been affected. He showed no emotion over the impact of the disaster.

Ten days after the spill, Exxon released full-page ads expressing concern and vowing to clean up the spill. Still, the company did not accept responsibility for the damage. Three weeks after the spill, the CEO went to Alaska, apparently no longer feeling technologically obsolete.

All oil companies operating in Alaskan waters now have crisis plans approved by the state. In 1989, Alyeska Pipeline Service Company's plan anticipated a much smaller oil spill and allotted only five hours for containment. A primary response in these plans was the use of dispersants as well as *in situ* burning for cleanup. The Coast Guard and the State of Alaska could not decide on the use of dispersants for the Exxon Valdez spill, and this debate prolonged the cleanup. A dispersant test was attempted on Monday following the Friday night spill, but harsh weather prevented it. In addition, the spill was so massive that there were not enough dispersants in Alaska to deal with it.

A month after the spill, Exxon finally had the equipment for a full-scale cleanup, which was completed in 1992. Some Alaskans say there is still evidence of the oil. In 1994 Exxon issued information to the media showing that predictions of long-term damage resulting from the spill were exaggerated, and that there was oil from other sources in Prince William Sound. Independent scientific studies seemed to confirm this, but oil from these sources was minuscule compared to that from Exxon.

There are still various controversies about the Exxon spill, but one thing is certain. The Exxon Valdez was a warning sign, a prodrome for other oil companies. Later, British Petroleum (BP) suffered an oil spill in the Pacific Ocean off the coast of Huntington Beach south of Los Angeles. BP reacted with haste, even getting underwater photographers to capture the hole in the ship for the media.

In a few days, the BP accident was no longer news. This spill, however, was in no way as massive or as difficult as the Exxon spill. It also must be noted that Exxon sent personnel and equipment to help work on the cleanup of this BP spill.

In 1994 a federal jury found that the Exxon Corporation and the captain of the Exxon Valdez, Hazelwood, were guilty of recklessness in the disaster.

Exxon was ordered to pay $287 million in damages to 10,000 commercial fishermen in Alaska who claimed their businesses had been severely hampered by the spill. Exxon also reached a $20-million settlement with Alaskan native groups who charged that the spill damaged their hunting and fishing grounds.

Exxon says it has paid more than $3.5 billion in cleanup costs and government fines. Rawl resigned in 1993, and Lee Raymond, second in command, took the CEO position. Cornet's position as public relations manager did not exist in 1989 and was arranged as a part of the organizational restructuring of Exxon under Raymond.

In the new organizational hierarchy, there are fewer layers between the CEO and the public relations department. Cornet reports to the head of public affairs who reports directly to Raymond.

For 1993, Fortune 500 revealed that the Exxon Corporation was number one in profit, number three in sales, and number two overall ("The Fortune 500," 1994, p. 220).

Discussion

It is frequently implied, if not actually expressed, that Johnson & Johnson, in the Tylenol tampering case, is the prototype of all that is good in public relations and business, and that Exxon is the prototype of all that is bad in business and public relations. Neither is true.

Johnson & Johnson has been widely praised—justifiably so—for being open and honest with the media. It had that reputation prior to its crisis. It had a company credo that was not just a piece of paper on the wall; the company's ideology was apparently guided by that credo.

This credo embraced concern for consumers, employees, communities, and stockholders, and all of these people wanted Johnson & Johnson to recover from the crisis. They wanted to believe in the products they had trusted for so many years, and they wanted Johnson & Johnson to be a victim, not a villain. It was almost a case of, "If Johnson & Johnson could distribute poison painkillers to the public, what companies and products can we trust?"

When Johnson & Johnson's crisis communications are compared to Marra's model of *excellent* crisis public relations, the company gets high marks in the area of strong and well-developed relationships with key publics, including the media and consumers, prior to a crisis. In living by its credo, the company also had organizational and communication ideologies that supported crisis management.

The company also deserves high praise for forming a crisis team made up of its CEO, its public relations head, and its legal head. They, essentially, were bound together to work on a common goal.

Nevertheless, the company had no crisis management or communications plan. It also had not anticipated such a crisis nor the need for tamperproof containers.

Johnson & Johnson is universally excused for not anticipating and not having a crisis plan because public relations programs were not as sophisticated in 1982 as they are now, and because the company reacted well when hit with the possibility that its products were murdering consumers. Also, there is the realization that hindsight has 20/20 vision. Companies will not be as readily excused in the future because Johnson & Johnson was their warning sign.

The Exxon Valdez crisis was a warning sign too. Nevertheless, public relations history has not excused Exxon. True, Johnson & Johnson was the victim of a psychotic killer. Its executives were not sure of the company's innocence in the beginning of the crisis. There was a fear that some employee may have snapped and poisoned the pills. When the impossibility of the company's guilt was established, Johnson & Johnson was in the best place to be while in crisis—it was blameless.

Exxon was not blameless at any point during the crisis or even later. However, Exxon may not be as guilty as the media—and consequently, the public—insist.

There are four charges for which Exxon must accept blame:

1. The oil emitted from the Exxon Valdez belonged to Exxon. Whether it was Captain Hazelwood's alcoholism, Third Mate Cousin's inexperience, recklessness or negligence of harassed and overworked employees, or just bad luck, the tragedy is still a blemish on Exxon's image.

Some theorize that had the tanker not borne the name "Exxon" on its bow, less attention would have been given to Exxon. With "Exxon" so prominently visible in films, photographs, and videos of the tanker, the public was, and is, constantly reminded of the company involved. If the name of the ship had been, for example, "Valdez Victor," one would have to wonder, initially, who owned the ship.

George Mason, a PR executive who was hired by Exxon to handle a portion of the crisis communications, points out that thousands of people died from a gas leak in Bhopal, India, in 1984. Many people recall what happened, but do not recall that it was a Union Carbide plant that leaked the poisoned gas.

2. Exxon CEO Lawrence Rawl did not take responsibility soon enough nor with the sincerity necessary to appease the media or the public. In a crisis of this magnitude, no one lower than the CEO will do. In Johnson & Johnson's Tylenol tampering crisis, CEO Jim Burke was up front and available to the media throughout the crisis. In the Exxon case, if the media had

captured, on video and film, the CEO on the site at Prince William Sound holding a oil-covered bird in his hand and looking as if he were crying, the entire story would be told differently today.

3. Employees have testified that in the corporate culture of Exxon, the push for productivity surpassed concern for human limitations. Also, Exxon Shipping President, Iarossi, did not consult with public relations staff members or do necessary preparations before holding a news conference.

These are violations of Marra's (1992) model of how *excellent* organizations handle crises. Exxon's communications ideologies did not champion crisis management preparations. However, it must be emphasized that the Exxon crisis was a wakeup call to other corporations. Although the Tylenol crisis was also a warning to other corporations, crisis communications did not become a growth industry until after the Exxon accident.

4. Also, according to the Grunig/Repper (1992) theory, Exxon committed several violations of *excellence* in public relations. The public relations head was obviously not an important part of top management since Iarossi and Rawl obviously made decisions independently. The company also ignored relationships with some of its key stakeholders: the media, customers, environmental groups, and employees.

Several business schools encourage top management to make independent decisions. This directly conflicts with public relations theory and public opinion.

Although Exxon must accept total blame in these charges, there are other elements of the oil spill crisis that must be considered. Even though Exxon is usually labeled the villain in the crisis, the elements discussed next point out the difficulties in handling the crisis management and the crisis communications of the megaevent. In some instances, there are indications that the notorious charges against Exxon should be tempered. Consider some of these indications:

1. Although the 1989 Exxon Valdez oil spill was America's worst oil spill ever, it was not the most oil ever inadvertently dumped from a tanker. In 1993, more than 20 million gallons of crude oil, twice as much as from Exxon, were spilled from the Braer onto the Shetland Islands.

Fierce waves were helpful in cleansing the waters, and all signs of the oil were gone in a few months. Nature did not help Exxon to the same degree. If the fault is in the initial spill, then the Valdez is less guilty than the Braer.

2. Jeff Wheelwright (1994) studied Prince William Sound for several years and claims that Exxon is *not* guilty of causing long-term damage to the Sound's fishing. He wrote the following:

Pink salmon catches broke records in 1990 and 1991, and herring catches broke records in 1991 and 1992. The last two seasons were very poor—the herring season never opened—as populations of both species fell sharply. If there was harm from the oil, it would have to be delayed harm, yet marine science cannot account for a delayed response from an oil spill. (p. 15)

3. Unlike the Johnson & Johnson case, there were many news sources in the Exxon Valdez oil spill—Exxon, Exxon Shipping, Alyeska Pipeline Service Company, the U.S. Coast Guard, Alaska state officials, local fishermen, VECO (the primary cleanup contractor), the Alaska Department of Environmental Conservation (ADEC), the National Wildlife Federation, the Environmental Protection Agency, the Natural Resources Defense Council, the American Petroleum Institute, Greenpeace, and others.

So many sources always create a possibility of confusion and error. For example, during the cleanup, Exxon told reporters that 96,600 gallons of oil were being recovered each day. On the same date as the Exxon announcement, the Coast Guard estimated the total at 42,000 gallons (Dietrich, 1989).

4. It is possible, even likely, that the national media was influenced by a local media conflict. Two major newspapers—the *Anchorage Times* and the *Anchorage Daily News*—were in a battle for readership in Alaska. The *Times* was purchased by VECO, Exxon's prime cleanup contractor, a few months after the spill. Its coverage was primarily supportive of Exxon's efforts to clean up the spill.

Conversely, the *News* wrote exposé-like articles that were critical of Exxon. Even Coast Guard officials complained that the articles were deliberately misleading. At any rate, the *News* articles were more appealing to the national media than those from the *Times*.

5. Sources close to the oil spill crisis claim that the reporters who covered the event had little knowledge of oil spills, the oil industry, or Alaska. Therefore, the reporters were forced to write stories in terms of what they and their readers could understand. Many observers say they felt the need to have a bad guy. Exxon was it, and there was little Exxon could say to redeem itself.

One editor who covered the spill, Bryan Hodgson of *National Geographic Magazine*, observed, "In Alaska, Exxon was the villain, and that was enough for most" (Smith, 1992, p. 94).

A public affairs official for ADEC who dealt with reporters following the spill said that 98% of the reporters had difficult tasks because the information came from "opinionated folks who didn't have a lot of facts early in the incident. The reporters, for the most part, had no way to distinguish opinion from fact and vice versa" (Smith, 1992, p. 86).

Because Exxon was the chosen villain, other organizations involved in the crisis were reluctant to support Exxon's position on any matter for fear that they would be categorized similarly or criticized for being "in bed" with Exxon.

6. The crisis was hampered by the remoteness of Valdez. The city is a 6-hour drive by car and a 45-minute flight by plane from Anchorage. There were only three flights each day into the city, only three hotels there, and few rental cars.

In addition, the spill was 65 miles from Valdez and could only be reached by powerful boats or helicopters. Mason recalls, "Several seasoned editors and reporters mistakenly thought they could just drive to the spill site as if it were in San Francisco Bay."

7. There were working conditions in the Exxon crisis to which reporters were not accustomed. There was limited office space. The telephone systems were inadequate for the flood of calls. Reporters had to wait for hours to get outside phone lines. This problem was exacerbated when some reporters, finally successful in getting outside phone lines, kept them open for hours so that they would not need to wait again.

The processing of film was a procedure that frequently required several days in Alaska, a process that is immediate in the most of the lower states.

8. The U.S. Coast Guard was accused of failure in following safety precautions governing oil tankers traveling out of the Sound. Outbound tankers were permitted by the Coast Guard to proceed faster than was considered safe. From 1980 until a few hours before the Valdez incident, several tankers had accidents and near-accidents in Prince William Sound. Some emitted oil, but none as crucially as the Valdez (Smith, 1992, p. 84).

Just prior to the Exxon crisis, two outbound tankers—the ARCO Juneau and the Brooklyn—took the same route as Hazelwood did. The Juneau traveled four knots faster than maneuvering speed. The Juneau, in 1988, had collided with a bridge in San Francisco Bay. The holes ripped in it were larger than those in the Valdez, but fortunately it had already dumped its cargo of oil.

On March 24, 1989, both the Juneau and the Brooklyn came within a half mile of Bligh Reef. Both had officers without proper Coast Guard certificates (Smith, 1992, p. 84).

9. There was a debate immediately after the spill over the use of dispersants to clean up the oil. The use of dispersants had long been the Alyeska's plan in the event of a spill. When permission was finally granted by the Coast Guard and the State of Alaska, 2 days later, bad weather grounded the planes that were to spread the dispersants. Then the weather blew the oil onto the beaches, further complicating the job.

Rawl (1989) said if the dispersants had been used, according to plan, 50% of the oil would have been broken up in the two days following the spill when the waters were calm. Lee Raymond, who became Exxon's CEO in 1992 when Rawl stepped down, said, "I guess if I had been there, on the first day, I would have put the dispersant planes in the air and they would have either had to get an injunction or shoot me down" (*The Big Spill*, 1990, p. 4).

An organization's image can be affected positively or negatively not only by the chief executive's actions or inactions, but also by each and every employee. If the image or the reputation is negative, the media and the public say "bad public relations" when they really mean "bad image."

Public relations practitioners do not *control* an organization's image; they communicate in an effort to try to improve or maintain it. In the end, the results may be out of their hands.

CASE 12: EXXON'S OTHER STORY: ANIMAL RESCUE CENTERS AND ALASKAN TOURISM

George Mason, APR, in 1989, was vice president of Bradley/McAfee Public Relations, Alaska's largest public relations firm. The firm was part of Bradley Advertising, the state's largest advertising agency. (The company name has since been changed to Bradley/Reid Communications.)

"Alyeska Pipeline Service Company was our largest account, and we'd held it for 14 years," said Mason, who was not personally responsible for the account but had, on occasion, handled crisis communications for the client.

When the Exxon Valdez ran aground on the night of March 24, Mason contacted Alyeska's public relations director, John Ratterman, to offer assistance. One of Alyeska's key public relations staff members was on vacation; two others were at the Valdez site. Mason, as he had on previous occasions, assisted the short staff with duties in Anchorage.

"What is often forgotten in the news stories," he said, "is that Alyeska Pipeline Company, a consortium of several oil companies (including Exxon), was responsible for initial response in the event of a spill."

Although Alyeska and Exxon realized damage had been done and the significance of it, Mason said, "No one knew how much damage had been done and what else *could* happen."

He said that when the Coast Guard arrived at the tanker just after the spill, there were thick fumes from the oil, thick enough to clog helicopter engines and prevent them from flying overhead. There was, therefore, a fear of onboard fires. In addition, he says, "Captain Hazelwood was smoking."

It was during this period that the media converged on Valdez. As Mason puts it, "In short order, the phones were jammed, and the small airport in Valdez was besieged. General public hysteria, the nightmare dimension of any crisis, was beginning, as was the media feeding frenzy."

In an effort to keep people informed, Exxon held briefings at the Valdez Community Center with representatives of the U.S. Coast Guard and the

State of Alaska participating. Frank Iarossi, President of Exxon Shipping, represented Exxon. "In an effort to fully cooperate and try to keep information flowing, it had been agreed to allow members of the local communities to participate in the briefings," said Mason.

One of these briefings exploded when angry fishermen shouted their concern and confusion. This was the briefing in which Iarossi was verbally attacked. There was a rumor that a member of Greenpeace planned to toss dead birds at the speakers. That never happened, but there was great concern when a woman with a bag of laundry tried to enter the room.

The day after the angry public meeting, Mason was asked to fly immediately to Valdez to meet with Don Cornet, Alaska coordinator for Exxon. "I flew out in an eight-passenger plane loaded with workers and contractors hurrying to the scene," said Mason. "I was met at the airport by Alyeska's onsite public relations staff members who gave me a quick tour of the mayhem in Valdez, then to the hotel that had been temporarily set up as Exxon's headquarters.

"The hotel was jammed with reporters and others trying to get a story. Security guards were stationed in the hotel's hallway in an effort to provide some breathing and working room for Exxon's staff."

Mason had never met Cornet, and their meeting was brief. As they talked, telephones rang persistently. One long angry caller, he remembers particularly, was the mayor of the seaport town of Whittier, many miles from the spill. "In my opinion," said Mason, "Mr. Cornet had already grasped the futility of the situation as far as the degree of damage Exxon's image had suffered. He seemed to accept this and had begun to look ahead to the long-term future."

At any rate, Cornet, while working on the cleanup of the spill, asked Mason to develop and implement strategies for three areas that he expected would be of future concern:

1. The tourism industry, Alaska's third largest industry. (Oil is the largest industry.)
2. The animal rescue centers Exxon had already begun to set up in Valdez.
3. The seafood industry, Alaska's second largest industry.

Mason said, "I agreed to handle the animal rescue issues and tourism. At the time, I was also the supervisor on the State of Alaska's tourism public relations account, and this arena was a natural one to handle.

"However, I explained that I would not directly handle the seafood issues because this was not my area of expertise. Also, the states' seafood public relations account was handled by another agency in Anchorage. I did agree to notify that agency and offer assistance if needed."

Mason then organized the next briefing in Valdez and met with Iarossi and others to plan a briefing strategy. He suggested two separate briefings—one for media, another for the public, including reporters who desired to attend. Prior to making the suggestion, Mason had consulted with reporters at the scene who said they were finding it increasingly difficult to get information over the shouting of the fishermen and environmentalists.

In assembling an agenda for the briefing, Mason included wildlife experts to address animal issues. Security guards checked press passes at the door to ensure that only credentialed reporters were admitted. Mason said that the briefing went smoothly. The media could pose questions without interruptions from persons with personal agendas.

Exxon's Animal Rescue Centers

After the media briefing, Mason went to the Animal Rescue Center where there was additional mayhem. Teams of wildlife professionals and their equipment had been flown into Valdez. They were trying to set up the center to help rescue some of the animals.

"Reporters and interested community people were given free access to the facility, again in an effort to cooperate," recalled Mason. "However, the result was impossible. On more than one occasion, eager reporters, mostly freelancers trying to make a buck, were in the way, and in some instances had stepped on injured birds being treated."

Again, Mason, in agreement with the head of the animal rescue center, put security guards to work. This time, it was the media and others not connected with the rescue effort who were kept out. The facility was roped off. Then media tours were arranged and guidelines were constructed to guarantee the protection of the animals.

With the protocols set up, Mason returned to Anchorage to set up long-term systems. He assigned a staff member of his firm, Suzanne Stolpe-Bishop, to the animal rescue effort. She worked in Valdez for 2 months and subsequently won the Public Relations Society of America, Alaska chapter's Aurora Award for her work.

Mason also subcontracted a staff member to do the same work with a second animal rescue center in Seward, Alaska. He also subcontracted others to act as community liaisons in other communities. "The purpose here," said Mason, "was to ensure credible connection between Exxon and the community, to assist Exxon's local claims offices, and to help in other ways."

Alaskan Tourism

Mason headed the tourism campaign himself. He already knew, from previous research, that the greatest concern was that the spill had occurred in spring, the peak time of year that tourists make plans for vacations.

"We suspected," he said, "that the televised reports of thick oil and dead animals would seriously impact decisions of tourists contemplating travel in Alaska. An early survey of vendors statewide confirmed our fears."

Mason said that the tourism industry telephoned from all over Alaska. The fear was that American tourists would think that the spill had marred all of Alaska. Cancellations were also rampant. Callers asked, "How deep is the oil in Fairbanks?" Fairbanks is a city nowhere near the oil spill.

Mason designed a crisis plan that was further developed and fine-tuned by a team of experts, including public relations heads of Westours and Princess cruise lines. The plan was quickly funded by Exxon and approved by the Alaska Tourism Marketing Council, a combined state and industry group.

The crisis plan involved bringing travel writers to Alaska to witness the conditions, and encouraging them to travel within the state in order to report what destinations were and were not affected by the spill.

News conferences were held in New York, Los Angeles, San Francisco, and Seattle with feeds to major television network programs. The news conferences in San Francisco and Los Angeles were organized by Ketchum public relations offices in those cities. Erik V. Peterson, APR, Senior Vice President at Communication Northwest, who was formerly Mason's boss in Alaska, did the groundwork for the Seattle news conference. The agency Padilla, Spear, Beardsley set up the New York press conference. Alaska Governor Cooper participated in the news conferences in Seattle and San Francsico and was a very credible participant because he had been so publicly critical of the spill. He said, "Alaska is beautiful," and people believed him.

A telephone hotline was also instituted for travel editors to get information swiftly.

At the same time, Exxon funded an advertising campaign developed jointly by Mason's agency and McCann-Erickson of Seattle. The public relations campaign reached an estimated 50 million Americans. The advertising campaign reached even more. Both were successful in diffusing negative travel publicity.

That season, Alaska's tourism set a new record. It was 5% higher than it had been the year before the spill. The public relations campaign won a Silver Anvil Commendation from the Public Relations Society of America as well as numerous other national and regional awards.

"None of it (the tourism and the animal rescue efforts) would have been possible were it not for the cooperation and support of Exxon," said Mason, who is now President of Corporate Communications Strategies in Anchorage and an adjunct professor of advanced public relations at the University of Alaska, Anchorage. "Exxon's cooperation and diligence after the spill is a fact that seems to have been lost in the myth of drunken sailors and dead wildlife," reflected Mason.

Mason continued, "The lesson I learned from that crisis and have since applied to other crises is that once the crisis begins and the public hysteria begins, it is too late to worry about your PR. All you can really do is hang on, get on with the work, and continue to do what you think is best and most honest.

"However, you must, immediately, plan for the future. Think to the mid-term and long-term future to start necessary preparations for those arenas, areas where you can begin to exert some logical controls and protections. Try to get ahead of the curve of events."

CASE 13: STARKIST TUNA
AND "SAVE THE DOLPHINS"

For years, in the eastern Pacific Ocean, massive fishing tuna boats have searched for tuna for months at a time. The vessels can hold up to 2,000 tons of tuna, the yellowfin we eat as canned light tuna.

The fishermen look out for seabirds that feed on the same smaller fish on which tuna feed. They also look for dolphins because tuna mysteriously swim beneath schools of dolphin. Therein lay the problem.

The nets that captured the tuna also captured dolphins. Although there were efforts to toss the dolphins back, some would get tangled in the nets, and because they are mammals, they drowned. Others died from shock after escaping the long arduous chase. Many were separated from family members or became severely disoriented from the loud noise of the engines. Hundreds, if not thousands of dolphins, were killed or maimed in each catch.

Environmental groups were irate. Dolphins, they cried, are not fish. They are the most humanlike, most intelligent of mammals. They have been known to save drowning humans. They protect swimmers from sharks. They should not be killed just to help the tuna industry reap profitable harvests.

The environmental groups began to pressure the tuna companies to cease the senseless fishing practices known as "setting on dolphin." The tuna companies were aware of the dolphin deaths but had viewed the process as a necessary sacrifice.

The activist groups were successful in getting the Marine Mammal Act passed in 1972 limiting, but not stopping, the allowed number of dolphins killed each year. They were not satisfied; they wanted visual footage to make a strong impression on the public, to arouse public opinion, and to get consumer pressure to force the industry to make changes.

The visual footage became available in 1988 when Samuel Lubudde, a biologist with the Earth Island Institute, posed as a cook on a tuna boat and shot 5 hours of video showing the slaughter of dolphins in tuna nets. The film exposed dolphins fighting for their lives, trying to get to the surface to breathe. It showed beaks and flippers breaking off their bodies. Some were crushed alive in the power block, a pulley-like device used to hoist mile-long nets back on board the vessel.

Lubudde said on the film, "I wanted to scream. It took an interminably long time to just get all the dead dolphins out of the net so we could get the tuna on board. After these hundred or so dolphins were cleared out of the net, there was only a single tuna fish caught" (Lubudde, 1988).

Lubudde's film began circulating through activist meetings, universities, and the public, touching hearts along the way. One of those hearts belonged to Ani H. Moss, a former model and wife of Jerry Moss, cofounder of A&M Records, who saw the film in June, 1989.

Mrs. Moss persuaded her husband to let her use a sound stage for a "Dolphin Awareness Evening." She showed Lubudde's film to actors, producers, directors, and others in the entertainment industry.

It is likely that the scene in "Lethal Weapon II" showing a character's wife and children screaming objections when he makes a tuna sandwich, as well as other scenes in television and film, resulted from Mrs. Moss' efforts.

In addition to planning the event, she persuaded her husband to try to meet with Anthony J. F. O'Reilly, chairman of H. J. Heinz, the parent company of StarKist Seafood Company, to discuss the dolphin situation. StarKist was headquartered in Long Beach, California; H. J. Heinz Company is located in Pittsburgh.

Jerry Moss finally met with O'Reilly in December. The two dined with Heinz Vice President of Corporate Affairs, Ted Smyth, at Heinz headquarters. While eating Weight Watchers entrées (a Heinz product), O'Reilly and Moss talked about their mutual fondness for horses. Moss had a thoroughbred running at Santa Anita; O'Reilly raises horses in Ireland.

Smyth said that Moss had "a lucid nonaggressive, nonantibusiness way" when he said, "People just want to let the dolphins alone. Period. And they're willing to pay the extra cost to do that."

Moss further declared that whereas many of the world's problems are too complicated to solve, this was one Heinz could solve in one move.

Moss was quoted as saying that he was impressed with O'Reilly's approach to leadership: "He was able to respond (to the interview questions) in a very generous manner; he wasn't holding back" (Parrish, 1990, p. D6).

By February, Moss had not heard from O'Reilly, so he mailed him a letter and a Scottish record entitled, "Nothing Ever Happens."

Shortly thereafter, something did happen. StarKist officials met with the H. J. Heinz board and indicated that at the next board meeting, on April 11, they would present a proposal for a dolphin-safe policy.

At the time, H. J. "Erik" Bloemendaal was the General Manager of Quality and Communications for StarKist. He was the company's spokesperson and, for the most part, its public relations department.

Most StarKist employees, like most Americans, were unaware for many years of the dolphin problem. Said Bloemendaal, "When I began to understand the extent of the tuna–dolphin issue, I was disappointed that more had not been done to address the needless deaths.

"In the early 1970s, some 400,000 dolphins were estimated to have been killed per year," said Bloemendaal, "By the time, I got involved, in the late 1980s, the number was down to under 20,000 per year. Still, I felt the lower number of deaths could have been achieved much earlier."

For StarKist and the rest of the tuna industry, it was primarily an economic problem. The "no dolphin-kill" system of catching tuna would be more costly, and the costs would be reflected in the retail price of tuna. There was a fear that consumers would not absorb the increase. Also, the new policy would mean a loss of jobs for tuna fishermen.

Costs or not, it became apparent that "zero-kill" changes would have to be made. The intensity of the environmentalists' movement had increased. The issue was popular in the U.S. Congress. Both the House and the Senate introduced bills to stop the dolphin slaughter. The grocery industry and the entertainment industry had also joined in.

A tuna boycott, considered small in the 1970s, expanded to include restaurants and school boards that eliminated tuna from their menus, and thousands of families that refused to eat tuna because of the way they were caught. A consumer tracking survey revealed that awareness of the dolphin issue had grown from 50% to 60% and would continue to grow.

StarKist's sales had been affected by the movement, although not seriously. Its image, and that of its competitors, was declining daily. The company was also aware that if it were the first tuna company to adopt a dolphin-safe policy, it would enjoy a brief economic advantage as well as a public relations advantage. It was sure that other companies would follow suit in a few months.

O'Reilly admitted that his own children begged him to change the policy. Children were a crucial part of the consumer public's quest to stop the killing of dolphins.

StarKist wanted to increase or, at least, maintain sales with its new dolphin-safe policy and to regain the trust of eight identified publics:

1. *Environmentalists*—who were organizing the boycotts and putting out information both negative and positive.
2. *Consumers*—who had stopped buying tuna and had to be persuaded to buy tuna products.
3. *Children*—who were urging parents not to buy tuna.
4. *Stockholders*—who could decline to own tuna stocks, causing a financial disaster.

5. *Retailers*—who would refuse to stock tuna if consumers refused to buy it.

6. *Employees*—who were concerned about the future of the industry and their jobs, as well as having the same concerns as other consumers.

7. *Fishermen*—who were afraid of losing their jobs.

8. *Canneries*—that were closing due to a decline in the usage of U.S. tuna vessels.

In preparation for developing its proposal, Starkist checked the basics of the plan with its most vocal public, the leading environmental groups. Chief among them was the Earth Island Institute, but other groups were also consulted.

The proposal was presented, as promised, before the executive committee of the Heinz board, and then to the entire board. It was approved. StarKist then became the first major tuna company to sell only "dolphin-safe tuna."

The policy had two key points:

1. StarKist promised not to buy tuna or any other fish caught in association with dolphins or other mammals, seabirds, or turtles.

2. StarKist promised to continue its practice of refusing to buy tuna caught by gill or drift nets, fishing methods known to be dangerous to dolphins and many other types of marine life (see news coverage in Fig. 6.2).

Communications

The plan was to announce the new policy through advertising, public relations, and merchandising with new "dolphin-safe" labels on cans of tuna.

Bloemendaal said that the company had only "a master crisis plan for dealing with the major issues judged to be a threat to the franchise," such as food safety, recall procedures, employee relations, and natural disasters. Environmental issues such as the dolphin problem were not specifically included.

As for the campaign, "We learned on the run," said Bloemendaal. "Since we didn't have much of a public relations department, it's safe to say we had little in the way of long-standing relationships with the media."

He continued, "Prior to April, 1990, we primarily dealt with the tuna–dolphin issue in a reactive manner. I would like to have said we developed a crisis plan without any pressure from the media and other publics, but that simply was not the case."

A plan for changing the policy and announcing it was finalized in early April, 1990. The company's public relations objectives were the following:

Los Angeles Times, April 13, 1990

Film Turns Tide for Dolphins At Star-Kist tuna

BY MICHAEL PARRISH

Over salads, Weight Watchers entrees, dry crackers and talk of racehorses, two corporate chieftains met at lunch last December to discuss the fate of the world's dolphins.

Two hours later, Jerry Moss, chairman of A & M Records Co., had become a catalyst to Anthony J.F. O'Reilly, chairman, president and chief executive of giant H.J. Heinz Co., who was pondering a change of policy for Heinz's subsidiary, StarKist Seafoods Co., the Long Beach-based tuna canner.

The new policy, announced Thursday to a surprised industry and jubilant environmentalists, is to no longer market tuna caught in ways that injure dolphins...

New York Times, April 16, 1990

'Epic Debate' led to Heinz tuna plan

BY ANTHONY RAMIREZ

Until last week, it was easy to describe relations between the H.J. Heinz Company, the world's largest tuna canner, and environmental groups trying to save dolphins tangled in tuna nets. "We were the bitterest of enemies," one defender of the dolphins said.

But on Thursday, Heinz's Star-Kist Seafood Company said it would no longer buy tuna trapped by nets that kill dolphins. Within hours, Star-Kist's leading competitors, the Van Camp Seafood Company and Bumble Bee Seafoods Inc. announced similar policies of buying tuna from fishermen using "dolphin safe" methods. These moves will affect nearly 70 percent of the canned tuna sold in the United States.

Anthony J.F. O'Reilly, the chairman of Heinz, attributed his company's decision to both external influences—lobbying by environmentalists and a consumer boycott of tuna—and an internal corporate debate. "There was an epic debate, almost theological in tone" about whether to adopt the dolphin-safe policy, Mr. O'Reilly said in a telephone interview.

The consumer boycott, which included a growing number of schoolchildren, seemed to argue for a dolphin-safe policy...

New York Times, April 18, 1990

How Youth Rallied To Dolphins' Cause

BY TRISH HALL

Although the tuna boycott has been in effect for years, even environmental groups were stunned by their apparently sudden success. Thousands of adults participated, but the efforts of young people were considered crucial, maybe because they showed that the issue had become important to ordinary people, not just professional organizers. "When young children approach boards of education to get tuna off the menu, companies have to listen," said Ms. Grunewald of the Humane Society.

Schoolchildren have been discussing dolphins and then talking to their parents about the issue. Senator Joseph Biden, Jr., Democrat of Delaware, was badgered about the dolphins by his 8-year-old daughter, Ashley. "She's been relentless," said the Senator, who has introduced a bill to require tuna labels to show whether dolphins were killed to catch the fish.

David Phillips, director of the Earth Island Institute, an environmental group in San Francisco, said that when he met with the Heinz company's chairman, Anthony O'Reilly, about the Starkist policy, Mr. O'Reilly told him his own children had been urging him to stop the killing of dolphins.

Indeed, when Mr. O'Reilly announced the company's change of policy, he read a postcard from a teenager who asked him when he and "the other jerks" were going to stop the dolphin slaughter...

FIG. 6.2. Headlines and leads representative of news coverage of the tuna/dolphin crisis.

1. Disassociate StarKist and Heinz from the killing of dolphins.
2. Promote a corporate image that pleases consumers and environmentalists.

Primary in the plan was a news conference strategically planned for April 12, "Earth Day." Chairman O'Reilly made the announcement, and a news release was distributed nationally (see Fig. 6.3).

StarKist Seafood Company

An Affiliate of H J Heinz Company

Heinz

180 East Ocean Boulevard
Long Beach, California 90802-4797
Telephone 213 590-9900

For release:
April 12, 1990

CONTACT:
H. J. Erik Bloemendaal
or
William M. Fallon
StarKist Seafood Company
213/590-9900

STARKIST ANNOUNCES NEW TUNA POLICY--
FIRST COMPANY TO SELL ONLY "DOLPHIN SAFE" TUNA

(New York, April 12) -- StarKist Seafood Company today announced it will adopt a sweeping new policy to save dolphin lives and protect dolphins from injury or harassment in association with tuna fishing. Starkist announced it would not buy tuna caught in association with dolphins. With this policy, StarKist, the world's largest tuna canner, becomes the first major tuna company to sell only "Dolphin Safe" tuna.

Under the new policy which StarKist will begin to implement today :

. StarKist will not purchase any tuna caught in association with dolphins.

. StarKist will continue its practice of refusing to buy any fish caught with gill or drift nets, which are known to be dangerous to many forms of marine life.

. Within three months, cans of StarKist tuna sold in the United States will carry "Dolphin Safe" symbols on the labels, with the message, "No harm to dolphins "

FIG. 6.3. A news release disseminated by StarKist announcing its new dolphin safe policy. (Printed with permission of StarKist Seafood).

StarKist Seafood Company

"In the future, StarKist will not purchase, process or sell any tuna caught in association with dolphins," said Dr. Anthony J.F. O'Reilly, chairman, president and chief executive officer of H.J. Heinz Company, Pittsburgh. StarKist is an affiliate of Heinz.

Dolphin mortality has declined dramatically since the passage of the Marine Mammal Protection Act in 1972.

"Our policy will have a dramatic and immediate effect on saving dolphin lives," O'Reilly said.

StarKist President and Chief Executive Officer Keith A. Hauge reminded consumers that the majority of StarKist tuna is already "Dolphin Safe." StarKist is the only major tuna canner that currently sells white meat albacore tuna that is not caught with gill or drift nets, an indiscriminate method of fishing that can trap many types of marine life along with the intended catch. Only a small percentage of the light meat tuna used by StarKist is currently caught by fishing techniques that involve dolphins.

"With today's announcement, StarKist continues to demonstrate its commitment to resolving the tuna/dolphin issue," Hauge said.

Within three months, StarKist cans bearing the new "Dolphin Safe" labels will appear on grocers' shelves in the U.S., Hauge said. The company's new policy regarding fishing practices applies to all its worldwide operations.

# # #

Printed On Recycled Paper

FIG. 6.3. *(Continued)*

O'Reilly, called "Dr. O'Reilly" by all Heinz employees, indicated that within three months "No Harm to Dolphins" labels would be placed on all cans of StarKist tuna and the Nine Lives brand of cat food containing tuna.

He advised that there would be a small price increase, but that the amount of available tuna would not decrease. He admitted his hope for an increase in sales. This was a risky announcement because internal marketing surveys were showing that half of all consumers were unwilling to pay higher prices for dolphin-safe tuna.

O'Reilly further told the media about alternative ways of catching tuna—sonar, for example. He said the company would rely on reports from federal observers to assure that it bought only dolphin-safe tuna.

StarKist and O'Reilly made no attempt to take credit for instituting the new policy. They clearly gave that credit to environmentalists, consumers and, particularly, children. O'Reilly even talked about a Maine teenager who had collected messages on postcards from students in his high school's science classes. The student got the home addresses of three Starkist executives and mailed each of them nine cards per day for 30 days. One card asked when StarKist and "the other jerks" were going to stop the dolphin slaughter.

Within hours of the StarKist news conference, "the other jerks"—Chicken of the Sea and Bumble Bee—announced similar policies.

A reporter from *The New York Times,* Anthony Ramirez, interviewed O'Reilly a few days after the news conference. In Ramirez's story, the chief executive again admitted that environmental groups, the consumer boycott, the concern of children, and an internal corporate debate had led to the new policy (Ramirez, 1990).

The article was a glowing tribute to StarKist and Heinz for being socially conscious. It praised O'Reilly's "sterling reputation on Wall Street," and the company's solid financial status (p. D6; see headline and lead in Fig. 6.2).

In addition to extensive coverage by newspapers, during the two days following the news conference, there was coverage on network and cable television news broadcasts, as well as local television coverage in, at least, New York, Chicago, Washington, DC, Los Angeles, Boston, Milwaukee, Detroit, Houston, Denver, San Diego, and Hartford. Combined, the media coverage of the announcement generated in excess of 1.5 billion impressions within 3 weeks of the news conference.

At the same time, ads were run in newspapers across the country with the headline, "Thanks, Kids" (see Fig. 6.4).

On June 9, a month early, cans of dolphin-safe tuna were delivered to supermarkets across the United States. The first 100 cases of dolphin-safe tuna, 4,800 cans, were donated to the Los Angeles Mission, a shelter for the homeless.

Again, a news conference was held to announce the deliveries and, once more, environmental organizations, consumers, and children were praised for bringing about the policy. Also, during the news conference, children from a LaHabra, California, elementary school and the "We Are All Children" youth council in Santa Monica, California, who symbolized environmentally conscious children all over the United States, were presented "StarKist StarKids" plaques by StarKist president and CEO, Keith A. Hauge, and Charlie The Tuna.

"Thanks, Kids"

- On April 12, 1990, StarKist® became the first major tuna canner to institute a policy that promises StarKist will not purchase, process, or sell any tuna caught in association with dolphins.

- To implement this policy, StarKist has asked U.S. government recognized observers to monitor boats in areas where dolphins are known to swim with tuna to certify that no dolphins are harmed.

- As a further part of this policy, StarKist will continue to refuse to purchase, process, or sell any tuna caught with gill or drift nets--a fishing method singled-out by environmental groups as being devastating to all marine life.

- StarKist has been working toward dolphin safety for many years, and we are pleased to have taken this leadership role in resolving a major environmental issue for all of us.

FIG. 6.4. An ad circulated in newspapers by StarKist after the new dolphin-safe policy was adopted. (Printed with permission of StarKist Seafood.)

The Heinz plan called for numerous public relations tactics: satellite media tours, press kits, an external and internal Q&A, a video for employees, a video for tuna brokers, a video news release, backgrounders, op-ed pieces, biographies of key people, numerous news releases, fact sheets, brochures, contacts. The plan also included direct mailings to food editors, food service companies, U.S. Congressmen and Senators, environmental groups, school principals, school district food managers, supermarket consumer affairs directors, and magazine editors.

Bloemendaal said that during the publicizing of the dolphin-safe policy, he worked "like hell to make all the pieces come together. In the days preceding the April announcement, I worked 16–18 hours per day. The days before the April 12 news conference, I slept a total of 4 hours."

A news release was disseminated on November 29 praising President George Bush for signing the Dolphin Protection Consumer Information Act. Hauge had urged passage of the law when he testified three times at congressional hearings. The law provides for U.S. government regulation of labels on canned tuna products. Only tuna not harvested in association with dolphin nets or drift nets can be so labeled.

StarKist received several commendations and awards for its pioneering policy. It won the Flipper Seal of Approval from Earthtrust, an organization that had championed dolphin safety for many years. The King of Sweden, Karl XVI Gustav, presented the company with the United Nations Environment Program's (UNEP) UN Global 500 Award.

Did anything go wrong? Bloemendaal recalled that he helped coordinate StarKist's public relations with Heinz public relations and the outside agency, Daniel J. Edelman. He said that, in his opinion, "Tremendous amounts of time and money were constantly wasted making sure the Heinz executives were pleased with the recommended plan of a action."

If he could do it over, Bloemendaal would have scheduled the 2 p.m. news conference an hour or two later so that Bumble Bee and Chicken-of-the-Sea could not have announced a similar policy on the same day. As it was, StarKist shared the limelight in news coverage with its competitors. "Timing is everything," he said.

Bloemendaal added, "I learned that public relations and corporate communications must be *proactive,* not *reactive.* Consumers want and deserve to know what a company is doing to address their concerns. Whether it's dolphins or nutrition-labeling or food safety, companies must act, not talk, to the issues."

Bloemendaal left StarKist in 1992 and is now working with the largest home builder in the United States as a corporate manager. He has remained in Southern California and said he has no regrets about leaving the public relations business.

StarKist's corporate headquarters moved to Newport, Kentucky in 1993, laying off hundreds of Long Beach employees.

Conclusion

Laws are constantly being written and passed to prevent environmental crises. Most are brought about by nongovernmental organizations—from neighborhood groups to consumer protection organizations and people like Ralph Nader.

The public expects businesses and organizations to be prepared for crises, to know in advance what they will do in the event of an ecocatastrophe or even a near-ecocatastrophe. When a company fails at that expectation, it loses loyal customers as well as its reputation.

REFERENCES

Averting a death foretold. (1994, November 28). *Newsweek,* Vol. CXXIV No. 122 pp. 72–73.

The Big Spill. (1990, February 27). Transcript of broadcast on WGBH in Boston.

Carson, R. (1962). *Silent spring.* Greenwich, CT: Fawcett.

Dietrich, B. (1989, April 11). A not so slick bureaucracy. *Seattle Times,* p. 1.

The Fortune 500. (1994, April 18). *Fortune.* p. 220.

Grunig, J. E., & Repper, F. C. (1992). Strategic management, publics, and issues. In J. E. Grunig (Ed.), *Excellence in public relations and communication management* (pp. 117–157). Hillsdale, NJ: Lawrence Erlbaum Associates.

Lubudde, Sam (1988). *Where have all the dolphins gone?* A film for the Earth Island Institute.

Marra, F. J. (1992). *Crisis public relations: A theoretical model.* Unpublished doctoral dissertation, University of Maryland, College Park.

Parrish, M. (1990, April 14). Film turns tide for dolphins at StarKist Tuna. *Los Angeles Times,* pp. D1, D6.

Ramirez, A. (1990, April 16). 'Epic debate' led to Heinz tuna plan. *New York Times,* pp. D1, D6.

Rawl, L. (1989, May 8). In ten years you'll see nothing. *Fortune, 119,* 8.

Smith, C. (1992). *Media and apocalypse.* Westport, CT: Greenwood Press.

Turning Point (1994, June 15). Transcript of telecast, p. 1.

What Chernobyl did. (1991, April 27). *The Economist,* p. 19.

Wheelwright, J. (1994, July 31). Exxon was right, alas. *The New York Times* (Late Edition Final), Section 4, p. 15.

## CHAPTER SEVEN

Natural Disasters

If you can say anything good about public relations campaigns after a natural disaster, it is that the disaster was caused by an external force. Neither your client nor anyone in your company or organization is responsible. Nature is.

Nevertheless, a natural disaster is often more pervasive than other crises. It can involve an entire city or region, like the 1993 floods did in the United States Midwest or the hurricanes that hit Florida and the Eastern Seaboard.

The public relations crisis occurs when the general public or specific publics criticize your company's reaction to the disaster. After experiencing an initial period of shock over the disaster, Americans do not want to be inconvenienced. They do not want to endure one day, even one hour, without the necessities, or even some of the luxuries of life. No power outages, no bridges down, no streets closed, no offices or businesses or stores closed, and no loss of cable television will likely be tolerated.

If people are inconvenienced and your company is the key to life as usual, it does not matter that you did not cause the disaster. If your company does not handle the disaster well and in a timely manner, you will have a crisis.

Following a natural disaster, the public relations professional and his or her company must frequently cope with irrational and traumatized customers and consumers. Sometimes the media, thinking of itself as representing the concerns of the public, will also be adversarial. However, in a natural crisis, the media is usually understanding at the beginning, realizing that your company had no control over the disaster.

In a natural disaster, the key goals are *health* and *safety*. The key question from publics is, "When will we return to normalcy?"

Some natural disasters can be expected and, therefore, crisis plans can be developed. Any Florida company realizes that hurricanes may occur and usually would have crisis plans. Floods occur in various locations regularly. Both floods and hurricanes generally are predicted by weather experts. If you live near a volcano, you know it can erupt. If your company is located near a wooded area, you know that forest fires can occur.

All Californians realize that earthquakes are imminent. Most companies there have contingency plans; some have crisis communications plans.

The cases that follow are of companies attempting to recover from the 1994 Northridge Earthquake in Southern California. It was a disaster exceeding all expectations for crisis planning.

CASE 16: CALIFORNIA STATE UNIVERSITY, NORTHRIDGE, AND THE 1994 LOS ANGELES EARTHQUAKE

At 4:31 a.m. on January 17, 1994, a 6.8 magnitude earthquake shook southern California for 40 seconds. Fifty-seven people died (Coffey, 1994, p. 7). Thousands were injured. Even more were left homeless. Unlike the wildfires a few months before and the 1992 riots, there was no one in Southern California who was not affected by this disaster.

The city of Northridge in the San Fernando Valley suffered the worst damage. About a third of the total deaths occurred when the Northridge Meadows Apartment collapsed into its underground parking structure. Northridge Meadows is located just across the street from the 353-acre campus of California State University, Northridge (CSUN).

Kaine Thompson was the campus' manager of public relations; Bruce Erickson is the director.

Thompson lived in Santa Clarita, 30 miles from campus and usually a 45-minute ride via I-5 and the Highway 14 freeway. "Highway 14 had collapsed and no one could get in or out of the neighborhood for a couple of days," said Thompson. "There was no electricity, no water. Outgoing phone calls were impossible, but incoming calls did come through."

Thompson used her car radio to find out what the general area damage was, but had no idea what had happened at the university. Fortunately, it was Martin Luther King Day, a holiday for staff members. Also, it was in the middle of winter break, the period beginning with the Christmas holidays and lasting through the month of January, when no classes are held.

Eventually, Erickson was able to get a phone call through to Thompson. He lives nearer to campus and had been able to see the damage firsthand. Erickson was later quoted as saying, "In a word, it's bad. It's unprecedented. Never has a university been hit this hard by an earthquake" (Hayes & Heller, 1994, p. 22) (see Fig. 7.1).

Students unsettled by quake
Northridge campus left damaged, in disarray

BY STEVEN KOSOY
STAFF WRITER

NORTHRIDGE - Passing classes and going to sporting events should have been Scott Gordon's biggest concerns during his senior year in college.

But one major earthquake later, Gordon, a 24-year-old from Glendora, had to deal with the added burden of not knowing where he would be able to finish his studies.

"Sixteen weeks away from graduating and we had to have a major earthquake," Gordon lamented. "And our campus had to be the epicenter."

When last month's 6.6 temblor rocked the Southland, one of the hardest hit victims was Cal State Northridge. Eleven on-campus structures suffered damage, as well as all 15 dorm buildings, CSUN spokesman Bruce Erickson said.

There were rumors spreading among students that the university might not re-open this year at all.

"The worst part's just not knowing," Gordon said.

Now university officials are making plans to start the spring semester on Feb. 14, about two weeks after the original date. Registration did resume on Feb. 1, Erickson said.

However, the college has not notified the students about all the changes.

"I've read it in newspapers," said Gabrielle Landau, 21, a junior. "They said they're going to send out new schedules, but I haven't got one yet."

Letters were sent out to students on Jan. 27 with registration and fee information, CSU Chancellor's office spokeswoman Colleen Bentley-Adler said.

"I think there's enough coverage in the media that students were already aware," Bentley-Adler said.

Despite the concern that the damage to the campus buildings would eliminate precious classroom space, Erickson said there should be enough room to house all of the classes.

Classes will be held in temporary buildings, Erickson said.

The university is also considering holding classes in such diverse locations as the Student Union, the Hillel house, the Satellite Student Union, the residence halls, and the new education and business buildings to make up for the lost classroom space, Erickson said.

There is also talk of holding classes at nearby community colleges - Pierce and Los Angeles Valley.

If classes are held off campus, the university may supply transportation, Erickson said.

FIG. 7.1. News story in the *Pasadena Star-News* (Feb. 7, 1994) about effects of the 1994 Los Angeles Earthquake on students at California State University, Northridge. (Reprinted with permission of the *Pasadena Star-News*.)

On that first day, the obvious damage was a completely collapsed parking structure (see Fig. 7.2), a science building burned extensively as a result of a chemical spill, and a lost roof over the majestic columns of the Delmar T. Oviatt Library with its support beams unstable. Later, it was discovered that of the 58 buildings, every major one was damaged or affected.

The most unstable building was the South Library, which housed the recently remodeled computer center with the computer data and main frame. The floors of the building were shifted laterally.

The public relations' temporary office building, a trailer, had fallen off its jacks; the ramp entrance had fallen and windows were broken. Like other campus buildings not actually damaged as far as structure is concerned, its furniture, computers, books, and papers were destroyed and disheveled.

On the day of the earthquake, the media was not concerned with the campus. The lead story in *The Daily News* (Tranguade, 1994, Jan, 18, pp. 1, 12), the major newspaper in the San Fernando Valley, had two paragraphs buried in the lead story of 57 column inches that read:

> Two miles northeast of the epicenter, several buildings on the California State University, Northridge campus—where students are still on winter break— suffered serious damage, including a science building that caught fire, spewing what firefighters believed was toxic smoke.
>
> The temblor partially collapsed a year-old, four-level parking structure on Zelzah Avenue, damaged portions of the Oviatt Library and froze the clock on the Sierra Tower at 4:31 a.m.

The hot stories were about deaths, fires, collapsed freeways, homelessness, and testimonials of "What I did and where I was when the earthquake hit."

The San Fernando Valley newspapers were also hampered. The building housing *The Daily News*, a paper specifically for San Fernando residents, was trashed.

Two Copley newspapers offered space: Editors and reporters worked from *The Santa Monica Outlook,* and printing was done at the *Daily Breeze* in Torrance. The offices of the Valley Edition of the *Los Angeles Times* were also damaged, and the staff operated from downtown Los Angeles offices.

On the day following the earthquake, *The Daily News*, in an entire first section about the earthquake, mentioned CSUN only in two paragraphs of a page 12 wrap-up story about damage in the San Fernando Valley. It was, again, a sketch of the obvious damage—the Oviatt Library, the collapsed parking structure, the science building that burned, and the clock in Sierra Tower that stopped at 4:31.

On the second day, press attention turned to the university. It was and is one of the largest institutions in the Valley with a student body of approximately 27,000 and a faculty and staff numbering 3,000.

FIG. 7.2. A CSUN campus parking lot after the 1994 Los Angeles Earthquake. Fortunately, the earthquake occurred during a semester break, on a holiday, and very early in the morning. (Photo by K. Fearn.)

Erickson began the day by trying to confirm with the coroner's office whether there were any CSUN student deaths.

Information was slow in coming. He relayed sketchy information about the status of campus buildings face-to-face with reporters who made their way through the city and campus rubble to find him. He was further occupied with the effort to get cellular phones to communicate with the media.

Orange County Search and Rescue set up tents to be used as the command center for the president, the primary spokesperson, and her executive staff.

Thompson packed as many belongings as she could in her car on the third day following the quake and drove for 4 hours on an alternate route to the CSUN campus. Rather than spend 8 hours daily on freeways, she stayed weekday nights at the homes of university staff. "My office was the trunk of my car," Thompson said. "I went home on weekends and even then, it took 3 hours to go 30 miles."

In addition to the media, the CSUN public relations department was charged with communicating with the following publics, segments of the university community:

staff,

faculty,

visiting faculty (faculty who planned to arrive for spring semester),

disabled students,

foreign students,

students who lived in the San Fernando Valley,

students who lived outside the area, and

hearing-impaired students.

The university president, Dr. Blenda Wilson, communicated with enabling publics—the regents, heads of alumni organizations, the governor, the mayor, and other officials. Normally, she would have had fact sheets and backgrounders at her fingertips. None was accessible. Erickson and Thompson had to create new documents from memory.

"This was especially difficult," said Thompson, "because the trauma had affected everyone's ability to recall such data. During the second week, I broke into the damaged and off-limits University Relations Building and retrieved valuable information on the campus and on media sources."

Dorena Knepper, the university's director of governmental (cq) relations, was later able to compile status reports, which were put on Internet.

Erickson and Thompson continued to research destruction, damage, and particularly, deaths. Many CSUN students lived in the Northridge Meadows Apartments and could have been among the fatalities in the building that collapsed. It was eventually revealed that two CSUN undergraduates died in the apartment collapse. One of them had just moved into the building the day before the earthquake and was spending his first night there when the earthquake struck.

Letters were sent to the families of the two students who died, and half-page ads in the form of a letter from President Wilson were placed in the *Los Angeles Times* and *The Daily News* to express sympathy, not only for families and friends of the two students, but for all who lost loved ones in the Northridge earthquake.

Assessing damage was difficult because aftershocks were constant for weeks after the quake. Following each aftershock of significant magnitude, buildings had to be reassessed. Damage estimates ranged from 200 to 350 million dollars. Most of the ruin was structural.

Telephone and electric lines were down. There was no water. The day was over when the sun set. Propane heaters were brought in for warmth. Books in the Matador Bookstore were in 3-foot mountains; bookcases were an awesome-looking mass of twisted metal.

"We also went in search of equipment," said Thompson, "We had nothing. Not even my rolodex, my fax numbers. We begged and borrowed whatever we could. 'Who has a functional telephone?' 'Who has a computer?' 'Who has a fax machine?' We had nothing. Then, we started working out of these people's homes. We had to travel from one home to another—through earthquake-torn Northridge—and back and forth to campus."

Getting information out was the primary task during this period. Student questions included the following: When will classes begin? Is the campus safe? Where will I park? Where will classes be held? Will commencement be postponed?

Many staff members did not know if they had work. They were asking these questions: Do I have a job? When do I report to work? Where do I report to work? Is it safe?

Some faculty members were even more insecure. Some had been at CSUN for 20 to 30 years and, according to Thompson, were completely disoriented.

"The students are used to new situations, like the first day of freshman registration, but some of the longtime faculty said they felt no personal emotion about the disaster until they saw what was left of their offices. Some lost their homes, but many of them had no serious problems at their residences. The experience of not being able to find even a pencil in their offices was traumatic," Thompson recalled.

"Everyone was traumatized, including me. I couldn't remember names, statistics that I use all the time—like how many people work here."

There was a real dearth of information within the community around the campus. Television cables were down, so there was little television service. Electricity was out in some places. People outside the "quake zone" knew more about what was going on than the people inside. Most of CSUN's publics lived inside the quake zone, in the blacked-out area.

Telephones

Pacific Bell was instrumental in setting up six phone lines that first week. Publics were able to call in for information. Hotline operators—some volunteers—were given scripts that were updated daily with new information for students, faculty, and staff. There was information about available phone numbers and cancellation of campus events.

An additional line was set up with recorded information that was updated daily. Also, a TDD line for the hearing-impaired student population was set up. Students learned about the telephone lines after the public relations department distributed news releases and PSAs to the media (see Figs. 7.3 and 7.4).

For outgoing calls, cellular phones were used. The San Francisco Earthquake of 1989 was a prodrome for CSUN in that San Francisco businesses, after the crisis, warned others of the importance of cellular phones.

Telephone Trees

To reach various key internal publics—school deans, department heads, and others—phone trees were organized.

The president's executive staff, the vice presidents, contacted their various staffs. Provost Louanne Kennedy called the deans of the schools and, in turn, the deans contacted the department chairs who called faculty and staff in the various departments.

"Nonessential personnel" (meaning they were not needed during the crisis, although they are quite valuable to the university when it is operational) were put on administrative leave. This information was communicated through newspapers.

Media

A backgrounder called the "General Information Guide" was written. It included names of university officials, details and statistics of the earthquake's effect on campus, degree programs offered by the university, makeup of the student population, location and physical information about the campus, as well as the history and achievements of the university.

At first, one by one, reporters were given tours of the campus as they requested. By Wednesday following the Monday earthquake, media coverage was intense and remained so until mid-February. Stories about the students who died in the apartment collapse, professors who lost years of research in the rubble, effects on students, aftershocks forcing new inspections of buildings, work crews laboring to repair buildings, rain soaking the already devastated campus, and estimates of damage were popular in nu-

CALIFORNIA STATE UNIVERSITY, NORTHRIDGE

Contact: Bruce Erickson
Kaine Thompson

PRESS RELEASE

SPECIAL INFORMATION FOR
CAL STATE NORTHRIDGE COMMUNITY

NORTHRIDGE- January 23, 1994 - Due to the Northridge Quake, the Cal State Northridge campus has been officially closed until all buildings can be evaluated and certified as structurally sound. Until this is accomplished, the Cal State Northridge community is advised of the following:

- Faculty and staff will be notified by phone or mail when to report to work.

- Registration (TTR) and classes have been postponed.

- Campus officials anticipate that Spring Semester will begin February 14.

- Intersession classes are postponed. Arrangements for completion will be announced when Spring Semester begins.

- Please do not come to campus until you have been notified.

- Call 818-885-3700, beginning Friday, January 28, for a pre-recorded message for the latest information.

FIG. 7.3. A news release from CSUN's University News Bureau written on a borrowed computer a few days after the 1994 Los Angeles Earthquake. (Printed with permission of California State University, Northridge.)

merous California newspapers, local television and radio stations, and national media like the television networks and news magazines.

The media was basically cooperative. There had been no hostility up to this point. Thompson and Erickson wanted it to remain that way.

"Sometimes the press seems to be out there to create sensation. Previously, we had had some civil unrest on campus and I was disappointed in the media's interpretation. But this time, when the sensation was created by Mother Nature, they were the public servants they are supposed to be. They did a good job of keeping the public informed," said Thompson. "I understand the press because I was a reporter. They don't want you to stonewall them. Sometimes academics don't understand the needs or the power of the press, and I enjoy serving as a bridge between the two worlds."

The *Los Angeles Times* ran an extensive story on February 11 charging that the relatively new parking structure that collapsed was not designed to meet seismic strength standards in building codes. The fallen garage had become what one builder called "a photographic icon" for destruction wrought by the temblor.

CALIFORNIA STATE UNIVERSITY, NORTHRIDGE

PUBLIC SERVICE ANNOUNCEMENT

To: News Director/City Desk
From: California State University, Northridge News Bureau

Re: **Information Lines available for**
       University's Faculty, Staff and Students

NORTHRIDGE: January 27, 1994 - Due to the Northridge Earthquake, the Cal State Northridge campus has set up several information lines for its students, faculty and staff.

For Cal State Northridge deaf and hard-of-hearing students and personnel, a TDD line has been set up with up-to-date information related to registration and classes . The number is (818) 885-4900 (TDD). The information line will be available 9 a.m. to 5 p.m., Monday through Friday. Cal State Northridge serves hundreds of deaf and hard-of-hearing students through its National Center on Deafness and its Deaf Studies Program.

For hearing students, the information line continues to be (818) 885-3700, providing up-to-date information on class registration.

For faculty, information may be obtained by calling (818) 885-4700 and for staff, (818) 885-2082.

FIG. 7.4. A public service announcement with pertinent information for students from CSUN's University News Bureau. (Printed with permission of California State University, Northridge.)

A San Diego-based consulting firm hired by the university had claimed, even before the structure was completed, that the columns were not adequately connected to the concrete floors and beams. There was no media clamor resulting from the story. Thompson said that so many parking structures were damaged, there was no need to single out CSUN's.

Also, because of the unusual variables that caused the collapse, federal agencies are reviewing the structure. Still, without doubt, had there been deaths or injuries—as there probably would have been if the quake happened during a school day—the story would have been front-page, top-of-the-TV newscast news. It is, therefore, a prodrome for CSUN should there be another disastrous earthquake.

On the Thursday following the quake, CSUN President Wilson held a news conference (see Figure 7.5). The media—TV, radio, print—was led en masse to the center of the campus and the Oviatt Library. The site was selected because of its visual appeal for camera persons and wordsmiths. It was the most dramatically damaged building.

On a platform erected in front of the building, President Wilson told the media the status of the buildings, that aftershocks prevented total assessments of the damage, that the necessity for reassessing buildings following aftershocks made it impossible to say, "This building is okay," and that the campus was closed.

FIG. 7.5. Photograph of CSUN President Wilson at a January 20 news conference. Bruce Erickson, CSUN Director of Public Relations, holds the microphone. Erickson said the photo was taken right after a serious aftershock. When the aftershock struck, two CSUN employees had gone into the badly damaged South Library by forklift to retrieve crucial backup computer files. President Wilson had, seconds before, learned that they were not injured. The media never knew about it. (Printed with permission of California State University, Northridge.)

She promised, however, that classes, scheduled to begin in 2 weeks on January 31, would begin only 2 weeks later on February 14. "We were still experiencing heavy aftershocks," said Thompson. "There were those who thought we would never open again, but somehow when President Wilson announced we would open on February 14, everyone believed her. Her leadership and strength of conviction infected many of us to make the impossible possible."

"People ask me how I managed to stay calm and I just laugh," President Wilson said. "I have a deep and abiding personal faith, and I believe that you can accomplish what you need to accomplish. We just worked step by step to get the campus ready for February 14. I knew my faculty and staff would support me.

"If the community at large and the campus community were to recover, we had to open. We owed it to our students to continue their education. We owed it to 7,000 students who were to graduate in Spring 1994. We owed it to the community organizations who helped us. We also owed it to our faculty and staff who needed to get back to work and find some normalcy."

After the university had promised to return to classes on February 14, Thompson knew there was a possibility that some hostility would develop if classes did not begin on schedule. She recalled, "I knew if our president wavered, the press would eat us alive. But she's dynamic and she stuck to her position. One or two journalists were a bit nasty, but overall, coverage was balanced."

The media not at the news conference were contacted by news releases or phone calls regarding the closing of campus and the reopening date. Full-page ads were taken out in local newspapers.

Student Newspaper

The *Daily Sundial*, the campus newspaper, normally publishes a special registration issue that is mailed to new students. The paper tells them about the campus, where services are, where buildings are. It is a general introduction to the campus.

The student-run paper, heroically, after the earthquake, published from the facilities of its sister campus, California State University, Los Angeles—35 miles away. The editors pooled their energies and skills, and the issue was out by the second week after the earthquake. The edition featured articles about the damage, measures being taken to assure safety, and plans to begin the semester with all courses previously scheduled.

The *Sundial* is credited with lessening the shock of what the students would see on campus and with helping them feel connected before they came to campus.

Campus Radio

Radio station KCSN normally operates from the theatre arts building at CSUN. This building was declared unsafe, so the staff set up a temporary headquarters in a tent on the soccer field.

Other radio stations donated thousands of dollars in equipment. A listener loaned a micro dish to receive the feed from National Public Radio.

The station's operations were hampered further by rain and the noises of helicopters, trucks transporting modular classrooms, and horses whinnying. In the next tent, there were horses being lodged by a search and rescue unit.

Nevertheless, the station broadcasted news updates to CSUN students. After a few weeks, the homeless station moved into a two-bedroom apartment in student housing.

The two PR practitioners set up two daily live broadcasts of interviews with various university officials, usually the president and one of the vice presidents. Sometimes they spoke themselves in the broadcasts. Radio talent also spoke from information disseminated from the public relations staff.

Campus Bulletin

The University Information Bulletin, nicknamed the "UIB," is normally disseminated weekly. With minimal phone service and subsequently little intercampus communication, it was crucial to distribute the UIB on a daily basis. "We kept the same format we had previous to the quake, but aesthetics went out the window. Printing was very limited," said Thompson.

The first issue after the crisis was distributed on February 25. It contained information about the library, mail, counseling, transportation services, cancellation of spring break, dates of final exams for spring semester, and a detailed map of the newly configured campus with shuttle routes, public transit stops, and parking.

Letters

A letter was mailed to faculty and staff from President Wilson. The letter reported damage sustained as well as progress and plans for restoring the campus and getting back to school.

Making the Deadline

A detailed plan to build a temporary campus was put into effect. The success of this plan was crucial to the public relations staff's desire to meet the deadline President Wilson had promised the media and thereby avoid media stories charging that "CSUN failed to open as scheduled." Meeting the deadline would also avoid calls and complaints from students and faculty displaced by the earthquake.

A sign went up at the campus entrance stating the goal of the plan and expressing the determination and spirit of the campus family: "Not Just Back, But Better."

President Wilson's plan included bringing in 400 trailers and tents for classrooms and offices as well as 29 portable bathroom trailers. The tents and trailers occupied open spaces on the campus and parking lots.

Two weeks prior to the scheduled opening date, 22 information stations were set up in tents at every major entrance point to the campus.

Each tent had 2 to 3 volunteers. Of the 350 total volunteers, many were faculty and displaced staff workers on administrative leave until they were called back to work. They just wanted to work, to help. The volunteers arrived on Sunday, February 13 for a tour of the newly configured campus and for training to be experts in the information link.

Inside each tent was a table and two folding chairs. All the tents were supplied with schedules of classes and maps of the new campus. There were also maps of sites such as libraries, computer centers, chemistry labs, music practice rooms, and so on. At nearby California State University campuses, the University of California campuses, and all the Los Angeles Community College campuses.

Eighty percent of the university parking space was lost because of the tents, so there was information about shuttle service to and from off-campus parking, classrooms, and resources.

A cherry picker went into the top floor of the seriously damaged computer center to retrieve computer files. The deed was heroic because, as feared, a major aftershock occurred during the rescue. There were no injuries, and the data were successfully retrieved and shipped to California State University, Fresno's computer system for registration.

During the fourth week after the quake, mail service was restored on campus. Prior to that, all mail had been put in storage. One by one, deans and heads of departments sent staff volunteers to retrieve the boxes of mail.

The public relations staff worked with the *Los Angeles Daily News* to help produce a special edition informing students and campus personnel as well as the general public about the new campus and how it would operate. The edition was delivered on Sunday, February 13 to subscribers. In it there were maps of the new campus and the schedule of classes. Copies of the section on the university were available in the information tents on Monday for students who did not get the Sunday edition.

President Wilson delivered on her promise. Classes began, as announced to the media, on Monday, February 14, 4 weeks after the earthquake, 2 weeks later than originally scheduled (see Fig. 7.7).

"There were minor glitches, but for the most part, things proceeded amazingly well," said Thompson. "Most students returned willing to take on the hardships in order to continue their education."

A highlight of that first day was a phone call from President Clinton. As preparations were being made for the opening day, Melkane Benton, a community relations specialist for KABC radio talk show host Michael Jackson, telephoned Erickson asking if the popular Jackson could broadcast from the campus on that day.

On Jackson's talk show, listeners call in. Erickson said his first thought was that having the broadcast on campus would present extra chaos to a naturally chaotic day. "But we always say 'Yes,' and never say 'No,' so it was approved."

It was then suggested that arrangements be made to have President Clinton telephone Jackson during the broadcast. Government relations staff members at CSUN made the arrangements through California Assemblyman Richard Katz.

When the White House call came in, President Clinton talked about the damage to the campus and the rebuilding process and said, "You can count on us. The federal government will do its share."

"We got that on tape," said Erickson. "The federal goverment is going to help us. The President said so. It was documented. We documented everything. You can't have too many photographers, too many slides, too many tapes, too many photographs. We also let anybody who wanted to photograph our damage do it. We wanted people to know we were hurt badly, so when federal funds came in, no one would question our need."

Then the President dropped a bombshell. He said that Vice President Gore would be on campus in 2 days. Everybody looked at somebody else. No one had heard that before. Then, later that evening, "These guys in jeans showed up at our president's RV and said they were Gore's advance team," recalls Erickson. "I said to myself, 'Sure they are!' But they were; I guess that's the new White House attire."

The Vice President arrived on campus as scheduled. Students and President Wilson greeted him. "He basically said, 'Good job!'," said Erickson, "and we got excellent media coverage from the visit." (see Figs. 7.6 and 7.7).

All classes originally scheduled were arranged. Even new courses were offered to take advantage of the disaster. There was a geology class that enabled students to get first-hand information about earthquakes and a social science course that dealt with counseling after a crisis. Thanks to Southern California's climate, some classes were held outside until trailers arrived.

Spring break was canceled, so classes ended only one week later than previously planned. Enrollment was 24,813, down about 2,000 students or 7%. Thompson said that a somewhat lower enrollment was expected anyway due to California's budget problems.

A month after classes started, CSUN was still in an emergency mode with limited access to telephones. There were about 100 workable telephones; one telephone serviced several departments housed in the same trailer. Where there once was a phone book, there was a phone list.

Thompson said the campus had an earthquake plan. "We even had an earthquake simulation with the press invited. It was done as if school was in session and a large part of it was evacuation and treating wounds. Fortunately, that was unnecessary. If the earthquake had happened when classes were in session, there might have been significant numbers of lives lost and injuries.

"What was worse was that no one anticipated having no access to any buildings, no phones, no power, no supplies, no access to any tools of communication and information gathering."

Wilson hailed as force behind recovery

BY CARMEN RAMOS CHANDLER
AND JIM TRANQUADA
DAILY NEWS STAFF WRITERS

NORTHRIDGE - CSUN president Blenda Wilson said her goodbyes to Vice President Al Gore on Wednesday and was dashing in her golf cart to another meeting when she spotted the two FEMA officials accompanying Gore boarding a van.

She ran to them, shook their hands and thanked them for the federal agency's help since the Jan. 17 Northridge Earthquake—the nation's costliest natural disaster—crippled her 353-acre university campus.

The men smiled and exchanged business cards with Wilson.

"We're going to need their help again, and I want them to remember us," Wilson said as she climbed back into the golf cart she uses to traverse the campus's patchwork of damaged buildings, portable classrooms and tents.

"CSUN needs to be personalized in the minds of the people who have the overwhelming bureaucratic task of helping Southern California recover with thousands of needs.

"They can't forget us," she said, flashing the cards. "They won't now."

Ultimately, what they may best remember is what some people liken to the Northridge miracle: CSUN's phoenix-like rise from the devastation wrought by the magnitude 6.8 earthquake that damaged nearly all of the major buildings on campus.

The quake-delayed spring semester at California State University, Northridge, opened Feb. 14, with the campus's 24,500 students returning to attend classes at more than 400 portable trailers or at satellite locations from Thousand Oaks to Westwood.

Government and university officials credit Wilson for her ability to pull together staff and tap into an extensive network of private and public agencies—from a local church to the White House—to get the campus up and running.

"What they have done at CSUN is absolutely incredible, and from what I hear, president Wilson had a large part to do with it," said U.S. Senator Barbara Boxer after a tour of the campus last week.

"You can see that she has this magnificent can-do spirit, and she has been able to transmit that can-do spirit to her staff and make them believe they can reach for the stars. And they've done it."

Rep. Howard "Buck" McKeon, R-Santa Clarita, said the makeshift campus is a tribute to Wilson's leadership.

"She did something I don't think anyone thought she could do—she created an entire university campus the size of a small city within the matter of weeks," McKeon said.

For her part, Wilson credits CSUN staff and faculty, many of whom worked 12- or 16-hour days, seven days a week—sometimes using their homes as temporary offices—to get the university operating.

She also cites the assistance offered by the California State University system and local colleges, as well as offers of help that ranged from donated computer equipment from IBM to classroom space at a Northridge church.

"I didn't pull off any miracles," Wilson said. "If anyone pulled off any miracles, it was our faculty, staff and students. They are the ones who did it... Especially our physical plant staff, who gave their souls to this campus."

FIG. 7.6. News story in *The Daily News*, February 18, 1994, about the rainstorm that hit the earthquake-torn CSUN campus as it was recovering. (Reprinted with permission of *The Daily News*, Los Angeles.)

Storm soaks CSUN in additional misery

BY CARMEN RAMOS CHANDLER
DAILY NEWS STAFF WRITER

NORTHRIDGE - To begin to understand the kind of day students and faculty had at CSUN Thursday, take a university campus, shake violently--and then add water.

The intense morning storm that triggered mudslides and knotted commuter traffic in the Southland forced course cancellations, turned dirt parking lots to mud and produced showers inside some portable classrooms on a campus hard hit by the Northridge Earthquake.

"What's a little rain after an earthquake?" said Bruce Erickson, a spokesman for California State University, Northridge, which opened its spring semester Monday--four weeks after sustaining as much as $350 million in quake-related damage.

Coping with disruptions has become academic at CSUN in the last month, but the rain Thursday delayed efforts by workers to finish retooling the campus for its 24,500 students.

More rain is forecast through the weekend, potentially pushing back the installation of the last 80 of 400 portable classrooms set up on the 353-acre campus.

"If the sun continues to shine Thursday and (today), then we'll be back in business and ready by Monday," Erickson said. "If it rains, then there will be more delays."

FIG. 7.7. News story in *The Daily News*, February 20, 1994, praising CSUN's president for leading recovery efforts. (Reprinted with permission of *The Daily News*, Los Angeles.)

Erickson and Thompson agree that the relationships they had established with the media helped to carry them through the crisis. Erickson said, "Absolutely, positively, the positive working relationships we had established with the local media helped us through the aftermath of the earthquake.

"There was a core group of local reporters we had dealt with before, plus many more we had never seen—some specializing in technical subjects, like seismology, even international reporters from Japan, France. All of them just fell in and took their lead from the regular crews."

It helped, the PR professionals said, that in 1992, there was extensive media coverage of a crisis on their campus in which Black students charged the university's athletic department with failure to adequately advise Black athletes. "I believe our effective handling of that crisis put us in good standing with the local media," said Erickson.

Asked about a crisis communications plan, Thompson responded, "There is a section in the university's Emergency Operations Center Manual on handling the media. It deals with phone trees, setting up a media center—all things we could not do. The phones didn't work. We had no furniture or equipment for the media center. We couldn't even get to our media guides. We're in earthquake country, so we expected an earthquake, but we never thought it would leave us without access to any materials. However, we found a way!"

Kaine Thompson resigned from CSUN in June 1994 and accepted a position in Boston. She said the Southern California earthquake of 1994 had nothing to do with her decision to move.

CASE 15: SOUTHERN CALIFORNIA GAS COMPANY AND THE 1994 LOS ANGELES EARTHQUAKE

For Richard Nemec, Manager of Special Communications Projects for the Southern California Gas Company, the public relations problem following the 1994 Northridge Earthquake was compounded because of three factors:

1. This earthquake struck in a densely populated area with 44,000 miles of natural gas pipeline.
2. His primary public was several million people near the epicenter and, ultimately, 16 million people who use natural gas through 4.7 million gas meters.
3. His secondary public was 9,000 employees.

Nemec lives near the Santa Monica-Los Angeles border. "When the earthquake struck," he said, "it was the most violent thing I have ever experienced. I just knew it was The Big One. I thought the second story of my house was coming down, but it didn't. The phones and the power were knocked out and my wife, daughter, and I listened to a transistor radio. When they started identifying the San Fernando Valley as the center of the earthquake, I couldn't imagine what it must have felt like there."

After about an hour and a half, Nemec's sister in Newport Beach was successful in reaching him by phone, so he realized that the phones were operational. "That's when I started to think about the job," he said. "First, there were phone calls to make."

The Gas Company, as it is popularly called, has the following departments involved in its communications department:

1. public affairs,
2. operating regions, and
3. advertising.

Each department reports to a separate vice president. Nemec's role in dealing with employee and news media communications is based in public affairs. Line public affairs people in five customer regions report to region managers, who, in turn, report to a vice president, customer regions. Advertising reports to the vice president of marketing.

Normally, Nemec would not have been required to head the communications crisis aspect of the disaster. It just happened that the person with that responsibility, the manager of public and employee information, had resigned the Friday before the Monday temblor. Even though this manager had 2 weeks more with the company, he was out of town and unreachable during the first 24 hours of the disaster. Nemec was a natural substitute because he had previously held the position from 1986 to mid-1992.

Nemec made phone calls to key personnel, including a news bureau representative who was on call for media purposes 24 hours a day. According to the company's disaster plan, an Emergency Operations Center (EOC) was set up in the downtown Los Angeles office within 1 hour after the earthquake. Nemec telephoned the EOC and offered to come in if necessary. Twenty minutes later he got the call that it was necessary.

Nemec described the commute to the office as "interesting." "The Santa Monica Freeway was down, so I took surface streets, principally Olympic Boulevard eastbound for about 10 miles. It wasn't as bad as it could have been because of the King holiday. Still, there were no traffic signals and a lot of traffic heading north and south at each major intersection."

Once Nemec arrived at the office, he discovered that the power had been out, and a backup generator for the EOC was also not working. Although telephones were working, personnel had worked in darkness for the first hour the EOC was open. The EOC was located one level below the lobby in the Gas Company's high-rise headquarters. Power for elevators and lights in the building was unavailable until around noon.

When Nemec arrived, power had been restored in the EOC, but the rest of the building was still without power. There was no access to his regular office on the 25th floor of the 52-story building.

The EOC was equipped with all the needed supplies and equipment, but not all the necessary personnel. "We couldn't reach some people because it was a company holiday. On a regular day, they would have been here," said Nemec. "The vice president of public affairs was there a little before I was, and the news bureau on-call person was there first." All members of senior management were called through a telephone tree.

Nemec said the company had rehearsed for disasters, specifically earthquakes, once each year. He felt that the hypothetical situations in the practice exercises were more disastrous than the real quake turned out to be. "The drill," he said, "is pretty well-known. It's automatic that once employees take care of their families, they report to their work location or to the company facility closest to where they live."

Other than personnel being away because of the holiday weekend, employees were also not available because they had sustained so much damage in their own homes that they could not come to the work site. Also, many people could not get to the work site because of damaged freeways.

The first task in the EOC, according to Nemec, "was to get a sense of where the damage was concentrated, which operations were impacted, and to what extent. We didn't have a lot of information, so we just decided to dive into the task of establishing contact with news media—answering and making phone calls and waiting for field operations to call in their damage assessments."

The initial concern was to determine if the Aliso Canyon gas storage facility and transmission pipeline infrastructure, the largest such underground facility in the United States, had withstood the temblor. Located 5 miles from the epicenter, it had sustained damaged. It was shut down immediately after the quake, according to design, but was brought back to near-normal operation within 2 weeks.

Fearful of fires, thousands of Southern Californians were turning off their gas, despite the fact that repairmen would be required on site to restore service. Ultimately, 150,000 homes were without gas. The original estimate was 70,000, but subsequent customer surveys indicated that thousands of additional customers were without gas service. Therefore, the estimate of homes without service was increased.

Only 15,000 gas services were turned off by The Gas Company for safety reasons. The rest were turned off by individuals unnecessarily. The Gas Company discovered later that some consumers managed to restore their own gas service.

In the mobilization of manpower, more than 400 volunteers from nearby gas companies—San Diego Gas and Electric, Southwest Gas, City of Long Beach Gas Department, Pacific Gas and Electric—worked out of field centers in tents. Beds were brought in for visiting crews.

Crews went from door-to-door to see if customers were safe and on-line principally in five impacted areas:

San Fernando Valley,
Simi Valley,
Santa Clarita Valley,
Santa Monica/West Los Angeles/Hollywood, and
South Central Los Angeles.

This impact area alone would constitute the sixth largest city in the United States. Several thousand miles of pipeline were surveyed, and 1,400 distribution leaks were located and repaired. As crews searched for leaks, aftershocks continued, some so strong that pipes previously examined had to be reexamined.

Only three dozen transmission leaks were found in the entire system, and all were restored within 24 hours after the quake. The number of transmission leaks would have been greater if the company had not replaced many older pipes prior to the earthquake.

Transmission pipelines are larger in diameter and the gas flows under higher pressure than in distribution pipelines. Service pipelines running from the distribution mains to customers' homes are smaller and have lower pressure. House pipelines, on the properties of residential customers, are even smaller and of even lower pressure than service pipelines.

Forty-nine fires were traced to gas leakage resulting from the earthquake. Although there were deaths attributed to the earthquake, no deaths were ever attributed specifically to natural gas fires or other safety problems dealing with gas. There were no deaths or major injuries among employees resulting from recovery efforts.

Approximately 172 mobile homes were destroyed by fire. Most burned because of fire spreading from one home to the next due to the unavailability of water to put out the fires. Main water lines to mobile parks were broken by the earthquake. Mobile home fires resulting from gas involved coaches that fell off foundations and broke gas risers as well as appliances, mainly water heaters, that fell and broke interior gas lines.

Communications

Communications during the crisis were directed to all major stakeholders: consumers, employees, mass media, elected officials, community leaders, and state and federal governmental officials.

Subsequently, customers and employee publics were segmented into a list of 9 target publics. Of the 9, 5 were gas consumers and 4 were employees. These 9 subpublics follow:

customers,
general public,
customers in the impacted areas,
customers in outlying areas,
news media,
employees and their families,
loaned employees from other utilities,
employees interfacing with customers, and
employees in command centers (like the EOC) and in the regions.

In the regions, staff members made initial contact with various stakeholders, including key government officials and community media. This two-way communications link continued throughout the 2-week recovery period.

Except for the first 2 days, the EOC and the eight regions worked separately in the area of public and employee communications.

During the first 2 days after the earthquake, the regions concentrated on identifying local operations problems and providing daily updates to employees. It was the responsibility of the regions to report operations issues, problems, and the scope of damage to the EOC.

Regions communicated with each other on a daily basis about the scope of the earthquake damage through telephone, fax report, and electronic mail.

Chance Williams, Region Manager, Pacific Region, recalls that later on, the EOC coordinated communications efforts between downtown headquarters and the regions. "This was done to provide consistent messages to the public and to employees," he said.

For advertising, radio was used along with print media, bill inserts, and direct mail. Radio spots were found to be most effective in both the early part of the recovery and the wrap-up. They can be conceived, placed, and changed most quickly. Various print advertisements were used to deliver thank-you and safety messages. Direct mail communications were targeted only to consumers in heavily impacted areas.

Regularly staffed 24-hour service bureaus in Chatsworth, San Dimas, and Redlands took calls from customers who dialed an 800 number.

From the downtown headquarters, the external messages (to consumers) spanned the 4 weeks following the earthquake and were as follows:

First Two Days

"The pipeline system is intact."
"Public safety is under control."
"Don't shut off the gas unnecessarily."

Rest of Week

"Individual customers should make safety checks."

"Call us if there is a problem and be patient."
"In aftershocks, don't shut off the gas unnecessarily."

Second Week

"Safety is our first priority."
"Call us if you have an emergency.
"Hold off on nonemergency calls.

Third Week

"Thank-you" to customers and employees.

Fourth Week

"Customers may have lingering problems from appliances and venting that shifted in the quake and aftershocks. Check. If so, call us or a plumber."

Internal messages included the preceding as well as the following:

First Three Days

1. "If an employee has suffered damage to his or her residence or injury to family members, the company is offering various assistance in getting aid, no-interest loans, donated goods and services."

First Week

2. "Employee efforts are extraordinary and they are truly appreciated by everyone: customers, top management, and shareholders, and so on."

Second Week

3. "Pride," "Appreciation," "Thank-you."
4. Recognition for loaned employees.

Third week

5. "Thank-you" to regular employees and families.

Later in February and March

6. Reward and recognition of all company employees.

On the first day in the EOC, the following five employees concentrated on media relations and communications to other internal-external stakeholders:

Tom Sayles, Vice President of Public Affairs,

Dick Friend, Senior News Bureau Representative,

Denise King, News Bureau Representative,

Mabel Solares, News Bureau Representative, (Spanish-speaking spokesperson), and

Richard Nemec, Manager of Special Communication projects.

In the regions, 40 assigned community affairs specialists also concentrated on media relations and community contacts in the operating regions.

The Los Angeles Times, Southern California's largest metropolitan daily newspaper, was physically knocked out itself with no power at its downtown Los Angeles city room until around noon on the day of the quake. Nemec recalls that his first contact with the newspaper was around 3 p.m. when he made the call to general assignment reporter, Larry Gordon.

On the second day of recovery, the company's MultiMedia Center had videotape crews dispatched to capture employees at work. A video titled "Relighting the Flame" was produced and distributed to numerous government, industry, and community groups. A longer version of the videotape eventually was given to all employees.

Within 48 hours of the earthquake, the public affairs staff operated in its normal mode. The EOC still functioned on the ground floor, while in the regular offices on the 25th floor, personnel took media calls and wrote news releases. The two offices communicated via special phone hookup.

"We used all available communications channels and determined which channels were best for the target publics (stakeholder groups) and the message," said Nemec. "For news announcements, by far, the most effective method was live broadcasts during the first 3 days. This was the best way to get timely information to customers and key stakeholders." Particularly effective were live phone-in interviews to major television and radio stations.

The staff also solicited the help of the broadcast media to disseminate key critical messages, and the stations complied willingly. Faxes to wire services and other news outlets were most effective, followed by pretaped broadcast information that was circulated routinely to all broadcast media. Later, in the chronic stage of the crisis, news advisories, news conferences, and in-the-field media contacts were more effective.

Numerous news releases were distributed. Following are the major messages they carried:

January 17, 2:30 p.m   Bills will be waived for customers in uninhabitable residences (see Figure 7.8).

January 17, 9 p.m.   The overall system withstood the earthquake. Repairmen will work around the clock to restore service.

January 18, 11:30 a.m.   Most incoming phone lines are inoperable. Do
                         not make nonemergency calls.

January 18, 8:30 p.m.   Most gas service will be restored by late tomor-
                         row night. (This turned out to be an overly op-
                         timistic goal. The Gas Company was unaware

The Gas Company™

News **Release**

Southern California Gas Company

CONTACT: Denise King
           (213) 244-3030

FOR IMMEDIATE RELEASE
2:30 p.m. Jan. 17, 1994

EARTHQUAKE REPORT FROM SOCALGAS

Southern California Gas Co. announced it will waive bills for any of its customers whose residences are uninhabitable because of damage caused by today's major earthquake. As of mid-afternoon, there was no estimate on how many customers fall into this category.

Gas Company officials are asking customers to be patient as utility workers respond to, and repair, breaks in gas lines.

The gas company reports that its overall system of 44,000 miles of pipeline has withstood today's 6.6 earthquake. As of 2:30 p.m., there were up to 5,000 customers without service, but the vast majority of the 16 million people served through 4.7 million meters were still receiving service.

Outages and damage to the gas system were concentrated in the northwest portion of Los Angeles County -- San Fernando Valley, Hollywood and West Los Angeles. Four transmission pipelines, 142 service and distribution lines sustained damage. All of these breaks are under control and repairs are under way in the impacted area. Eastern and Southeastern parts of LA County and neighboring Orange, Riverside and San Bernnardino counties sustained little or no damage to the natural gas system.

However, the overall damages were more severe than the Whittier quake in 1987 and other major quakes in recent years.

We will restore services as soon as repairs to major pipelines are completed. At this time, we don't know how many services are affected. Lack of electrical service may impact how quickly service is restored. Customers are asked to be patient. Customers in the Val Verde area may experience outages lasting up to one week. The Gas Company has 600 employees in the field performing pipeline repairs or providing service at individual customer premises. (Extra crews have been brought in from outlying area, such as Riverside and Orange Counties ties for repair work in the Los Angeles basin.)

Customers are reminded of the following:

•   Don't automatically shut off your gas service.
•   First, check to determine if you smell or hear a hissing gas leak.
•   If you do, check to see if you can isolate the leaks at a given appliance. If you can, turn off the valve on the gas line serving that appliance.
•   If you cannot do this, and you still suspect a gas leak, go to the meter an turn the valve cross-wise with the pipe to shut off service.
•   Don't try to restore the service, call the gas company.
•   You can call the number in the white papers of the telephone directory, the · number on your gas bill or an 800 number: 1-800-427-2200.

# # # #

FIG. 7.8. News release distributed by the Southern California Gas Company on the day of the earthquake. (Printed with permission of Southern California Gas Company, Los Angeles.)

that thousands of customers had shut off their service in fear of fires.) (see Fig. 7.9. Figures 7.10, 7.11, and 7.12 are examples of other news releases and ads distributed).

January 19   Two service restoration centers open in San Fernando Valley.

The Gas Company⁻

News **Release**

CONTACT: Ron Owens - (213) 244-8908

FOR IMMEDIATE RELEASE
8:30 P.M., TUESDAY, JAN. 18, 1994

GAS COMPANY HOPING TO RESTORE SERVICE

TO MOST EARTHQUAKE VICTIMS BY TOMORROW NIGHT

Southern California Gas Co. believes that most of its customers who lost gas service because of broken gas pipes will have that gas turned on by late tomorrow night. Homes that received major damage will not be restored until the house or building has been declared safe by building officials, however.

Only about 35,000 of the company's 4.7 million customers had their gas service disrupted during Monday's earthquake and aftershocks. All of these were located in the immediate quake area of the San Fernando and Santa Clarita valleys, Simi, Hollywood, Los Angeles and Santa Monica.

The utility assigned 1,700 workers to the quake area to repair pipelines and restore customer service. As pipeline breaks are repaired, employees go block-by-block, house-to-house, to restore customers' gas service. Because of this, routine service calls in most every other area of Southern California have been delayed. In addition, technical problems impaired the ability of The Gas Company's telephone lines to accommodate the large increase in the volume of customer service requests. As a result, some callers received recorded messages indicating they had reached a disconnected number.

Callers still are asked to phone only for emergencies and call 1-800-427-2200.

Customers in the earthquake area without telephone service can reach the company at two temporary walk-in stations, between 8 a.m. and 5 p.m. They are located at Santa Clarita City Hall, 23920 Valencia Blvd., and the City of San Fernando Park at 208 Park Ave. In other areas, payment offices remain open; addresses are located on the customer's bill or in the telephone directory.

The Gas Company announced that it is making a $10,000 donation to the Los Angeles County Chapter of the American Red Cross to assist in earthquake disaster relief. Also, gas company employees are volunteering to work at various community shelters.

####

FIG. 7.9. News release distributed by the Southern California Gas Company the day after the earthquake announcing plans to restore gas service by the next night. (Printed with permission of Southern California Gas Company, Los Angeles.)

The Gas Company‾

Contact: News Bureau
             (213) 244-3030

News **Release**

<u>FOR IMMEDIATE RELEASE</u>
<u>2:30 p.m., Jan. 24, 1994</u>

<u>GAS COMPANY URGES CUSTOMERS TO MAKE SURE</u>

<u>APPLIANCES ARE SAFE TO OPERATE</u>

In the aftermath of the recent earthquake and aftershocks, Southern California Gas Co. is urging customers to check their natural gas appliances to ensure they are safe to operate.

"During one of the many temblors, appliances may have shifted and vents may have become separated or damaged," said Lee Harrington, senior vice president of operations for The Gas Company. "It's important that customers inspect their furnace and water heater venting systems, and other appliances to ensure they are functioning properly. Customers should also look for visible signs of damage to walls near gas appliances that might indicate an unsafe condition."

Harrington added that during the company's field inspections following the 6.6 quake, the company found a number of homes with unsafe conditions, such as damaged vent pipes.

"Obvious signs of unsafe conditions would be moisture on the inside of windows or the presence of an unusual odor when the appliance is in operation. These would be good indications of an improperly-vented appliance," he said.

If any of these conditions are found, customers should shut off gas to the individual appliance, if possible, and call The Gas Company's 24-hour number, 1-800-427-2200, or a qualified heating/plumbing contractor.

MORE

FIG. 7.10. News release distributed by the Southern California Gas Company a week after the earthquake urging customers to check appliances for safety. (Printed with permission of Southern California Gas Company, Los Angeles.)

January 19, 4:30 p.m.	Gas service restored to 10,000 customers, a third of all customers who were estimated to be without gas at the time.
January 20	Media advisory for a news conference.
January 20, 3:30 p.m.	Gas service restored to 20,000 customers; more outages discovered.
January 21	Service restored to 30,000.

Some of the most serious earthquake damage may be invisible.

Here's how to spot it.

The effects of an earthquake aren't always obvious. Carbon monoxide may build up in living spaces if gas appliances have moved or been damaged. Although colorless, tasteless and odorless, exposure to carbon monoxide can cause nausea, drowsiness, and other flu-like symptoms. Prolonged exposure can be serious. In the event of an earthquake, The Gas Company wants you to know about a few simple steps you can take to make sure your gas appliances are working safely and efficiently:

Check appliances to see if they've moved or come loose from gas connector lines.

Check venting systems on hot water heaters, furnaces and gas logs to make sure they haven't separated from the appliance, wall or ceiling. If your furnace has moved, check for gaps at the base.

If you have a forced-air unit, make sure the fan compartment door fits snugly and is tightly shut.

If you suspect your natural gas appliances are not operating properly, please have them inspected and serviced by a qualified agency. Contact The Gas Company at 1-800-427-2200, your heating/plumbing contractor or service agency.

The Gas Company™

FIG. 7.11. Ad circulated in newspapers by the Southern California Gas Company during the earthquake recovery period. The ad was part of the company's public service effort to provide consumers with crucial information. (Printed with permission of Southern California Gas Company, Los Angeles.)

The Gas Company⁻

Contact: News Bureau
              (213) 244-3030

FOR IMMEDIATE RELEASE
2 P.M., JAN.26, 1994

GAS CO. RESTORES SERVICE TO 120,000; MANY STILL WITHOUT

GAS BECAUSE WORKERS UNABLE TO ENTER CUSTOMERS' HOMES

Southern California Gas Co. has restored natural gas service to more than 120,000 customers since last week's earthquake. However, the company reported there are still several thousand customers without gas because service personnel could not gain entry into homes and businesses to check appliances to ensure they are safe to operate.

"We've almost completed restoring service to all customers, with the exception of those where we weren't able to get into the premises," said Lee Harrington, senior vice president of operations at The Gas Company. "It's important that customers who are still without service make arrangements to have someone at home, or leave a key with a neighbor, and call us at 1-800-427-2200.

"For customers whose homes have been damaged by the recent temblors, we may not be able to assist you until the building is safe," Harrington added.

The company deployed employees from throughout Southern California into the heavily damaged earthquake areas. These crews are being released from earthquake duty as restorations are completed. Within the next few days, they will be returning to their home bases.

"We hope to begin phasing into a normal work schedule next week and thank all of our customers for their patience and understanding during this emergency," he said.

# # #

vcedoc:quake26
94-020

FIG. 7.12. News release distributed by the Southern California Gas Company nine days after the earthquake when the company realized its efforts to restore service was more difficult than anticipated. (Printed with permission of Southern California Gas Company, Los Angeles.)

Communications directed to employees during the recovery period stage were the following:

1. The Gas Company's weekly employee newsletter, "Sendout"—both regular and special editions—kept employees up to date on the recovery.

2. The daily bulletin, "FYI," informed employees of press coverage of the company's efforts at recovery.

3. A special 14-page issue of the company's monthly tabloid, "Energy," provided both photographs and copy of the efforts of employees in the recovery.

4. Two letters—one to employees at work locations, one to their families at home—were sent by CEO Dick Farman. They were "thank-you" letters for hard work, support, understanding, and dedication.

5. Four issues of "Epicenter," a special publication in the area nearest the earthquake's epicenter, were distributed to employees involved in recovery work. It praised employees for quality work under extraordinary situations. This publication originated with the region's emergency operation center in Chatsworth.

Evaluation

The Gas Company's self-critique admits that it "over-promised" customers on service requests and underestimated the extent of customer outages. Nevertheless, its communications efforts did not reach a crisis point. The company was not a *major* target of the news media, consumers, community groups, or government officials.

The largest problem during the recovery period occurred when Channel 11 News, a Fox Broadcasting station, and a few community leaders, charged that service to poorer neighborhoods was not a priority. The charges were quickly diffused by Williams, a former manager in public relations for the company who headed the Pacific Region, as well as by government and community affairs employees at the downtown headquarters.

Williams explained the process: "We contacted all important community-political leaders in the inner city. We explained our priorities in terms of getting services restored for the public. We gave them an overview as well as insights into resources available.

"We offered to meet and satisfy any significant request from community or political leaders. We provided resources, donated drinking water, blankets, food. We held mini-earthquake service fairs at our service districts in the inner city.

"We had meter readers going door-to-door in what we called 'neighborhood sweeps,' asking the public if they had damage and following through with appropriate action. We made daily contact with local politicians to head off any problems."

The effort worked.

Williams says that the company's relationship with the media and the general public was enhanced by the way the earthquake was handled. "We maintain an ongoing effort to establish rapport with all news media outlets in our service territory," said Williams.

"This is a constant effort that is built to the way we do business and not solely on crisis management. Perceptions were that we were responsive, very open with the issues and we kept the public informed of the progress of restoration projects."

Nemec (seen in Fig. 7.13) said he agrees with Williams, "We sometimes fall short of our desired results in the more proactive, creative, nonemergency stories we try to pitch to the news media; but we are known to be responsive and responsible in a crisis, and we always seem to get results in these situations."

The Southern California Gas Company received a resolution from the California Public Utilities Commission praising its work on the earthquake recovery. In the resolution was a compliment regarding dissemination of information: "Southern California Gas representatives provided continuous, clear, and helpful information to emergency officials and the public about public safety and the resumption of service."

Discussion

The two cases of crisis communications described here are only two of many stories—each with comparative similarities and differences—during the 1994 Southern California earthquake.

One public relations department (at California State University, Northridge) had only two professionals, whereas the other (Southern California Gas Company) had large staffs. Despite their difference in size, both had the same task of protecting the company's image, showing that the company was doing all it could to recover from the disaster, and returning its constituents to normalcy.

Because they are located in Southern California, both departments were well aware of the likelihood of earthquakes. The Gas Company, a company that stresses reports on every aspect of its operation, was better prepared. Thus, the earthquake did not incapacitate its employees as it did those at the university.

The Gas Company, since the earthquake, has evaluated its actions and then the evaluations themselves. There have been meetings to plan things it might do differently—next time. The university also learned from the experience, but its staff is so small that an actual crisis plan may be a long time in coming. One of its public relations professionals (half of the staff), Kaine Thompson, has left the university, so it does not have the benefit of her memory of the disaster.

Both organizations were lucky in that they were not responsible for any deaths. The CSUN students who died in the earthquake lived in off-campus housing.

FIG. 7.13. Scene from the Southern California Gas Company's Emergency Operations Center (EOC) during the 1994 Los Angeles Earthquake. Richard Nemec, Manager of Special Community Projects, sits on desk at top left of photo. Dick Friend, Senior News Bureau Representative, stands top right. Frank Ayck, EOC manager, sits at center. Lee Stewart, vice president, Engineering, is at bottom of photo. (Printed with permission of Southern California Gas Company, Los Angeles.)

Both organizations, like most of Southern California, had underestimated the possible damage of an earthquake. As one professional said, "I thought we would either be able to do business as usual or the entire city would be rubble and there would be no need for public relations." Although no one in the area was unaffected by the earthquake, life did continue and, therefore, so did public relations.

REFERENCES

Coffey, S. (Ed.). (1994). *Images of the 1994 Los Angeles earthquake: 4,* 31. Los Angeles: Los Angeles Times Syndicate.

Hayes, D. W., & Heller, P. J. (1994, February 10). In a word, it's 'Bad,' A president stands her ground. *Black Issues in Higher Education,* Vol. 10, No. 25, pp. 20–23.

Tranguade, J. (1994, January 18). 6.6 Temblor cripples southland, 24 killed. *The Daily News,* pp. 1, 12.

Crises of Violence

Robberies of taxi drivers are the most common type of workplace violence, although the incidents of violence at the U.S. Postal Service facilities are the most notorious.

Actually, nearly anyplace where violence occurs, except perhaps in private residences, is somebody's workplace. In some instances, even private residences could be described as workplaces when you consider the house-keepers, plumbers, repairmen, and others who labor there.

Numerous violent acts have made headlines. In 1984, James Huberty entered a McDonalds restaurant in San Ysidro, California and shot 40 people, killing 21 of them. He was then shot and killed by the San Diego Police's SWAT Team. The victims were McDonalds' employees and patrons.

The incident was called, by the media, the McDonalds Massacre, although McDonalds was the victim, not the gunman. Unfortunate headlines also used terms like "Big Mac Attack" and "McMurder."

The McDonalds crisis team reacted to media calls by expressing "shock," "sympathy," and "disbelief." It presented the company as a grieving organization concerned about its employees and patrons. All ads were pulled, as airlines do in tragedies. McDonalds paid for hospital bills, assisted with funeral arrangements, and consoled families.

The restaurant at the site of the murders was closed. To avoid media coverage, Communications Officer Richard Starmann said he made arrangements for the distinctive golden arches to be removed at 3 a.m. It was not a news photo or news video footage that the company wanted to be seen. That footage would not console the bereaved families, the community, nor the company.

The decision was made to reopen three blocks from the original site. McDonalds left it up to the public relations staff to make the determination of when and how to reopen. Starmann said it was decided to open with little fanfare and just local media coverage: no calls to the media, no news releases (Starmann, 1993).

A similar incident occurred in October, 1991 in Killeen, Texas, when George Hennard drove his vehicle through a window of Luby's Cafeteria. He opened fire on customers having lunch, killing 23 customers and employees, wounding others. Then Hennard took his own life.

The CEO and the public relations representative arrived from the San Antonio corporate offices within 2 hours of the crime. The media was already there. The presence of the Luby's executives showed concern.

While a communications center was being established in a nearby motel, there was a concentrated effort to count employees. One was missing. His family was contacted; hospitals were checked. He was eventually found hiding in a dishwasher.

There was a lot of time spent searching to see if the gunman was ever a Luby's employee or if he was a frequent customer. He was found to be neither.

To disseminate information, the motel communications center staff used a loaned cellular phone and the motel's fax machine to communicate with media and board members. In San Antonio, the public relations personnel also distributed information to the media and answered media questions.

The media was kept up to date as information was gathered. Among the news was that Luby's legal department halted the trading of its stock on the New York Stock Exchange.

Employees who witnessed the massacre were offered counseling and assistance and were assured they would suffer no loss in salary (Barton, 1993).

These two incidents were isolated incidents of violence. The two cases that follow include one organization that suffered from a serial killer and another organization that suffered several incidents of violence. The cases describe how public relations was used to rebuild morale internally and image externally.

The University of Florida's crisis was a case of students murdered. The incidents did not actually take place on campus, but the entire campus was affected by the crimes. The U.S. Postal Service, the second case, involves an extensive program to stop the violence among employees.

CASE 16: UNIVERSITY OF FLORIDA
AND CAMPUS VIOLENCE

On May 4, 1970, the National Guard, attempting to disperse an anti-Vietnam war demonstration at Kent State University in Ohio, opened fire on a gathering of 1,000 people, primarily students. When it was over, four protesters were dead.

On August 1, 1966, a lone sniper mounted the tower at the University of Texas, Austin, and from a vantage point at which he could spot people in a large radius, shot at will until 14 were dead.

Those two tragedies were the most memorable incidents of campus violence until August 1990, when students living near the University of Florida campus in Gainesville were the targets of a serial killer. Unlike the Ohio and Texas incidents, which began and ended on one day, the Florida tragedies kept the students, faculty, and staff of the university, as well as the residents of Gainesville in a state of fear and panic for weeks. During those days, the number of victims of the unknown assailant increased and rumors were rampant.

The crisis communications job fell on the shoulders of a university crisis team made up of faculty, staff, and students, including the university's law enforcement officials.

On the team was the staff of the Office of News and Public Affairs. Linda Gray was and is the Assistant Vice President and Director. Frank Ahern was Associate Director and directed contact with the broadcast media. Charlie Tuggle was Broadcast Section Chief and worked under Ahern's direction.

The President of the university, John V. Lombardi, participated with the crisis team, which was headed by Student Affairs Vice President Art Sandeen. At the time of the tragedies, Lombardi was new to the campus, having been hired 6 months before from Johns Hopkins University.

Sunday, August 26

Classes were to begin Monday, August 27, for the Fall 1990 session. On that Sunday, August 26, Gainesville police discovered the brutally attacked bodies of two female students in their apartment four blocks away from campus. Gray learned of the murders from University Chief of Police Everett Stevens, and then notified Ahern and the rest of the staff. Stevens also notified Lombardi and Sandeen.

Gray recalled later that her first thought was to imagine how awful the incident had to be for the parents of the coeds. Her next thought was hope that the murderer was not affiliated with the university.

Monday, August 27

The crisis team was called together by Sandeen on Monday, August 27. At the time, most people believed the murders were an isolated incident. Gray said they learned later that police suspected, after the first murders, that it might turn out to be the work of a serial killer.

On Monday morning, police discovered a third mutilated body, another female living in an off-campus apartment two miles away from the other murdered students. Police felt that the same person had killed all three students.

The university's crisis team began organizing and enhancing safety measures including arrangements for students to make free calls to their parents from the Alumni Office. Frightened students living off campus were invited to move into on-campus housing if they would feel safer there. The long-established Student Nighttime Auxiliary Patrol hired additional members, and its operational hours were increased to 24 hours a day.

Following the second incident, local and national reporters and broadcast news crews began to converge on Gainesville. Among the interviews they sought was one with President Lombardi who, before the murders, had planned to drive his daughter to Michigan for her first year in college.

Gray's office staff scheduled a news "availability" for August 28 in their campus television studio. "We are careful to make a distinction between news conferences and news *availabilities*," she said. "An *availability* is making a person or persons available for the media to answer questions. A *news conference* is for making an announcement."

Tuesday, August 28

The location for this event, she admits in hindsight, was a bad choice. Many more media attended than expected, and the room was too crowded to contain all of them (see Fig. 8.1).

Lombardi was, however, well received. He told of the various campus security and safety services and increases in such services. *The Miami Herald* wrote of his "stabilizing force," "a calming voice in a crisis," and (he is) "engaging and deadly intelligent" (McGarrahan, 1990, August 31, p. 1A; see Fig. 8.2).

The campus was numb as two additional bodies were found on Tuesday morning—a male student and a female student who lived a half-mile from campus. Lombardi was quoted as saying, "It's clear this part of the country has some maniac on the loose" (Morgan, 1990, August 29, p. 10A).

Tom Brokaw on the NBC Nightly News called it "an unnatural disaster, one that goes beyond comprehension. A person described as a maniac, apparently a serial killer, has been paralyzing a Florida college community. There have been five gruesome murders in Gainesville since Sunday" (CASE, 1992).

The dead students were Sonja Larson, 18; Christina Powell, 17; Christa Hoyt, 18; Tracy Paules, 23; and Manuel Taboada, 23. All were Floridians and all except Hoyt were UF students; Hoyt attended nearby Santa Fe Community College and planned to attend UF (see Fig. 8.1).

The university students lived and slept in fear. One student said she was sleeping with steak knives. Parents pulled their children out of school. Other

Third Student is Slain in Gainesville

By Curtis Morgan
Miami Herald Staff Writer

GAINESVILLE — A third young woman was found brutally slain in her apartment Monday, turning this normally quiet university town into a caldron of fear and terror.

Less than eight hours after Gainesville police found two roommates murdered in their off-campus apartment, a third body was discovered, that of an 18-year-old woman. When she didn't show up for her midnight shift at work, deputies went to check on her at her apartment, in the 3500 block of Southwest 24th Avenue.

The first two bodies were found Sunday afternoon about two miles away at 4 p.m. Sunday at the Williamsburg Apartments, 12 blocks from the University of Florida campus.

Authorities would not immediately identify the victims, but the first two were believed to be incoming UF freshmen and the third was a student at nearby Santa Fe Community College.

The three murders were the most sensational crime in Gainesville since the mysterious disappearance of Tiffany Sessions, daughter of a prominent South Florida developer, two years ago. It harkened to the two savage slayings 12 years ago at Florida State University's Chi Omega sorority by Ted Bundy.

Thousands of UF students were adjusting their schedules at the old Florida Gym at the 34,000-student campus Monday and the slayings were a hot topic.

"It's another Ted Bundy on the loose," said Jana Walters, 18, a freshman from Longview. "Some sicko. It's frightening, really."

Tina Kovar, a junior who just transferred from Boca Raton Community College: "I knew about Tiffany but I really didn't think about it too much," she said. "This does make me nervous. I definitely won't walk alone at night."

Alison Grooms, 20, a sophomore from Tampa, lives about three blocks from the Williamsburg Apartments and heard about the killings Sunday evening. A few hours later, she woke up with a nightmare that someone was trying to get her.

"I'm not usually nervous and nothing like this has happened to me before," Grooms said. "Every little noise just totally threw me off and really frightened me."

UF spokeswoman Linda Gray said the university was besieged by frantic calls from parents. President John Lombardi and other officials spent Monday morning trying to soothe their fears. The university was advising students to make reassuring calls home.

"My parents were calling all weekend and they couldn't get me because I was out," said Lainie Gold, 20, a North Miami junior. "My father was a basket case. Everyone I've talked to is very nervous."

FIG. 8.1. News story in the *Miami Herald*, August 28, 1990, relating the third of the five murders in the frightened University of Florida community as the Fall 1990 semester began. (Reprinted with the permission of the *Miami Herald*.)

FIG. 8.2. Scene from the August 28, 1990 "news availability" at the University of Florida. Gainesville Police Chief Waylon Clifton is at the podium. The university's president, John V. Lombardi, stands between the flags. (Printed with permission of the University of Florida.)

universities opened their doors to University of Florida transfers. Fewer than 500 students of the 35,000-plus student body left. Nearly all of the 500 returned the following semester.

On campus and in Gainesville, unfounded, untrue rumors circulated that there were more bodies and that officials would not admit it for fear of panic, that the killer was a pizza deliveryman, and that the killer was wearing a stolen police uniform.

Three Guiding Principles

The UF crisis team's work centered on three guiding principles:

1. concern for the students, faculty, and staff and the ways the tragedy had impacted them and their families;
2. the need to respond quickly to events as they were revealed and not permit other agencies, such as the police, to assume total responsibility for responding to the crisis;
3. the need and desire to present to the media effective communications, a clear, consistent message of the university's response (CASE, 1992).

Strategies and Tactics

Said Gray, "We knew that by dealing with it (the tragedy) we had a chance to control it. I'm talking about getting our message out, our message that we were protecting the students, faculty, and staff. We were not a university in paralysis" (CASE, 1992).

One crisis team discussion was about the best way to communicate with parents and students around the state and the country. The members tried to consider what they would want to hear if they were parents of students. The essential task was to answer the question, "What could I, as that parent, be told that would make me feel secure that my child is safe at the university?"

Lombardi wrote a letter to parents of each of the more than 35,000 students at the University of Florida. In the letter, he offered parents the opportunity to telephone the student affairs office for information, especially if they could not reach their children. The office would track down students and ask them to telephone their parents.

The letter also outlined all the precautions and safety procedures the university had taken in response to the tragedy. Lombardi said he felt the letter was crucial to the success of the crisis campaign (see Fig. 8.3).

After the fourth and fifth bodies were found, Gray said, "The level of tension was so thick, it was palpable" (CASE, 1992). She called a news conference with Lombardi, the president of Santa Fe Community College, the university police chief, the Gainesville police chief, the county sheriff, and staff members.

This time, to be sure the room was large enough, the staff held the conference in a ballroom in the Student Union Building. More than 20 television crews and 40 print reporters attended. Figure 8.4 describes television coverage of the event. Still, another problem occurred.

"Probably the worst mistake we made in dealing with this tragedy was that we scheduled a safety meeting for students within an hour of the major news conference" (CASE, 1992).

Before the news conference had ended, students began to arrive for the safety meeting. Already in an emotional state, they attempted to take over the conference. They fired questions primarily at Gainesville Police Chief Wayland Clifton, who was reluctant to reveal too much about the investigation and, therefore, provided only sketchy answers (Tuggle, 1991).

Twenty satellite trucks from all over the United States were parked on campus, and reporters roamed the campus searching for students who would graphically describe their fears.

One student appeared on CBS "This Morning" with President Lombardi. The student had been ordered by her parents to return home that day, but instead went with friends to the beach.

The Cable News Network announced, in error, that the university would suspend classes. Ahern telephoned CNN asking them to correct the infor-

UNIVERSITY OF FLORIDA

Office of the President

226 Tigert Hall
Gainesville, FL 32611-2073
(904) 392-1311

August 28, 1990

Dear Parent:

No doubt by now you have seen or heard in the media of the recent tragic deaths of several young people in the Gainesville area. I know you join with us in mourning the senseless loss of these young people. I write to let you know that we at the University of Florida are doing all we can to protect our students and other members of the university community. Their safety is our primary concern.

We offer a variety of security, psychological, housing and food services to students and others. Many of those services have been expanded, with increased hours of operation and numerous additional personnel. As just one example of the expanded array of services we are offering, we are providing food and housing on our campus for those of our students who do not wish to remain in off-campus residences. We are encouraging everyone to take advantage of these services.

We have publicly encouraged all UF students who have not called home since the tragic deaths occurred to do so immediately. To make that easier for the students, we have established a phone bank at our Office of Development and Alumni Affairs where students can call home for free and let their parents know they are safe.

Our University Police Department is working closely with the Gainesville Police Department, the Alachua County Sheriff's Office, and the Florida Department of Law Enforcement to do all we can to mobilize our law enforcement services in the area and provide the best protection and safety possible.

Our Office for Student Services is available to help students at any time. Students who have questions or concerns are encouraged to call the Office for Student Services at 392-1261, and they may call the University Police Department at 392-1111 24 hours a day.

We hope you will encourage your child to do everything he or she can to preserve personal safety and to use the services we are providing. We appreciate your thoughtful concern, and assure you that we are mustering the considerable resources available to us to sustain a safe and supportive environment.

Sincerely,

John V. Lombardi
President

Equal Opportunity/Affirmative Action Institution

FIG. 8.3. President John V. Lombardi wrote this letter to parents of members of the University of Florda student body in an effort to assure them that the university was concerned about the security of the students. The following day, police announced the fourth and fifth murders. (Reprinted with permission of the University of Florida.)

Tragic UF Story Fills TV Dial

BY JUAN CARLOS COTO
HERALD STAFF WRITER

South Florida television news operations responded to the Gainesville student murders with swiftness – and some onscreen histrionics – Tuesday. But as the story unfolded, the news staffs seemed to realize that a heavy-handed sell was unnecessary – and inappropriate.

All four of the area's English-language stations and one Spanish-language station prepared half-hour "special editions," packed with live reports from Gainesville, interviews with UF students and parents, and comments from psychologists on the nature of fear.

WSVN-Channel 7 ran two live specials at 4:30 and 7:30 p.m. The first program, hosted by Penny Daniels, splashed on the screen with the title Campus Killings...Horror in Gainesville and Channel 7's trademark sensational window-dressing. A scratchy image of UF's bell tower was accompanied by ominous music and a death knell in the background.

Tastefulness prevailed through the station's afternoon news block and at the 7:30 p.m. special hosted by Rick Sanchez. The title was changed to Tragedy in Gainesville and accompanied by Channel 7's regular news theme.

The strength of Channel 7's coverage was in its reporters in Gainesville, Michael Williams and Patrick Fraser. Williams managed a moment of poignancy in front of a sign at the Gatorwood apartments – where two of the students were killed – which described the complex as "The Place to Be!"

Williams said: "The sign behind me appears now to be only mocking in tone."

WTVJ-Channel 4 reporter Sue Corbett was not so eloquent. She only raised the station's level of hype when she noted at the top of the 5 p.m. newscast that Archer Road in Gainesville, near the murder scenes, is "a street that would more aptly be called Elm Street, because it's a nightmare here."

Channel 4's Terror on Campus special at 7 p.m. seemed disjointed and rushed, and was further hampered by a technical snafu that cut the anchors off from Corbett.

Spanish-language WLTV-Channel 23 worked through the particulars of the murder investigation early in the expanded 10 p.m. newscast. Reporters Mercedes Soler and Rafael Orizondo filed touching profiles of the Miami victims, while Alicia Ortega and Lissette Campos added strong perspective from parents and family of UF students.

WCIX-Channel 6 anchor Barbara Sloan had done a series on campus crime in February, where she showed the lack of security at UF. The piece was re-cut for a 7:30 p.m. special, and Sloan complemented it with sharp anchoring. Especially notable: her live interview with UF president John Lombardi, whom she confronted with the school's efforts to downplay previous campus crime.

WPLG-Channel 10, which dedicated its entire 6 p.m. newscast to the tragedy, provided coverage that was positively somber. Even rock-steady anchor Ann Bishop seemed shaken by the story, especially when she asked the reporter in Gainesville, Eliott Rodriguez, if there could be more murders.

"Is this the end?" Bishop said. "*Please, God,* is this the end?"

Bishop's attempt to sum up the story seemed contrived, though, as she commented: "We can only share our sorrow with the families, hope police find this madman, and try to go on with our lives, looking over our shoulders into the frightening shadows and praying this will never happen again."

FIG. 8.4. Account in the *Miami Herald*, August 31, 1990, of television news coverage of the murders. (Reprinted with permission of the *Miami Herald*.)

mation. Some parents did want classes suspended; Lombardi refused, but said that students who wished to leave could do so without financial or academic penalty.

"The university thought long and hard about suspending classes," said Lombardi. He said, however, because many students *could not* return home, it would be better to keep the campus fully operational with the additional safety precautions (Morgan, 1990, August 29, p. 10A).

Professors were asked not to require class attendance or hold exams. That way, students could go home for the Labor Day weekend without jeopardizing their status at the university. Deadlines to pay fall fees and to drop and add classes were indefinitely postponed.

Labor Day Weekend

There was an eerie kind of calm on the campus during the Labor Day weekend. There was concern on the part of a few students that, perhaps, they would not return, that they and their parents would talk and decide to wait out the term or arrange for them to attend another university.

The crisis team met and recommended a news conference to be held on Sunday, September 2. The strategy was that the students could watch the televised conference, discuss it with their parents, and make a decision on whether to return by Labor Day.

During the conference, Lombardi, responding to a reporter's questions about the safety of the campus, said he felt it was safe and that if his daughter were a student there, he would feel secure enough to allow her to stay on campus. Gray recalled the student body president, Mike Browne, encouraging fellow students to return noting, "We now know it's not safe anywhere."

On Monday evening and Tuesday morning, students returned without incident. There were no more murders.

Other Flaws

Gray said, "The crisis was handled successfully, but some things could not be predicted." Politicians running for local office appeared at the news conferences just to be seen on camera. (An election was to be held soon after.)

Phil Donahue and representatives of other talk shows asked Gray for President Lombardi and others to appear on their shows. Gray said that she and Lombardi agreed, "There is a fine line between news and entertainment on such shows and the university would not be involved in entertainment."

Lombardi said, "We simply said under no circumstances would the president of the University of Florida participate in such a show. This is not an entertainment for us. This is not a publicity device for us. This is not something we choose to commercialize, to glorify, to pander to—because this is a tragedy which is our personal tragedy" (CASE, 1992).

Post Tragedy Actions

On the Thursday following Labor Day, Ahern suggested a special 30-second television announcement to be delivered by Lombardi during the half-time of the first football game. Normally, the announcements are planned video pieces that describe the university's programs, campus, students, and achievements. Instead, Ahern proposed that Lombardi issue a message of "thank-you" to alumni, friends, parents, and other supporters who stood by the university through the tragic days.

A memorial service was planned. The central problem in the planning was what would be done with the media. Some wanted to bar reporters and news crews, but Gray disagreed saying, "After seeking the media's help to get out information on safety services, how could UF then refuse to include the media?"

Instead, Gray suggested that a certain area be designated for television cameras, another for still photographers, and that there be rules for everybody in attendance. She believed that if all were treated fairly and equally, the press would cooperate.

Tuggle drafted a memo to the media asking them to remain in designated places, to use no artificial light during the ceremony, and to do no standups until after the ceremony (see Fig. 8.5). Ahern distributed the memo to all attendees at the afternoon news conference.

All reporters and camera crews followed the rules and understood why they were necessary. Gray was especially relieved and proud because she had essentially gone out on a limb on behalf of the media.

The ceremony itself provided a formal ending, a closure for the university community. There had been no murders for a week, so there was a prevailing sense that it was over. People could speak of the tragedy in the past tense.

Evaluation

Tuggle recalls that an essential problem during the crisis was that many reporters had only a superficial knowledge of the state and the university. UF media relations personnel had to help them with the details of the story and assist them in getting accurate information.

Some media wanted to relate the situation to Ted Bundy's rampage at Florida State University and did not realize that this is a separate and distinctly different institution. FSU is in Tallahassee; UF is in Gainesville (Tuggle, 1991).

Memorial Service Guidelines

To: Media Representatives

From: Information and Publications Services

During today's memorial service, we ask that you adhere to a few simple guidelines to help insure the dignity of the service.

• Do not use any artificial light source, including flash photography.

• Do not shoot stand-ups during the ceremony, or do live pick-ups with reporters in the O'Connell Center.

• Remain in place or on the photo platform until the conclusion of the service, which is expected to run 30-40 minutes.

(Please note that no one will be allowed to set up after 4:20 p.m.)

Thank you for your understanding and professionalism during what has been a difficult time for us all.

FIG. 8.5. Linda Gray, head of the university's public affairs department, argued with other university officials who, afraid of a media circus, did not want reporters and broadcast news crews media to attend the memorial service to slain students. She insisted media would adhere to guidelines designed to ensure a dignified ceremony. Gray's suggestion worked well. (Reprinted with permission of the University of Florida.)

Gray said, "One of the things I did was take notes. I didn't know how valuable those notes would be later because I had the details of when things occurred and numbers and times that were very useful" (CASE, 1992).

All agree that a crisis plan developed prior to a crisis is mandatory. Gray developed a new crisis plan, taking into consideration what she had learned from this crisis (see Appendix C).

A suspect, Danny Rolling, was charged with the murders in June, 1992. He was already incarcerated for life for numerous other crimes. His plea was not guilty. In early 1994, in a surprise move, he admitted to all five murders. A jury unanimously recommended the death penalty, and the judge concurred.

CASE 17: U.S. POSTAL SERVICE AND WORKPLACE VIOLENCE

Roy Betts, media representative for the U.S. Postal Service, stands in the little square-shaped cubicle that is his office and disseminates information about the new electricity-powered postal service trucks. If his cube were situated just a bit differently, he could see a magnificent view of Washington, DC, from the office windows of the headquarters building nicknamed the Pink Palace, but he is not concerned with views just now.

In addition to the outgoing news on trucks, he is thinking about a story already in the local papers about a gunman on the rampage in San Francisco. "My first thought when I heard about it," he said, "was 'I hope he's not a postal employee.' But even though he's not, I guarantee you I will get at least one phone call from the news media about the incident."

Many Postal Service employees are experts on violence, particularly workplace violence. Between 1983 and 1993, there were ten incidents of violence in which postal employees or former postal employees murdered 34 people, most at a worksite.

The most notorious incident, staff members simply call "Edmond." Part-time letter carrier Patrick Sherrill, about to be terminated from the Edmond, Oklahoma post office, brandished a gun and shot 14 people. When it was over, all of them were dead and Sherrill killed himself. It was August 20, 1986.

"Edmond," said Betts, "seemed to be a bizarre, rare incident. I believe institutions, like individuals, go through a period of denial before reality sets in. The Postal Service was in denial after Edmond, but Royal Oak shocked us into reality."

Royal Oak happened on November 14, 1991, when Thomas McIlvane killed four people in the Royal Oak, Michigan post office, injured eight others, and killed himself (see Fig. 8.6).

Violent tendencies targeted
Postal chief orders screening, replaces Royal Oak director

BY WYLIE GERDES AND MIKE BETZOLD
FREE PRESS STAFF WRITERS

In the wake of a fired worker's rampage that left four employees of the Royal Oak post office dead, federal officials on Friday ordered a sweeping review to pinpoint current and former employees with violent tendencies.

The toll from the Thursday shootings reached five Friday as postal supervisor Rose Marie Proos, 33, and the gunman, 31-year-old Thomas McIlvane of Oak Park, died at William Beaumont Hospital in Royal Oak. Five other people remained hospitalized.

McIlvane's shooting spree was the fifth such assault at a post office in the last six years. His attack, sparked by his firing for swearing at a supervisor, came just over a month after four people were killed in Ridgewood, N.J. by a fired postal employee,.

At a news conference in Birmingham, U.S. Postmaster General Anthony Frank said the five shootings formed no pattern. Nevertheless, he said, records of nearly 750,000 current postal employees, along with those of former employees, will be examined.

In addition, the Postal Service will review its hiring process and begin contacting law enforcement and military agencies about potential employees.

Local police and postal inspectors had investigated allegations of threatening behavior by McIlvane, who had a history of aggressive behavior while a marine, officials said.

Frank also has asked for an examination of the circumstances that might lead up to such violence, and directed postal officials to contact private firms that have had similar tragedies.

"Together, we begin the long process of healing. And we are resolved to do all that we can to assure that senseless carnage never again strikes our postal family," he said.

FIG. 8.6. News story in the *Detroit Free Press*, November 16, 1991, about a gunman's shooting rampage at a U.S. Postal Service facility in Royal Oak, Michigan. (Reprinted with permission of the *Detroit Free Press*.)

"Once the trigger is pulled, you've lost; the battle is over," Betts said. "You go through posttrauma and then do what you can to prevent another incident." (Violent incidents from 1983–1993 are charted in Fig. 8.7.)

"You can't erase the incident from people's minds or delete words from the media. The media is very interested whenever there's an incident of violence." (Examples of communications with employees and the media are shown in Figs. 8.8 and 8.9.)

Following Royal Oak, the "Joint Statement on Violence and Behavior in the Workplace" was issued to employees. It was a response, not only of Postal Service management, but also of the unions and the management associations—all working together to prevent further tragedy (see Fig. 8.10).

Fourteen departments report to Postmaster General Marvin Runyon. Each department has somehow dealt with the issue of preventing workplace violence.

Betts reports to the Manager of Media Relations, Frank Brennan, who reports to Corporate Relations Vice President Larry Speakes (yes, the same Larry Speakes of the Reagan Administration), who reports to Runyon (see Fig. 8.11). Among its other duties, the media relations department is faced with getting information to the media and to employees about violence prevention programs and has also been instrumental in keeping the media away from grieving employees, families, and eyewitnesses of incidents of violence.

One floor down, Ann Wright, Manager, Employee Health and Services, collaborated with others to set up the national strategy for violence prevention.

Dave Cybulski, Manager of Management Association Relations, is a liaison with four principal unions of postal workers and three management associations. Workplace violence has been a point of unusual accord between the labor associations and the Postal Service. "We have very collegial relations with the unions on this issue," said Cybulski.

Employee Relations Specialist Bradley Johnson was hired by former Vice President of Employee Relations Suzanne Henry, to coordinate all the various violence prevention efforts. He is responsible for the development and implementation of the Postal Service's corporate strategy on prevention programs for workplace violence.

He developed a leadership awareness program on workplace violence prevention for 40,000 supervisors, managers, postmasters, and local union officials.

To develop the program, Johnson said, "The issue is too massive and the credibility of the program too important for me to do it alone. So, I consulted with several of the nation's leading clinical psychologists in their field. These consultations provided me with the strategic direction and foundation for the development of this program."

```
┌─────────────────────────────────────────────────────────────┐
│              Post Office Violence                            │
│                                                             │
│  Date and Location        Gunman              Victims       │
│                                                             │
│  1. August 19, 1983       Perry B. Smith      1 dead        │
│     Johnston,SC                               2 injured     │
│                                                             │
│  2. Dec.2, 1983           James Brooks        2 dead        │
│     Anniston, Ala                                           │
│                                                             │
│  3. March 6, 1985         Steven Brownlee     2 dead        │
│     Atlanta, GA                               1 injured     │
│                                                             │
│  4. August 20, 1986       Patrick Sherrill    14 dead,      │
│     Edmond, Okla                              plus himself  │
│                                                             │
│  5. Dec. 14, 1988         Warren Murphy       3 injured     │
│     News Orleans                                            │
│                                                             │
│  6. Aug. 10, 1989         John Taylor         2 dead        │
│     Escondido,CA                              plus himself  │
│                                               plus (not on  │
│                                               site)his wife │
│                                                             │
│  7. Oct. 10, 1991         Joseph Harris       4 dead        │
│     Ridgewood, NJ                                           │
│                                                             │
│  8. Nov. 14, 1991         Thomas McIlvane     4 dead        │
│     Royal Oak,MI                              plus himself  │
│                                               8 injured     │
│                                                             │
│  9. May 6, 1993           Mark Hilburn        1 dead        │
│     Dana Point,CA                             plus (not on  │
│                                               site)his      │
│                                               mother        │
│                                               1 injured     │
│                                                             │
│  10.May 6, 1993           Lawrence Jaison     1 dead        │
│     Dearborn,MI                               plus himself  │
│                                               1 injured     │
│                                                             │
│  Since 1983, ten incidents of violence at U.S. Postal      │
│  Service locations left 34 employees and two family members│
│  dead.                                                      │
└─────────────────────────────────────────────────────────────┘
```

FIG. 8.7. Statistics on U.S. Postal Service violence.

News break

10 p.m. (EDT) postal shootings update

Three postal employees were killed and three others wounded today in two separate shooting incidents at facilities in Dearborn, Michigan, and Dana Point, California. Crisis response professionals are on the scene in both locations providing counseling and support for all employees and their families.

At approximately 9 a.m., employee Lawrence Jaison, 45, allegedly entered the main floor of the Dearborn, MI, Vehicle Maintenance Facility (VMF) and opened fire on fellow employees with two small-caliber handguns, killing automotive mechanic Gary Montes and wounding two others before taking his own life.

VMF employee Sandra Brandstatter was critically wounded with gunshot wounds to the head and back while VMF Manager Bruce Plumb is in serious condition after being shot in the back. Another VMF employee, Glen Gay, suffered an injured hip in a fall while fleeing the facility and also reported chest pains. All three were admitted to Oakwood Community Hospital.

Jaison, a 26-year postal veteran, had filed an EEO complaint alleging discrimination on the basis of sex in the selection of Brandstatter for a position he had applied for at the VMF. The final decision denying Jaison's EEO claim was issued on April 19, 1993.

Almost four hours after the first incident, former postal employee Mark Richard Hilbun entered a rear door of the Dana Point, CA, Post Office. He allegedly shot and killed letter carrier Charles Barbagallo and wounded a clerk, who was grazed in the head by a bullet. The clerk was treated and released.

Hilbun, who was fired last September and had been arrested previously for assault, then went to the postmaster's office and fired a shot through the door, failing to wound the postmaster. After shooting at, and missing, a private citizen outside the building, Hilbun escaped and still is being sought by Orange County Sheriffs. A search of Hilbun's mother's home following the shootings led to the discovery of his mother and her dog, both dead. The stabbing of Hilbun's mother occurred approximately one hour before the post office shootings.

 UNITED STATES POSTAL SERVICE

PLEASE POST ON ALL EMPLOYEE BULLETIN BOARDS

Published by Corporate Relations, U.S. Postal Service Headquarters, Washington, DC 20260-3100

FIG. 8.8. Announcement to inform U.S. Postal Service employees about a shooting incident in Dearborn, Michigan in May, 1993. (Printed with permission of U.S. Postal Service.)

UNITED STATES POSTAL SERVICE Washington DC 20260-3100

Media Advisory

Who: Postmaster General and CEO Marvin Runyon

What: The Postmaster General will discuss actions to be
                        taken by the Postal Service in the aftermath of yesterday's
                        tragedies at the Vehicle Maintenance Facility in Dearborn,
                        Michigan and the Post Office at Dana Point, California.

WHEN: Friday, May 7, 1993

TIME: 10:00 a.m.

WHERE: Hyatt Regency Dearborn
                        Fairlane Towne Center
                        Franklin Suite, 2nd Floor
                        East Atrium
                        Dearborn, Michigan

BACKGROUND   At the Press briefing also will be Ken Hunter, Chief Postal
Inspector, Washington, D.C.; Joseph Mahon, Vice President of Labor Relations,
Washington, D.C.; Ormer Rogers Jr., Area Manager, Customer Services,
Chicago, Ill.; and Jim O'Beirne, Postmaster will be in attendance.

A press briefing on the investigative aspects of the Dearborn tragedy will be
conducted at the Dearborn Police Headquarters at 11 a.m. In attendance will be
local and federal law enforcement officers.

CONTACT: Jim Mruk, (313) 271-0041

FIG. 8.9. Media advisory urging press to attend briefing in which U.S. Postal
Service officials would discuss the violence in Dearborn, Michigan, and Dana
Point, California, on the same day in May, 1993. (Printed with permission of
U.S. Postal Service.)

Ask any one of them about the violence and you will be told that the
incidents, although tragic, are not as common as they seem. The U.S. Postal
Service is the largest civilian employer in the United States (at times, General
Motors is larger) with 730,000 employees. When you have that many employees, problems develop, conflicts occur, and violence can happen.

The media seems especially interested if the incident takes place in a
post office. The crimes committed by postal workers make much greater
food for the news-hungry than crimes against postal workers. Mail carriers
are mugged, shot, stabbed, and bitten by dogs. Rarely does it make news.

JOINT STATEMENT ON VIOLENCE AND BEHAVIOR IN THE WORKPLACE

We all grieve for the Royal Oak victims, and we sympathize with their families, as we have grieved and sympathized all too often before in similar horrifying circumstances. But grief and sympathy are not enough. Neither are ritualistic expressions of grave concern or the initiation of investigations, studies, or research projects.

The United States Postal Service as an institution and all of us who serve that institution must firmly and unequivocally commit to do everything within our power to prevent further incidents of work-related violence.

This is a time for a candid appraisal of our flaws and not a time for scapegoating, fingerpointing, or procrastination. It is a time for reaffirming the basic right of all employees to a safe and humane working environment. *It is also the time to take action to show that we mean what we say.*

We openly acknowledge that in some places or units there is an unacceptable level of stress in the workplace; that there is no excuse for and will be no tolerance of violence or any threats of violence by anyone at any level of the Postal Service; and that there is no excuse for and will be no tolerance of harassment, intimidation, threats, or bullying by anyone.

We also affirm that every employee at every level of the Postal Service should be treated at all times with dignity, respect, and fairness. The need for the USPS to serve the public efficiently and productively, and the need for all employees to be committed to giving a fair day's work for a fair day's pay, does not justify actions that are abusive or intolerant. *"Making the numbers" is not an excuse for the abuse of anyone.* Those who do not treat others with dignity and respect will not be rewarded or promoted. Those whose unacceptable behavior continues will be removed from their positions.

We obviously cannot ensure that however seriously intentioned our words may be, they will not be treated with winks and nods, or skepticism, by some of our over 700,000 employees. But let there be no mistake that we mean what we say and we will enforce our commitment to a workplace where dignity, respect, and fairness are basic human rights, and where those who do not respect those rights are not tolerated.

Our intention is to make the workroom floor a safer, more harmonious, as well as a more productive workplace. We pledge our efforts to these objectives.

_____
D.C. Nurses Association

_____
Federation of Postal Police
Officers

_____
National Association of Letter
Carriers

_____
National Postal Mail Handlers
Union

_____
United States Postal Service

_____
National Association of Postal
Supervisors

_____
National Association of Postmasters
of the United States

_____
National League of Postmasters of
the United States

_____
National Rural Letter Carriers'
Association

Dated: February 14, 1992

PLEASE POST ON BULLETIN BOARDS IN ALL INSTALLATIONS

FIG. 8.10. The Joint Statement on Violence and Behavior in the Workplace, a document issued to employees of the U.S. Postal Service after the Royal Oak, Michigan incident. (Printed with permission of U.S. Postal Service.)

FIG. 8.11. Roy Betts (left), media relations representative at U.S. Postal Service headquarters in Washington, D.C. gets advice from Media Relations Vice President Larry Speakes.

At the same time, there are crimes committed on other worksites that also are unreported, under-reported, or reported as something other than workplace violence.

Cybulski reminds us about one such tragedy in which an irate airlines employee walked onto a plane, shot his supervisor, and caused a fatal crash. The story was reported as a plane crash, but it was also an act of workplace violence.

Postmaster Runyon has maintained that, despite news media concentration, postal workers have a lower rate of violent worker death than industry in general (Fields, 1993).

Betts said the staff thinks of the Postal Service as a family operation despite its large numbers of employees. "At some point in time, somebody in every family works for the post office," he said. "Most of the postal workers are mail-handlers—sorters, clerks, carriers, truck drivers—in all the various facilities around the country. As we talk, they are collecting and delivering the mail.

"When we go home, the night shift is going to work. Mail approximating 580 million pieces a day (177 billion in 1993) is being dumped on conveyer belts, sorted, and sent to its destination the next day. These people are valuable to us. The purpose of this organization is to get the mail out, and they do it."

To protect these valuable employees, Runyon and other Postal Service officials first admitted that violence is a problem. Violence in the workplace is increasing. The Bureau of Labor Statistics reveals that more than 1,000 workers were murdered at work in 1992, and these were not just postal workers.

Most were victims of robbery, but the prevailing publicity centers on the U.S. Postal Service. The staff believes that the Postal Service mirrors society, so the problems of American society are the problems of the U.S. Postal Service.

Cybulski said he input four key words into the Nexus computer program: employee, violence, homicide, and workplace. "The printer kept going and going and going. It's what's going on in society," he said.

"Violence is a part of everyday life," said Betts. "Either you are victimized by violence or you recognize it for what it is and develop strategies to cope with it." To prevent the growth of violence, the Postal Service has developed a six-part national strategy for violence prevention.

The strategy was developed by a national committee consisting of postal management, union officials, and management associations. Rank and file employees were also consulted through focus groups to determine their ideas on the issue.

The result was a prevention strategy with these six sections:

1. selection,
2. security,
3. policy,
4. climate,
5. employee support, and
6. separation.

Selection

The Postal Service wants its hiring procedure to result in the selection of the right person for the right job. To that end, one outside firm is contracted to do thorough background checks of all job applicants.

The firm has access to national data bases to investigate job applicants' criminal, credit, and driving histories, credit records, and physical and mental health backgrounds.

Wright, an experienced postal manager who has had several high-level management positions, said, "Because we have a unique population in that we're across the entire country and we have mobile people, it's been difficult for personnel to do thorough checks on the local level" (Anfuso, 1994, p.70).

Wright says that the outside firm frees up Postal Service workers to do other screening processes, such as getting references from former employers.

Competency examinations are used, but the agency has declined to use behavioral tests in the screening process. Management looked into the possibility and could not identify a test that was effective for the agency's purposes. Critics of behavioral tests say they invade privacy and may not be a predictor of violent behavior.

Security

Wright said, "To protect people from homicide and other violence, a certain amount of security is necessary."

Security procedures vary at the various U.S. Postal Service facilities. There are 47,000 such facilities nationwide. Some have a single employee, others have as many as 4,000 employees and operate on a 24-hour basis.

There is an established Postal Inspection Service, the law enforcement department of the Postal Service, which coordinates security measures with the management at each facility.

Some facilities have security guards. Some require badges for admittance to their premises. Some have surveillance cameras. There are also awareness programs with guidelines on the way to report incidents.

Policy

A policy of "no incident of violence," not even a minor incident, is promoted at Postal Service locations. All such incidents are to be reported. No weapons are permitted on Postal Service premises, including parking lots. There are to be no threats of any kind and no pushing, cursing, yelling, or other aggressive behavior.

"We're trying to promote a clear, direct, absolute, and well-known policy related to violence," Wright said. She said that seemingly small incidents are forbidden because they can escalate into something major.

"An employee's chances of being terminated for bearing firearms are greater than ever before," said Betts. "We cannot afford the risk."

Climate

Positive changes are sought in the culture of each postal service facility that will produce an environment conducive to good work and a calm atmosphere. Managers and supervisors participate in a series of training sessions designed to make them knowledgeable about conflict resolution, positive reinforcement, and employee empowerment.

The postal workers unions are also working with the Postal Service to improve the process of addressing workers' grievances. Both the unions and the Postal Service officials agree that alleviation of stress is the key to improving the relationships between employees and management.

The American Postal Workers Union represents 340,000 postal employees, who join voluntarily. Tom Fahey, communications director of the union, said, "The relationship between labor and management of the Postal Service has not been good at all, to put it mildly" (Browning, 1994, p. 24).

Communications publications emanating from Fahey's office are still concerned with employees' complaints of a militaristic management style which, they feel, has contributed to the violence.

Henry says progress has been made, although the complaints and the stress have not been totally eliminated. "We're doing a lot of things jointly with our unions that wouldn't have been possible before," said Henry (Browning, 1994, p. 24).

There is also an annual employee-opinion survey that measures employee satisfaction and promotes positive interaction between employees and management. In the 1994 survey, half a million employees participated and expressed that they had better authority to do their jobs, that they were kept informed on important matters, that union and management worked better together, and that the quality of service had improved. They were happy with their salaries and job security, and were enjoying their work.

They were concerned that improvements be made in job safety, that the pace be quickened in changing the work culture and preventing problems like sexual harassment. As an example of changes resulting from the survey, one third of performance compensation for managers is now based on employee satisfaction.

Employee Support

The Employee Assistance Program (EAP) was founded in 1986 as a program for the recovery of alcoholics. Dr. John Kurutz is manager of the EAP, which is currently a short-term counseling and referral source to help employees overcome any problem dealing with work or personal issues that can cause stress or physical, mental, or emotional duress.

The EAP has counseled more than 600 employees.

Also, improvements have been made in teaching employees how to use the EAP. All Postal Service employees participate in some kind of orientation program that includes an explanation of the EAP.

Two 24-hour hotlines and toll-free 800 numbers were installed for employee use in reporting threats or concerns to headquarters. One line connects to the U.S. Postal Inspection Service, the law enforcement section, and is for the reporting of threats or any illegal activity. The second line takes calls reporting almost anything employees want to vent. Wright said all calls are taken seriously.

"Employees know about the hotlines," said Betts. "A worker can talk too loud and another will call the hotline. This can be an early sign of a crucial problem. We try to do this without a witch-hunt atmosphere. But we use common sense in defining acceptable and unacceptable behavior. We do not ignore any calls.

"Sometimes people just call with personal problems," Betts said. "And that's okay. If a caller contacts us and needs some sort of counseling, then counseling is available on that phone line."

The U.S. Postal Inspection Service investigates threats from both hotlines. During the first year of operation, the hotline logged 1,790 calls. Paul Griffo, national spokesperson for the Postal Inspection Service said, "If you are threatening others or if you are exhibiting threatening behavior, it's going to be followed up on right away" (Browning, 1994, p. 23).

In certain regions of the Postal Service, crisis intervention teams have been organized to address threats and behavior believed to be potentially violent.

Jim Merrill, a human resources executive with the Pacific Area, heads such a team in California. Each district created its own crisis intervention team made up of key employees as well as others from outside sources. "The teams provide an organized way of addressing potentially dangerous situations so that we can have control and respond appropriately," said Merrill (Anfuso, 1994, p. 76).

Merrill recalled an incident in which a former employee wrote a threatening letter and sent it via computer to the Antioch, California, post office. The letter read, "I have posttraumatic stress disorder. I haven't been properly treated; I'm enraged and I wake up at night thinking that I want to kill the postmaster" (Anfuso, 1994, p. 76).

The crisis intervention team went into action. The man had an attorney to deal with the issue, so the team met with the attorney. A physician on the team met with the man's therapist. A permanent restraining order was filed against the former employee. Additional security was added. The postmaster was temporarily moved to a different site.

"You don't have control of that person (the former employee) because he's outside your work force," said Merrill, "but through these efforts we were able to put him on notice, determine that he wasn't dangerous, that he was just blowing off steam, and defuse the situation" (Anfuso, 1994, p. 76).

Also, in California, 5,000 managers were trained in how to report threats and how to recognize the warnings of violence.

Separation

"We're trying to make the point with our managers and supervisors that firing people doesn't necessarily solve the problem," said Wright. "Quite a few of our most violent incidents have been terminated employees who come back and shoot people" (Anfuso, 1994, p. 69).

The employee who places all hope in his or her job is one type of worker at risk for violence. This employee, if terminated after many years on the job, suddenly realizes loyalty is a myth, or at best a one-way street.

Nevertheless, termination is sometimes necessary, so the Postal Service has created policies and procedures for terminating employees effectively and for making assessments of potentially violent consequences.

Dearborn

In addition to the programs emanating from headquarters, any state and any facility may have its own programs. Following the incident of violence in Dearborn, Michigan, its postal staff adopted the following programs:

1. A suggestion box was installed in the four post offices to promote employee ideas.
2. Two work teams were formed: a communications committee and a leadership committee. Each consists of 8 to 10 workers, a union representative, and a manager. The work teams discuss suggestions made by employees and make recommendations to the joint labor-management committee.
3. The joint labor-management committee was set up consisting of representatives for the three unions and postal managers along with the Dearborn postmaster. It meets monthly to evaluate the recommendations of the leadership and communications committees. An employee newsletter has resulted, as well as the institution of employee evaluations for new acting supervisors.
4. An employee picnic helps to raise funds for victims of the shooting incident. The city police and firefighters are invited.
5. An Employee of the Month Program was initiated in which the selected employee is presented with an engraved plaque, a gift certificate for movies and dinner, and a special parking place.

Communications

Without question, employees are the target public for the Postal Service's violence prevention program. How do policies and programs developed at headquarters in Washington, DC get communicated to nearly three quarters of a million employees?

Betts says there is competition for the attention of employees on the issue of workplace violence. There are Postal Service communications along with the communications from unions, the media, and peers. "Each may have a different slant but the messages are the same," Betts said. "It would be naive to expect anything different. Our best bet is to communicate early, often, and accurately. Credibility is all we have."

Various newsletters and bulletins are circulated nationwide. There is *Postal Life* (formerly *Focus*), a national newspaper for postal employees. There are also newsbreaks posted on bulletin boards nationwide.

A video, *Video Focus,* is issued monthly describing new policy decisions. There are television monitors in rooms where employees take breaks and have meals. The supervisors ensure that everyone has the opportunity to view the videos.

There are also special Town Hall meetings once every three or four months at various locations. Postmaster General Runyon heads the two-hour session attended by about 250 employees. Issues pertinent to the employees are discussed and questions are answered by the postmaster general. Videotapes of each session are distributed to facilities throughout the country.

One-on-one meetings with supervisors are important, as are group meetings with supervisors.

The unions have made it possible to segment the employee public further. Cybulski says all the unions and management associations have newsletters and bulletin board messages widely read by their particular workers. The American Postal Workers Union communicates with approximately 330,000 window clerks and mail processors. The National Association of Letter Carriers communicates with 300,000 people who deliver mail. The Mail Handlers Union communicates with 51,000 workers who do heavy lifting, loading, and unloading of mail. The National Rural Letter Carriers Association communicates with 60,000 workers in rural areas—carriers who deliver to street boxes.

Cybulski said that the three management associations also are a source of communications with their members. The three associations are the National Association of Postal Supervisors, the National Association of Postmasters of the United States and the National League of Postmasters of the United States.

Cybulski said that the Postal Service formed a leadership team in April, 1993 on which, "Every officer of the Postal Service and the presidents of the unions and management associations meet for a full day, twice a month. There are no substitutes for the presidents because we need the person with authority to make commitments and decisions. Workplace violence is a subject all members of the team believe is crucial, and participants take information and decisions back to their members."

Other Efforts

The U.S. Postal Service, in December 1993, sponsored a symposium on workplace violence in Washington, DC. It was attended by academic and professional experts on the subject, in addition to corporate and government executives.

There is also a National Committee on Workplace Behavior headed by Joseph Mahon, the Postal Service's vice president of labor relations.

The Postal Service's communications program got a boost when The Centers for Disease Control and Prevention (CDC) in August 1994 published statistics that said despite extensive media coverage to the contrary, neither the Postal Service industry nor postal occupations are among the groups at increased risk for work-related homicide.

The report further found that "the occupational fatality rate for U.S. Postal Service workers is approximately 2.5 times lower than that for all workers combined" (Center for Disease Control and Prevention, 1994, p. 594).

Furthermore, the report also said, "Although the occupational homicide rate for the Postal Service is similar to the national rate for all industries, co-workers appear to be disproportionately responsible for homicides that occur in the Postal Service."

The two statements were good news and no news respectively to Betts and the rest of headquarters staff. "We were aware that people from employee relations had been working with the CDC on the study," said Betts.

"The results confirmed what we were saying all along." When released to the media, the information was more credible to the public coming from the CDC than from the Postal Service. If the Postal Service had released the information, it could have been accused of attempting to improve its image with questionable data. The CDC, however, had nothing to gain from the release of the information.

The information was used in a report on the Associated Press wire and appeared as a positive story in many newspapers on or soon after August 19, 1994, including the St. Louis *Post-Dispatch* (August 21, 1994), *The Washington Times,* the Denver *Rocky Mountain News, The Commercial Appeal* (Memphis), *The Houston Post, Newsday* (New York), the *Orange County Register, The Sacramento Bee,* the Newark *Star-Ledger, The Denver Post,* and the *Seattle Post-Intelligencer* (see Fig. 8.12).

An employer does not cause violence. Circumstances on a job can, however, contribute to stress levels which cause violence. The Postal Service is looking for solutions and, by these efforts, it is making significant contributions to corporate America.

Betts says of the Postal Service, "We are coming of age. We are an organization which tries to define and redefine our mission, our purpose. We are looking for new innovative ways of handling mail, but 80 cents of every dollar in our budget is spent for labor. Our operations remain labor-intensive."

In the middle of these words, Betts got a phone call from a California reporter. He was checking the possibility of doing a series of articles on violence and wanted suggestions and cooperation from Betts. "See what I told you," Betts responded after the call. "I knew that the incident in San Francisco would cause some media connection to us. I knew it!"

From the Newark **Star Ledger**, Friday, August 19, 1994

Postal workers' death risk found to be low

ATLANTA (AP) – The risk of death on the job for postal workers is far less than gory headlines about post office shootings would suggest, federal health officials said yesterday.

In fact, the risk of death for the U.S. Postal Service's 892,000 employees is 2.5 times less than that of all workers nationwide, according to the Centers for Disease Control and Prevention.

Taxicab drivers and dispatchers have the most risky occupation, with a death rate of 26.9 per 100,000 employees, said CDC epidemiologist Dawn Castillo. The Postal Service rate is 2.1 per 100,000.

The rate for all U.S. industries combined was 5.4 per 100,000 in the period studied by the CDC, 1983-89. The CDC has not yet compiled figures for the 1990s.

The CDC researchers found that motor vehicle-related accidents were the leading cause of death on the job both nationally and in the Postal Service.

From 1980-89, 43 percent of the postal workers killed on the job died in motor vehicle accidents. Nationally, the figure was 23 percent.

Murder was the second highest cause of death on the job for postal workers and the third leading cause for all workers, the CDC said. Machine-related injuries are the second leading cause of death on the job for all workers.

Firearms were the most common murder weapon, and postal employees were more likely to be killed by a co-worker than by people not employed by the Postal Service, the researchers found.

From the New Orleans **Times-Picayune**, June 16, 1993

Postmaster ponders rash of violence

WASHINGTON (AP) – Postmaster General Marvin Runyon is trying to pin down the causes and solutions for workplace violence.

Recent killings by postal workers in Michigan and California are just the most recent of many such incidents that have affected the post office and other businesses around the nation.

"Images of grieving family members and shocked employees during my visits to the sites of both tragedies will remain with me forever," Runyon said in a commentary Monday in the Los Angeles Times.

Runyon said he is considering trying to organize a panel of corporate executives and researchers "to explore what the nation's businesses can do to curtail workplace violence."

In addition, he said, the Postal Inspection Service is launching a study to try and determine what connects workers who turn to violence.

Runyon said his agency has tightened screening procedures for job applicants, operates hotlines to report threats and is trying to improve communication.

"All kinds of jobs in our economy come with built-in stress. Yet the vast majority of managers don't push employees too hard. Moreover, 99.99 percent of postal employees don't do violent things to fellow employees when they face job disappointments and frustration," wrote Runyon.

As for the causes of specific incidents, Runyon concluded, "I don't have all the answers and probably never will. I wish I knew what causes irrational behavior by irrational individuals."

FIG. 8.12. News stories with a positive slant about violence at the U.S. Postal Service. (Reprinted with permission of the Associated Press.)

Discussion

The University of Florida murderer was a person not connected to the university, who wrecked havoc on its publics: students, parents, faculty, staff, and community. The crisis communications team's effort was to restore calm and peace to all publics.

The U.S. Postal Service's continuing campaign is to eliminate problems internally. Employees are the essential public, but the Postal Service is also concerned with its image as an institution. Media relations were used to project that image to that vast general public.

REFERENCES

Anfuso, D. (1994, October). Deflecting workplace violence. *Personnel Journal, 73*(10), 66–77.

Barton, L. (1993). *Crisis in organizations.* Cincinnati: South-Western Publishing Co.

Browning, D. L. (1994, April). Stamping out violence. *Human Resource Executive.* pp. 1, 22–24.

Center for Disease Control and Prevention. (1994, August 14). *Morbidity and Mortality Report,* Vol. 43, No. 32.

Council for Advancement and Support of Education (CASE). (1992). *The worst of times* (a crisis training video).

Fields, G. (1993, December 17). In '92, 750 were slain on the job. *USA Today,* p. 1.

McGarrahan. E. (1990, August 31). UF President is 'the person we needed.' *Miami Herald.* p. 1A, 14A.

Morgan, C. (1990, August 29). Terror grips Gainesville as 2 more bodies found. *Miami Herald,* p. 1A, 10A.

Starmann, R. (1993). Tragedy at McDonalds. *In* J. A. Gottschalk (Ed.), *Crisis response* (pp. 309–321). Detroit: Visible Ink.

Tuggle, C. (1991, summer). Media relations during crisis coverage—the Gainesville student murders. *Public Relations Quarterly, 36*(2), 23–28.

CHAPTER NINE

Celebrities and Crises

When a famous person is involved in a crisis or brings on a crisis, the public relations professional who represents the celebrity or the organization associated with the celebrity is on a hot seat. All of the strategies, tactics, and rules of crisis communications are needed and even more because anything out of the ordinary with celebrities is likely to be interesting to the media.

Reporters will quote the First Amendment to the U.S. Constitution—"freedom of the press," "the public's right to know." The First Amendment says that the U.S. Congress shall make no law "abridging the freedom of speech, of the press; of the right of the people peaceably to assemble, and to petition the Government for a redress of grievances."

The Supreme Court has ruled that the First Amendment applies to newspapers, broadcasting, books, magazines, and film.

On the other hand, the Fourth Amendment to the U.S. Constitution guarantees privacy. An individual has a right to be left alone, to be protected from intrusion, from publicity that places him or her in a false light, and from publicity that discloses private and embarrassing facts (Johnston, 1978).

Every United States citizen has this right of privacy except "public figures." Public figures sacrifice that right, that protection, when they become celebrities: sports stars, actors, entertainers, political figures, or elected officials.

Public relations and advertising agencies must obtain permission from celebrities to use their likenesses or names in promotional materials that imply endorsement. However, the news media has carte blanche to divulge information about celebrities as long as it is legitimate news. "Legitimate" is a vague word. Because "inquiring minds want to know," few in the media worry about the word "legitimate."

Debates ensue over what rights of privacy a celebrity should enjoy. The media say "few" or "none," depending upon what they want to do. Celebrities argue "more." In the meantime, celebrity stories sell newspapers and help broadcast shows win ratings, so the stories continue big time.

True enough, some celebrities are responsible for their own bad news. Others are innocent victims of rumor, hearsay, and viciousness. Nevertheless, one must remember that all celebrities are humans with emotions and problems, that their fame has not eliminated the usual woes of life.

The question is this: How do celebrities impact public relations practitioners, who sometimes find themselves compassionate for celebrities and, at other times, critical of them?

Celebrity Spokespersons

Public relations practitioners are affected by celebrity crises when the celebrities are spokespersons for product endorsements or the voice of a public service project.

The problem with celebrities as spokespersons is that there is disenchantment when the heroes fail, either by their own deeds, shortcomings, or by society's accusations. The greatest risk is that there will be some negative publicity, embarrassment to an organization or product, or decline in the credibility of the product.

Magic Johnson was the perfect spokesperson for various companies: Nestle, Converse, Kentucky Fried Chicken, and Pepsi—until he announced that he had contracted the HIV virus. Then he became a powerful spokesperson for AIDS.

The campaign to fight the spread of the disease needed a spokesperson like Magic. The campaign could not have asked for a better spokesperson—a popular star athlete with a reputation as a heterosexual. Even though his sexual promiscuity was, admittedly, a negative factor, his engaging personality and rapport with youth, a key target for the campaign, were considered extremely positive.

Some frequent celebrity spokesperson crises are the following:

1. Spokespersons inform the public that they do not use or support the product they endorse.
2. Spokespersons are charged with a crime or are publicly associated with illegal or immoral activity.
3. Spokespersons are charged with encouraging crime related to the endorsed product or service.

Spokespersons Who Do Not Use
or Do Not Support Products They Endorse

Actor Don Johnson, spokesman for Pepsi, was seen in a popular magazine drinking a Diet Coke. Cher, although promoting Bally's Health Club, never attends a Ballys; she has her own. Former Philadelphia 76'er Darryl Dawkins shocked Nike, with which he had a contract, by appearing at the 1982 playoffs wearing Pony sneakers. It seems he had contracts with both companies (Horovitz, 1992).

Olympic Silver medalist Nancy Kerrigan embarrassed the Walt Disney Company when, under a million dollar contract and in a parade with Mickey Mouse, Disney's in-house star was heard saying, "This is so corny. This is so dumb. I hate it. This is the most corny thing I've ever done" (Bloomberg Business News, 1994).

American Express endured similar chagrin when actress Meryl Streep, after collecting $3 million for an appearance in a commercial, told a newspaper reporter that she didn't believe in the company (Bloomberg Business News, 1994).

Pepsi was not upset, however, when the information was made public that the King of Pop, Michael Jackson, prior to accusations of child molestation, did not drink Pepsi. He acknowledged drinking only vitamin-fortified liquids. Barry Holt, Pepsi spokesman, said, "It's not important to us whether he drinks it. He has millions of fans who drink it. . . . What's more, Jackson has a Pepsi vending machine at his home that we supply. We presume he serves it to his guests" (Horovitz, 1992, p. D6).

Spokespersons Charged With Crimes
or Immoral Activities

In 1994, Jackson—reportedly suffering from prescription drugs he was taking in the midst of accusations of child molestation—canceled a performing tour sponsored by Pepsi. At that point Pepsi did cancel his contract.

Scandals, as well as criminal charges, are usually fuel for cancellation of spokespersons' contracts. Even though the contracts may be canceled and the courts may or may not decide guilt, the negative image generated by the scandal is often too much for companies and organizations to bear.

Former football star-actor, sportscaster, O. J. Simpson, was dropped from the Hertz contract he had since 1975 when he was charged with murdering his ex-wife and her companion. Hertz was criticized and picketed after the murder charges were filed for not canceling the contract when Simpson pleaded "no contest" to spousal battery charges in 1989. Until that time, Simpson had been a prime asset to the company and ranked first in a poll of 40 favorite sportscasters (Bloomberg Business News, 1994).

Tennis star, Jennifer Capriati, under contract to Prince, the tennis racket-maker, and Diadoro sportswear, was arrested for drug possession (Bloomberg Business News, 1994). Ringo Starr spoke on behalf of Sun Country wine coolers and subsequently entered an alcohol rehabilitation center (Tom, Clark, Elmer, Groch, Masetti, & Sandhar, 1992).

Seagrams wine cooler dropped actor Bruce Willis after he went into alcohol rehabilitation. Seagrams said the contract was canceled because Willis' "lifestyle was perceived to be incompatible with the image Seagrams wanted to project" (Pendleton & Winters, 1987, p. 74).

Companies sometimes put morals clauses in spokespersons' contracts as a protection should they stray into illegal or immoral lifestyles. The clauses may serve as warnings to celebrities seeking contracts and may offer some legal recourse for the company, but the court of public opinion does not respond to such clauses. If they associate the celebrity with the product, and the celebrity errs, the product may still suffer despite what the contracts stated.

Spokespersons Charged With Encouraging Crime

Another type of celebrity-caused crisis is not *clearly* the fault of the celebrity—or, for that matter, the product, the manufacturer, or the advertising agency.

Furor rages in minority communities over incidents in which celebrities are used in the target-marketing of products seen to promote antisocial or addictive behaviors which are already at crisis levels.

Cigarettes are touted by African-American celebrities on billboards, in magazines ads, and in television commercials when statistics show that African Americans suffer a cancer rate 58% higher than that of whites. Alcoholic beverages, like malt liquor, are promoted by famous people, such as actor Billy Dee Williams, while African Americans have high rates of cancer of the esophagus and cirrhosis of the liver, both caused by the drinking of alcoholic beverages (Fearn-Banks, 1994).

Similarly, basketball star, Michael Jordan, and other athletes have been involved in crises connected with their positions as spokespersons for manufacturers of athletic shoes. Nike experienced two such crises in the summer of 1990 (see Case 18).

Research

A large percentage of advertising, both print and broadcast, uses celebrity spokespersons. Advertising experts point to three advantages:

1. Celebrities tend to be highly appealing, likable, dynamic, and sometimes beautiful individuals. As Aristotle said, "Beauty is a greater recommendation than any letter of introduction."

2. In a sea of advertising messages, celebrities get the attention of the public, so that viewers recall the message better than in commercials without celebrities.

3. Celebrities affect the credibility of the advertiser's claims, in that they provide a positive effect that could be associated with the product they endorse.

Several studies are not so positive on the use of celebrities to promote products and services.

Some research shows that it is not recognizability or the talent in sports or entertainment of the spokesperson that helps sell the product; it is credibility. A study by Sternthal, Phillips, and Dholakia (1978) revealed that highly credible sources are more effective in print advertising and commercials than less credible sources. Other studies reveal that highly credible sources produce favorable attitudes toward the products (Craig & McCann, 1978; Woodside & Davenport, 1974).

Ohanian (1991) conducted a study that reveals the characteristics of credibility as the following:

1. *Trustworthiness:* The consumer has confidence in the spokesperson, believes the spokesperson is honest and objective when speaking of the product.

2. *Expertise:* The consumer believes that the spokesperson's ability and knowledge of the field is high.

3. *Attractiveness:* The consumer thinks the spokesperson is physically appealing.

Ohanian's study reveals that trustworthiness is not an important determinant of a consumer's likelihood to purchase the advertised product, that the consumer does not trust persons who get paid large sums to promote a product. She finds that expertise is a stronger factor, and that it is not necessary for a spokesperson to be a celebrity.

She suggests that celebrity spokespersons should be knowledgeable, experienced, and qualified to talk about a product. She also suggests that people who have direct connections with the endorsed product are more believable, persons such as Lee Iacocca for Chrysler.

Kamins, Brand, Hoeke, and Moe (1989) concurred when they concluded in a study on the impact of advertising effectiveness and credibility, "Believability has not always been observed to be enhanced by the use of celebrity appeal" (p. 4).

Walker, Langmeyer, and Langmeyer (1992) built on Ohanian's work and found that the celebrity spokesperson passes on an image to products with undefined images—products that have never been associated with a celebrity—more readily than to products that already have established images.

These researchers say further that the endorsers may have certain attributes that are desirable for endorsing the product, but they may also have inappropriate attributes for a specific product. As an example, they cite Madonna and Christie Brinkley. Both, they say, are sexy, but Brinkley projects a classy, soft, conservative image compared to Madonna's outlandish, hard, unsophisticated image. Similarly, Misra and Beatty (1990) said there must be a "match-up" between characteristics of a celebrity and of a product.

This finding leads advertisers and companies to look more closely at the celebrity than merely to his "Q" rating, the widely used method of measuring popularity and recognizability.

Frieden (1984) found that celebrities are good spokespersons for awareness and goals, whereas actual experts are good for trust and positive effect. Klein, a Senior Vice President of "7-Up" said, "Celebrities are an unnecessary risk unless they are logically connected to the product" (Watkins, p. 41). This also supports Misra's theory that there must be a match-up, congruency between celebrity and product.

Tom, Clark, Elmer, Groch, Masetti, and Sandhar (1992, fall) found that created spokespersons are an effective alternative to celebrities. They say that the created spokesperson can build up character recognition, desirable traits, and a public persona in much the same way as a celebrity.

However, such public personas cannot damage a product's image. If they are portrayed by actors, no one knows their names. Their fame lasts only as long as the advertising campaign or the product.

Created spokespersons can be animated characters such as the Pillsbury Doughboy and the Jolly Green Giant or actors playing characters such as Charmin's Mr. Whipple, Madge, the Palmolive manicurist, and the little boy who for many years has sung about his bologna for Oscar Meyer.

Fighting Image Problems

Sometimes, celebrities fight scandals with their own public relations campaigns. Television celebrity, Bob Barker, host of the game show, "The Price is Right," and a top television personality since 1956, is a long-time spokesperson for animal rights. He closes each show with advice to have pets spayed and neutered. He was one of the most vocal and visible spokespersons responsible for the fact that fur coats are rarely seen on television shows.

When a former model on the game show accused him of sexual harassment and threatened to sue, his publicist, Henri Bollinger, said, "a decision was made early on to just tell the truth."

Bollinger said the original problem was to get Barker, whose private life had never been made public, to agree to go public and tell the nature of his relationship with the woman.

"He was embarrassed," said Bollinger, "but he said 'Okay.' We decided to go out and tell the story, and we decided not to limit our answers."

A news conference was held to announce the situation and to tell the story. A second news conference was held to answer questions. Then the decision was to pull back and grant no more media interviews. One exception was made when "Dateline NBC" had a story about a witness close to the former model who was supportive of Barker. Barker participated in the story and was interviewed.

The tabloids, televised and print, continued to cover the story. Kevin McDonald, the CBS publicist for the series, said the reaction from the public was supportive of Barker. In late 1994, a judge threw the case out. In 1995, the model dropped the suit too.

CASE 18: NIKE, ITS SPOKESPERSONS AND OPERATION PUSH

Liz Dolan, who in 1990 was director of public relations for the Nike Company, said she will never forget the summer of 1990. "It was a bad summer," she said. Nevertheless, she feels that the relatively young company and its public relations program grew stronger as a result of the summer's challenges.

The first challenge was the crisis that erupted over kids and violence and Nike athletic shoes. The second was the furor that erupted when Operation PUSH (People United to Save Humanity), an African-American organization headed by the Reverend Jesse Jackson, attempted a boycott of Nike. In each case, Nike's celebrity spokespersons were key to the public relations campaigns.

Michael Jordan, then a Chicago Bulls basketball star, was among the notables who have had a contract with Nike. An athletic shoe called the Air Jordan was marketed to basketball players, both pro and amateur. It was hot immediately. Jordan's name on the shoe and in the advertising added credibility to the image of shoes that cost, in 1990, $125 a pair. The Air Jordan was the highest priced basketball shoe made by Nike.

There lay the rub. Children, from low-income minority neighborhoods, whose parents could not, or would not, afford the shoes, were committing violent acts, even murder, to gain ownership of other kids' Air Jordans.

Jordan had not committed any illegal or immoral act. He had not been accused of taking drugs, abusing alcohol, or committing crimes.

Defending Nike's position in the matter, Dolan emphasized that the company does not target youth in its marketing; it targets all basketball players. "It was the best basketball shoe we could make and we targeted players," she said. "We didn't care what race a person is or where he lives. There were no billboards in low-income African-American neighborhoods, no ads in African-American publications." There were television commercials during basketball games, and the youth saw professional players wearing the shoes. "It was understandable," said Dolan, "that Michael Jordan, the hero, wore 'cool shoes'."

The violence spurred loud objections and complaints among African-American community leaders. They said few children will make it to the pros, that there is an over-fascination with athletes in all of America, that in poor, predominantly Black America, children see excelling in sports as their only ticket out of the ghetto. If Air Jordans will make them like Michael Jordan—in any way—they *must* have them. These objectors said Nike was promoting the problem when it promoted the shoe.

There were persons who supported Nike's use of the athletes. Lon Rosen, president of First Team Marketing, which represented Magic Johnson of the Los Angeles Lakers, was indicative of this support when he said, "An athlete has a responsibility, but if people are getting killed for shoes, it's a society problem, not a marketing problem" (Colford, 1990, p. 64).

The number one objector was Reverend Jesse Jackson who criticized athletes who endorsed expensive athletic shoes by saying, "They are exploiting mindless materialism" (Woods, 1994, p. 76).

Later, the Reverend Jackson telephoned Phil Knight, Nike's CEO, and announced that his Operation PUSH, based in Chicago, wanted to meet with Nike, based in Beaverton, Oregon, regarding its investment practices. This was the beginning of the second crisis which, Dolan said, was not linked to the first.

Operation PUSH charged that African Americans spent $200 million each year on Nike shoes, whereas the company did not have African Americans in high executive positions and did not do business with Black-owned businesses (Woods, 1994; Jackson & Schantz, 1993).

To address Nike's minority hiring statistics and the company's philanthropic record, Dolan wrote a news release that would be available whenever questions arose about the subject. The release was distributed frequently, included all the facts from the records, and reinforced Nike's determination to increase minority hiring.

Dolan said that she did not like to use percentages because, by Nike's figures, 13.5% of its sales were to minority groups (PUSH later charged that the number was 30%), whereas 16% of the workforce was from minority races. She also said that because most of Nike consumers (80%) were men, the same kind of logic would dictate that 80% of Nike's employees should be men too. Actually, the company was 53% female, and many of those women would be out of work if sales fell.

Dolan also distributed information about the company's $10 million philanthropic budget, but PUSH responded with "We want parity, not charity."

July 25, 1990

A meeting was held in Chicago. Jackson and the Reverend Tyrone Crider represented PUSH. Scott Bedbury, Director of Advertising; Dolan; and newly-named President, Richard Donahue, represented Nike. There was much clashing of heads and PUSH. The Reverend Crider would challenge the athletic shoe industry to give African American communities a share of the profit African American consumers brought to the companies. Also at issue were the places where Nike did and did not advertise and in what banks it did business.

Dolan said she found the charge that Nike did not advertise in Black publications odd in that if Nike had advertised in such publications, the company would have been further charged with target-marketing, and would have been more severely criticized in the murders. At the time, Nike only advertised in *Sports Illustrated.*

July 30, 1990

Nike President, Richard Donahue, and Crider met in Chicago where Crider gave Donahue a long questionnaire to complete. The responses would establish how committed Nike was to minorities. Dolan said Nike felt that the information requested was "highly proprietary, information even our shareholders do not have." Nike later gave PUSH a questionnaire seeking to establish PUSH's credibility.

Then PUSH distributed a flyer that said Nike had no Black on its board of directors, no Black vice presidents, dealt with no Black public relations or advertising agencies and had no deposits in Black banks (see Fig. 9.1).

At one point, a reporter asked Donahue who was the highest paid Black person in the company. He said he did not know and the response was used later on CNN. "It was unfair," said Dolan. "He didn't know anything; he had only been with Nike a week when this crisis occurred."

August 10, 1990

PUSH called a boycott. Dolan responded by reissuing the news release prepared earlier after adding more employment information. The information included the following:

1. Of 1,000 new employees hired in the previous seven months, 21% were from ethnic minority groups.
2. Nike had a $200 million line of credit with 15 banks, and Nike would use a Black-owned bank capitalized to that level. "In fact," said Dolan, "we agreed with the basic point here and had even tried, in 1986, to do this and there was no Black-owned bank that could carry that line of credit."

'Stay in School,' but 'Buy Nikes'?

By Elizabeth Brown
Christian Science Monitor

"Operation PUSH. Say No to Nike." That's how they answer the phone in the Chicago office of this social activist group (People United to Serve Humanity). They have started a boycott against the athletic shoe giant Nike Inc.

The 14-week-old boycott will continue "until Nike decides to put money in black-owned banks, advertise with black-owned media, do business with black-owned businesses, and put a black on the board of directors," says Rev. Tyrone Crider, national executive director for the group that was organized in 1971 by Rev. Jesse Jackson to fight for economic justice for blacks.

Critics have charged that Operation PUSH is unfairly attacking Nike while accepting ads in its own magazine from Nike's closest rival, Reebok.

"We're dealing with the No. 1 company first. When we challenge industries, we start with the No. 1 company," says Reverend Crider.

Nike says only 14 percent of its sales are to non-whites, but PUSH's Crider says basketball shoe sales to blacks amount to $200 million dollars a year—40 percent of such sales. Last week, in its first move to meet PUSH's challenge, Nike hired a minority-run advertising firm in Los Angeles. "We are the largest minority employer in the state of Oregon," adds Liz Dolan, director of public relations at Nike.

Nike and Reebok have launched "message ads": Reebok is running an anti-racism campaign; Nike is targeting inner-city black youths with a $5 million "Stay in School" campaign.

As part of the campaign, Nike has made thousands of "Bo Knows School" book covers for distribution to schools. Jackson appears in a graduation cap and gown, a band uniform, a scientist's white lab coat, and a Greek philosopher's toga. "Bo knows all this stuff because he stayed in school," the jacket reads. Also prominent: Nike emblems.

No one argues the merits of sending the message out, but some question the commercial tie-in: "To keep these black boys in school is wonderful," says Eric Perkins of the Educational Testing Service in Princeton, N.J., "but when they [see these book covers] they're going to want to buy Nike sneakers."

FIG. 9.1. News story in the *Christian Science Monitor*, November 23, 1990, about Nike and the Operation PUSH boycott. It mentions Nike's use of black athletes as spokespersons. (Reprinted with permission of *Christian Science Monitor*.)

3. PUSH was only interested in the advancement of African Americans, not other minority groups.

Nike announced, by news release, that it would increase the number of minorities heading departments by 10% and name a member of a minority group to its board of directors within a year and another as a vice president within two years.

August 19, 1990

PUSH said the response was not enough. "It didn't take 24 months to find Michael Jordan," said Crider. On August 26, Crider announced that retail stores selling Nike shoes would be picketed.

In a brief time, a Gallup national survey revealed that 20% of the public planned to buy fewer Nike products. Sixty-four percent were planning to make no changes in their buying of Nike products, and 39% believed that a company is not obligated to return profits to the communities it markets (Jackson & Schantz, 1993).

Still, for the first two weeks of the boycott, Nike stock fell $12.75 a share to $61.50, a drop of 17.2% (Jackson & Schantz, 1993).

There was disagreement over the causes of the drop, but there was agreement that the boycott was casting a negative image on the company. Nike did not want the negative image, even if the boycott was not affecting sales or stocks. It did not want to appear racially prejudiced to employees, media, and other publics.

Early September, 1990

Most of the day-to-day media questions were handled by Dolan. The primary media covering the issue were local crews and reporters and local offices of the wire services.

"It was decided that Knight would not be the day-to-day spokesperson because we were getting up to 100 calls each day," said Dolan. "It was just not a good use of his time.

"Donahue, on the other hand, had deep roots in the civil rights movement, was more involved."

Then in early September, a news conference was held at the Heathman Hotel in Portland. At the conference, Donahue and Knight were the speakers. They revealed statistics showing that of Nike's 3,703 employees, there were the following from ethnic minority races:

African Americans	7.2%
Hispanics	2.5%
Asians	4.8%
American Indians	0.48%

Out of 622 persons in management positions, there were 18 Asians, 10 African Americans, 9 Hispanics, and 2 Native Americans. PUSH was not impressed because the statistics showed that, although Blacks were the predominant minority group in the company, they were not the predominant minority group in management.

September 17, 1990

At a Nike shareholders' meeting held at the Multnomah Athletic Club in downtown Portland, attendees enjoyed the news that the company was experiencing good sales. There had been word that Operation PUSH would hold a demonstration at the event.

"We expected the group to demonstrate at the question-and-answer session. We thought they would then pose their questions," Dolan said. It didn't happen that way. Dolan said that Donahue was addressing the shareholders when the Reverend Crider and about 20 people entered the room and demanded the opportunity to pray.

"Donahue," Dolan said, "said it was not the time or place." Local television cameras were there expecting the demonstration. A shouting match ensued between the PUSH demonstrators and the shareholders.

Nike announced, shortly afterwards, that it had already opened an account at Portland's only Black bank.

Also in mid-September, after the shareholders' meeting, Coach John Thompson of Georgetown University arranged two meetings. One was with Jackson, Crider, Knight, and Donahue with Thompson as mediator. Dolan said "Nothing resulted." Jackson was never seen or heard from again in the crisis, according to Dolan.

A second meeting followed with Michael Jordan in which Spike Lee (also a Nike spokesperson) represented Nike and Crider represented PUSH, again with Thompson as mediator.

October 23, 1990

Nike expanded its relationship with African-American leaders and organizations. Nike had already supported the United Negro College Fund (UNCF) and had an internship for African-American college students.

"All our employees were in Oregon and Memphis," said Dolan. "We felt we had a positive image in those communities and an extremely loyal following in the African American community. Representatives of the local Black organizations said PUSH never asked them about Nike's record in the community," said Dolan.

She also said that the company was proud of its relationship with its role-model spokespersons: "Michael Jordan and Spike Lee made public statements on behalf of Nike, though I must admit that both had problems making statements that were against the Reverend Jackson."

According to Dolan, Nike "decided we needed to get to know the movers and shakers in other national organizations, like the Urban League."

Muse, Codero & Chen, a multiethnic agency based in Los Angeles, was hired to handle an advertising campaign targeted to Hispanic, Asian, and African-American communities.

November 15, 1990

An African-American man was hired to head the employment department. A minority advisory board was organized internally to review recruitment and training programs.

January 31, 1991

An external minority affairs board was also organized to advise executives on employment goals and other minority issues.

March 16, 1991

The boycott was never really called off. Crider left PUSH. A spokesman for the organization said she felt that some goals of the boycott had been achieved.

David Robinson tells kids drugs aren't allowed in Mr. Robinson's Neighborhood in Nike's new advertisement.

FIG. 9.2. Nike ad featuring sports figure David Robinson with an anti-drug message. (Printed with permission of Nike.)

NIKE. Inc.
9000 S. W. Nimbus
Beaverton. Oregon 97005
Telephone 503·644·9000

For release July 9, 1990   Contact: Liz Dolan, Nike PR
                              7/9 & 10: The Columns, NYC, 212-941-9464
                              After 7/10: 503-644-9000

NIKE'S NEW ADS TELL KIDS TO JUST DO IT IN SCHOOL

"Don't be stupid. Stay in school."

That is the theme of a new series of ads that Nike will be running on national television this year starting on Tuesday night's Major League Baseball All Star Game. Nike has devoted $5 million to the campaign.

The company has completed three of the news ads: one featuring Bo Jackson and two featuring David Robinson. By the time the school year begins, a fourth will be added to the series. That ad will feature Michael Jordan and Spike Lee.

"The purpose of the ads is to take our "Just Do It" campaign to a higher level", said Nike's CEO and founder Philip Knight. "In the past we have addressed athletic achievement by using great Nike athletes. Now we are addressing academic achievement as well."

The Bo Jackson spot features Bo in a variety of athletic and non-athletic guises. Not surprisingly, the question is what Bo knows. The multi-talented athlete tells kids that Bo knows Shakespeare, Bo knows calculus, Bo knows philosophy because Bo stayed in school.

The two Robinson spots take place in Mr. Robinson's Neighborhood. In one, the NBA Rookie of the Year says that those who use drugs are "garbage", and he doesn't like garbage in his shoes or in his neighborhood. In the second, Robinson is joined by his mother and by Coach John Thompson of Georgetown. David warns kids that it is stupid to ignore Coach Thompson, really stupid to ignore your mother and really, really stupid to drop out of school. The close is the same as the Bo Jackson spot. "Don't be stupid. Stay in school."

The commercials will run in regular rotation with other Nike spots for the next year. Nike's purpose in producing them was to use the great role models that appear in their sports commercials to deliver an even more pressing message. David Robinson is a graduate of the United States Naval Academy with a degree in mathematics. Bo Jackson is currently finishing a degree in child development at Auburn. Michael Jordan went back to the University of North Carolina in 1986 to finish his degree in geography.

"David Robinson, Bo Jackson and Michael Jordan are all good citizens in addition to being great athletes. We began major television advertising just three years ago, and since then it has become clear to us how powerful these athletes are as role models," said Nike VP/Director of Marketing Tom Clarke. "We began to plan this campaign last year when we introduced the first "Bo Knows" spots. We will continue for as long as we can to use our athletes to talk to kids in a positive way about achievement and excellence."

FIG. 9.3. Nike news release announcing its new ads starring celebrity spokespersons. (Printed with permission of Nike.)

The "Stay in School" campaign will supplement Nike's successful "Just Do It" advertising that began in August 1988. That corporate campaign is designed to inspire Americans to get involved in sports and fitness. Nike also has developed a series of "Just Do It" grants to support innovative grassroots efforts to keep kids in school. The cash grants, which will be administered through the National Foundation for the Improvement of Education, go to teachers who develop their own local programs to prevent kids from dropping out..

Nike, Inc., based in Beaverton, Oregon, is the world's leading manufacturer of authentic athletic footwear and apparel.

FIG. 9.3. *(Continued)*

Shoe sales were never affected by the boycott, only Nike's image in some minority communities. Nike still uses African-American athletes as spokespersons in targeting the Black consumer, as well as sports fans. Nike's "Bo Knows School" featuring Bo Jackson was well received. Paid television ads featuring Bo Jackson, Jordan, and David Robinson have also been received well (see Figs. 9.2 and 9.3).

Criticism still abounds about the use of African-American athletes to sell expensive shoes. Criticism also abounds about philanthropy buying approval of minority organizations.

Dolan said that Nike had no crisis plan, that it "stumbled" through the early days of the crisis. "We were not good at the slick response. The company," she said, "knew what it stood for and had defined its values" much as Johnson & Johnson had prior to the Tylenol crisis. "You can't make that up," she said.

Dolan said Nike's instincts were good in handling a crisis it had not anticipated. She said the company was "stunned" when the situation was "laid at their doorstep."

"The number one lesson we learned is that once a crisis happens, it is too late to get a good reputation. Your friends must rally around you." said Dolan.

Dolan is now vice president of marketing at Nike.

CASE 19: SWEDISH MEDICAL CENTER AND THE FAMOUS DEAD PERSON

It is standard operating procedure at Seattle's Swedish Medical Center that when newsworthy people are admitted through the hospital emergency room at night, the nursing supervisor will notify the head of media relations.

At midnight not very long ago, Jane Anne Wilder, then media relations director, received the call she had dreaded for all the years she had been at the hospital. She had trained each of the six nursing supervisors to recognize the occasions that warranted such off-hours phone calls—multiple calls from the media, patients who are well-known, and so forth.

The nurse on the phone said, "Jan, somebody's here. He's dead and everybody says he's famous."

Trying to wake up, Wilder asked, "What's his name?"

The nurse spoke his name, but we shall call him "Mr. Famous Dead Person."

Wilder, then awake, replied, "Yes, he's famous," and rolled out of bed to get the telephone number of the CEO. Telephoning the CEO is also standard operating procedure.

Then she drafted a "very fast, very brief news release." "The hospital had a notebook for a crisis," Wilder said, "a very sophisticated emergency management plan, but there was no crisis communications plan as far as the media was concerned."

Wilder said that she also had a "good working relationship with the Seattle press," which was about to pay off.

In minutes, a member of Mr. Famous Dead Person's family telephoned Wilder from an out-of-town airport. She inquired about the possibility of a news conference and asked him if he would be comfortable with information she would include in a news release.

"The family member was very media savvy, which helped a lot," she said. "I told him what information I planned to reveal and asked if he and the rest of the family were comfortable with it and with the news conference." She got the go-ahead to proceed with both.

Having taken care of the crucial tasks, Wilder went back to bed. She planned to go to the office an hour earlier than usual; there would be phone calls. The news conference was to be in the afternoon. There would be plenty of time to plan for it.

"That was the big mistake," she said. "I should have taken a shower and gone to the office immediately." It was about 1 a.m.—4 a.m. in New York—and the morning network news-interview shows were gathering information.

"It was a bigger story than I estimated," she said. "I had never dealt with the national media in a situation like this. When I arrived at the office, all the morning talk shows were over. I should have been available to handle those East Coast calls—even though there wasn't much I could tell them."

Because Wilder was a one-person department, it was necessary to have another's active presence. There were so many simultaneous events and so many media calls that one person could not adequately do the job. An experienced professional from an agency would be better than volunteers from other positions in the organization because volunteers require considerable training for crisis communications. It was not just a matter of "someone to answer telephones." The situation needed someone who was skilled and experienced in what to say, what to do.

First, Wilder telephoned Dave Endicott, Vice President of the Communication Northwest firm, who had been a public relations consultant to the medical center for media training of physicians and administrators.

"Endicott," she said, "flew to the hospital. He helped me, the attending physician, and the CEO draft the perfect press release." He also helped to organize the day, made efforts to blend the wishes of all parties, and assisted in planning media strategies.

Wilder distributed a news release by PR Newswire. The release mentioned the celebrity's name, age, and apparent cause of death. "I kept a skeletal fill-in-the-blanks news release on file that merely needed the pertinent data," said Wilder (see Fig. 9.4). The news release was distributed with a full-page statement from the family about the celebrity's life and career. The family members wanted no other information revealed.

The wishes of the family are paramount. Washington state law governs the maximum amount of information a hospital may release without the permission of a patient or a patient's family.

"Only name, age, and condition. That's the maximum. You cannot even reveal addresses without permission," said Wilder.

Hospitals in other states are governed by both federal laws and state laws that vary from state to state. In California, for example, the code says, that public figures should not be afforded less privacy than others with regard to release of medical information, and that hospitals should work with public figures or designee to answer media inquiries with minimum disruption for all concerned and to provide the appropriate cooperation with the media (California Association of Hospitals and Health Systems, 1991).

Ron Wise, Vice President of Public Relations and Marketing for Cedars-Sinai Medical Center in Los Angeles, said that by federal law no hospital can acknowledge drug or substance abuse, attempted suicide, or mental problems. The hospital has its own policy and does not divulge a lot of specifics, only medical information. Wise, who is also the medical center's spokesperson, said police matters are reportable.

The Washington law is a protection to the patient, the family, and actually to the public relations practitioner.

Newsworthy patients are sometimes hospitalized under suspicious, sad, or tragic circumstances. For example, a married person might suffer a stroke while in an intimate situation with someone other than the person's spouse. Public relations practitioners, fortunately, cannot admit or deny this information, so the law lets them and the patient off the hook. Family members may reveal additional information, but it is their call.

The press called the public relations office of Wilder's hospital all morning, but they respected the fact that the celebrity's family had asked that no more information be revealed until the afternoon news conference.

When the family arrived for the news conference, the media was already at the site. Reporters were there from numerous national publications, the wire services, and national radio programs, not to mention all those from local television, radio, and newspapers. Some of the national and international outlets were represented by Seattle-based stringers.

NEWS RELEASE

For Immediate Release

Date_____

Contact: Jane Anne Wilder, 555-5555

         __(NAME OF CELEBRITY)____**DIES**

    (Seattle) _____(Full name and title)_____ **died today of** _____(cause of death) **at** ____(time of death)____ **at Swedish Hospital Medical Center in Seattle.** He/She was _____(age)_____.

    Further details will be released by ___(name of person to make announcement--family member or professional contact)_____ **at a news conference scheduled for**_____ (time of news conference)_____, **at Swedish Hospital, Glaser Auditorium, 747 Summit Avenue.**

              ###

FIG. 9.4. Sample fill-in-the-blanks news release.

Family members requested to see the deceased first and were accommo-dated by a clergyman. The media was anxious—"chomping at the bit" was the way Wilder described it. However, she kept the family in a separate place where no reporters could reach them.

The family members were such public people, but this was a private occasion" said Wilder recalling the task of briefing the family, "This was a very special situation. I tried hard to remember that we had a grieving family. True, it was a media event, but somebody died—a father, a brother, a husband. You cannot just say, 'Here, stand in front of this podium and this is what you say'."

The doctor who pronounced Mr. Famous Dead Person dead appeared at the news conference, as did the hospital's CEO.

Wilder told the family what questions would probably be asked. She said that some questions might be very personal. She asked if there was any information the family members were worried about reporters seeking and advised them to take some time to decide how they would handle difficult questions.

As the conference began, Wilder introduced the family members, the physician, and the CEO. "There was a great deal of interest," she said, "in what he died of, of course. Was he dead on arrival? What did medical personnel do? What measures were taken?"

Wilder said the reporters were "lovely and respectful to the family, but less lovely to me. They asked me questions a lot more personal than they asked the family. 'What were the circumstances?' 'Who was with him?' I knew the answers to the questions, but I said absolutely nothing. Absolutely nothing. I had the state law and patient privacy to fall back on.

"I believe strongly in patient privacy, so it was easy for me. I know how I would have felt if I were involved. I wouldn't want a hospital spokesperson telling anything about my family that I didn't want them to know."

The media concern was enormous. It was a front page story all over the world. "It thrilled my relatives out of state," said Wilder, "because I was quoted in their local papers saying, 'Yes, he died last night.' "

At Swedish Medical Center, families of newsworthy patients have the option of having Wilder serve as a liaison between them and the media. If reporters want to interview patients or family members of patients, they must first contact Wilder, who said, "This happened often, and it worked well, especially when there were unusual circumstances."

It was no different in the case of Mr. Famous Dead Person. Calls came in for several days after the news conference. The family requested that Wilder handle the media calls and be the spokesperson for the family.

As days passed, the calls became more and more personal. Said Wilder, "It got to the point where I couldn't tell anybody anything. I kept wishing that we had been able to revive him. Not only would he still be alive, but it would have been quite a story for the hospital. But, it was too late for wishing.

"I had worked with many of the reporters before, and I always had tried—to tell them everything I could, to be as clear as I could, and to say when it was necessary, 'I can't tell you that. I'd like to be able to say more, but I can't.' "

Wilder eventually had to tell the family that another spokesperson was needed, one who could relay more information than she could, and one who could, at least, share the burden of the numbers of requests for information and interviews. A lawyer accepted the task for the family; apparently, there was no public relations representative.

Even a year later, a magazine reporter telephoned asking for permission to speak to the nurse who brought Mr. Famous Dead person to the hospital. Wilder responded with, "Look, I'll tell you everything I can, and I'll tell you exactly where I have to stop." She said that she and the reporter "got along great, and I basically didn't tell him anything he didn't know already. He had already learned a lot of personal family things."

When the reporter indicated that he would keep digging for more information on his own, Wilder replied, "You're doing your job." She said, "I realize that people in the press are doing their job just like I'm doing mine. But I did not tell him what he wanted to know. Not that I knew anyway."

Sometime later, another celebrity whom we will call Mr. Famous Sick Person was admitted to the hospital's emergency room. The celebrity, a rock star, fell ill at a radio station while doing an interview, so the public knew about it before he arrived at the hospital.

Wilder said her previous experience with the deceased celebrity was a benefit in determining her actions. "As soon as I had the information, I just whipped the news release out over PR Newswire and set about to get the news conference going. Also, by that time, I had designed an internal crisis communications plan which we followed."

This celebrity was surrounded with his entourage whom Wilder remembers as being very nice and cooperative. Persons in the entourage realized that many times the media and the public jump to conclusions about entertainers, especially musicians, and their first thought is "drug abuse." "There was no drug abuse involved here, and they wanted to make sure that was clear," said Wilder.

They agreed to the news conference and the publicist, Wilder said, "encouraged the interest of the media."

Within 2 hours, the news conference was underway. The publicist and the physician appeared at the press conference. "The physician was boring compared to the publicist," said Wilder. It seems that Mr. Famous Sick Person was malnourished and exhausted. None of the reporters pushed for an interview with the celebrity, who stayed in the hospital several days and then was released.

Wilder said that she looked at her role as public relations director as one of putting the hospital in the best possible light. "And some of it," she acknowledged, "was to make sure some information did not get out. Anything that would be negative or damaging to the hospital, to the patients, or to the patients' families would be protected. Now, morally, I suppose if there was a danger to the community or malfeasance, it would be another matter. Luckily, I never had that problem."

Wilder said that she did persuade the media not to do two stories—one was about a bomb threat. Two reporters knew about it. She told them she "could neither confirm nor deny it." She added that the police policy is to not alert the community because it causes panic, that she did know that the hospital was not being evacuated. "Was it really newsworthy?" she asked. The reporters did not do the story.

"I respected them a lot for that," said Wilder. "And it was a good thing for the hospital. We would have had all the cameras all over the place and a controversy could have come up over whether or not we should have evacuated."

Wilder now has her own firm and specializes in small business marketing.

REFERENCES

Bloomberg business news. (1994, July 16). *Financial Times, 83*(29), B1(2).

California Association of Hospitals and Health Systems. (1991, April). *Consent Manual and Guide to Public and Private Release of Patient Information.*

Colford, S. (1990, March 19). Athlete endorsers fouled by slayings. *Advertising Age, 61*(12), 64.

Craig, S., & McCann, J. (1978). Assessing communication effects of energy conservation. *Journal of Consumer Research, 3*, 82–88.

Fearn-Banks, K. (1994). The ethics of marketing to ethnic minority publics. In A. F. Alkhafaji (Ed.), *Business Research Journal* (pp. 81–85). Lanham, MD: University Press of America.

Freiden, J. B. (1984, October/November). Advertising spokesperson effects: An examination of endorser type and gender in two audiences. *Journal of Advertising Research, 19*, 63–71.

Horovitz, B. (1992, Feb. 11). It may be hard to swallow some endorsements. *Los Angeles Times, 111*, D1, D6.

Jackson, J. E., & Schantz, W. T. (1993, January/February). Crisis management lessons: When push shoved Nike. *Business Horizons, 36*(1), 27–35.

Johnston, H. M. III. (1978). *Invasion of privacy in law and the writer* (p. 32). Cincinnati: Writer's Digest Books.

Kamins, M., Brand, M., Hoeke, S., & Moe, J. (1989, Spring). Two-sided versus one-sided celebrity endorsements: The impact on advertising effectiveness and credibility. *Journal of Advertising, 18*(2), 4–10.

Misra, S. M., & Beatty, S. (1990). Celebrity spokespersons and brand congruence. *Journal of Business Research, 21*, 159–173.

Ohanian, R. (1991, February/March). The impact of celebrity spokespersons' perceived image on consumers' intention to purchase. *Advertising Research, 31*(1), 46–54.

Pendleton, J., & Winters, P. (1987, Jan. 5). Cooler ads in turmoil as Gallo, Riney split. *Advertising Age, 58*(1), 74.

Sternthal, L., Phillips, L., & Dholakia, R. (1978). The persuasive effects of source credibility: A situational analysis. *Public Opinion Quarterly, 42*(3), 285–314.

Tom, G., Clark, R., Elmer, L., Groch, E., Masetti, J., Jr., & Sandhar, H. (1992, Fall). The use of created versus spokespersons in advertisements. *The Journal of Consumer Marketing, 9*(4), 45–51.

Walker, M., Langmeyer, L., & Langmeyer, D. (1992, Spring). Celebrity endorsers: Do you get what you pay for? *The Journal of Consumer Marketing, 9*(5), 69–72.

Watkins, A. (1989, May). Simply irresistible? Pepsi learns there's a downside to signing up rock stars. *Beverage Industry, 1,* 41.

Woods, G. B. (1994). The gym shoe phenomenon: Social values vs. marketability. In P. Patterson & L. Wilkins (Eds.), *Media Ethics* (pp. 75–77). Madison, WI: Brown & Benchmark.

Woodside, A., & Davenport, J., Jr. (1974). The effect of salesman similarity and expertise on consumer purchasing behavior. *Journal of Marketing Research, 11*(2), 198–202.

Generic Crisis
Communications Plan

Contents

itions

Crises:

Crises are unplanned events that directly or potentially threaten our company's reputations; the environment; the health, safety or welfare of employees; and the health, safety or welfare of citizen in communities surrounding our plants.

Events that fall into this category include: fires, explosions, bomb threats, civil disturbances, equipment malfunctions, environmental impacts, widespread illness, hazardous material spills, and other types of incidents.

Minor Crisis:

A *minor* crisis is confined to a limited area of a building; results in minimal, if any, disruption of operations; is quickly brought under control; does not require evacuation other than by a few employees in the immediate vicinity; and causes a minor injury or none at all. Media inquiry is possible with events in this category but apt to be minimal.

Major Crisis:

A *major* crisis may involve significant injury or less of life, prolonged disruption of normal operations, substantial property damage, or a significant environmental impact--or holds potential for any of these. Media inquiry is more likely to occur with events in this category, especially if other municipal emergency response groups have been called in for assistance.

Communication Objective

In the event of a minor or major incident on any of our sites, every effort will be made to communicate as appropriate to employees, management, surrounding communities, other target publics, and the news media promptly and accurately. The appropriate division communications staff will be the primary information source available to the news media.

When a crisis occurs, it is necessary for communications personnel to gather facts and data quickly, including the nature of our response to the crisis. The following communication efforts will strive to alleviate employees' concerns, minimize speculation by the media, and to ensure that our position is presented.

It should be noted, though, that many incidents occur that are relatively minor in nature and are consequently not covered by the media. Nevertheless, it is essential to gather facts about the incidents and have them available to communicate, if necessary to appropriate audiences.

The nature of that communication is outlined in the following plan.

Roles and Responsibilities

Each site's Crisis Committee (at the various sites) is responsible for the following: identifying, confirming, investigating crises; developing strategies for managing crises; and developing strategies for recovering from crisis incidents.

As a member of the Crisis Committee, communications personnel will:

- Provide a representative at the Emergency Operations Center (EOC) if activated

- Control the release of information to employees, surrounding communities, and to the news media

- Maintain contact with media representatives

- Establish and maintain a news conference center, if necessary

Two, and in some cases, three communicators may be required for adequate crisis communications response. Those communicators will function in the following roles: Public Relations (PR) Lead, Incident Command (IC) Interface, and PR Backup.

The responsibilities for each communication role are outlined as follows:

- PR Lead
  - Received initial notification
  - Designates staff member as IC Interface
  - Designates staff member as PR Backup (if necessary)
  - Receives initial facts and updates from IC Interface
  - Prepares initial statement for release
  - Fields media inquiries to office
  - Briefs executive identified as spokesperson
  - Joins Emergency Operations Center team, if activated
  - Provides updates to senior executives

- Incident Command (IC) Interface
  - Joins IC team
  - Gathers and documents facts as they become known
  - Shares initial facts and updates with PR lead in main office
  - Prepares initial statement for release (if necessary)
  - Briefs affected organization management and employees
  - Fields media inquiries (if necessary)

- PR Back-Up
  - Updates corporate personnel as necessary
  - Fields additional media inquiries to office
  - Fields employee inquiries to office
  - Conducts in-field interviews with media (if necessary)
  - Sets up media conference room (if necessary)

Notification of a Crisis

Notification is an extremely important process in managing crises and sending the right messages to all audiences. When notification goes well, it makes the rest of the crisis communications job more streamlined and effective than when it doesn't.

Notification of incidents and crises (both major and minor) have been examined by an Ad Hoc Committee to the Corporate Crisis Committee for the past year. Members of this Ad Hoc committee included PR/Communications, Fire and Security, Facilities, and Emergency Response Coordinators.

This committee has reviewed the entire notification process from the moment a crisis begins to the point that a crisis warrants informing senior corporate executives, including the chief executive officer. This committee has endeavored to determine the most reliable notification process for each site Crisis Committee to use.

Notification Process in Brief

Notification is initiated from the area where a crisis has occurred or been identified. The person who discovers the crisis or incident calls the site emergency number, which goes to the site Fire Station Dispatch office. A senior Fire Officer is then dispatched to the incident site, evaluates the magnitude of the crisis, and then contacts the Fire Dispatch to notify additional emergency response organizations. From that point on, notification occurs according to defined call lists and through chain-of-command channels.

Site Communications personnel are now notified directly the respective site Fire Dispatchers. Once that initial notification occurs, the Communications representative receiving the call should, in turn notify Corporate PR offices and the company switchboard operators as soon as he/she obtains information about the incident, and then follow the procedure noted on pages 5-9.

Communications Procedure for Handling a Minor Crisis

Minor Crisis:

1. ____ *Division Communications* receives notification from the Fire Dispatcher and compiles the basic facts and chronology of the event (possibly using an Incident Information Sheet).

2. ____ Division Communications representative becomes the *PR Lead* and informs other communications team members.

3. ____ *PR Lead* determines if more information is necessary and if a communicator should be dispatched to incident site (*Incident Command Interface*).

4. ____ *PR Lead* calls Incident Commander (this is usually the senior Fire Officer at the incident site).

5. ____ *PR Lead* notes more details about the incident (type of incident, when and where the incident occurred, chemical involved and potential chemical reactions, emergency response personnel on site, number of employees evacuated, any injuries, work performed in the building, what is being done to mitigate the incident, and who the appropriate contacts are and how to reach them).

6. ____ On hours, *PR Lead* notifies and confers with *PR Manager* (or backup). Off hours or on weekends, *PR Lead* notifies and confers with *PR Manager* and *PR Duty Officer* when practical. If the *PR Lead* determines that the off-hour incident is likely to generate media inquiries, such notification must be made immediately. The *PR Duty Officer* should notify the *Switchboard Operators* (555-1000) and tell them to direct media inquiries to the person serving as *PR Lead*.

7. ____ *PR Lead* and *PR Manager* agree to key messages and response to query statement.

8. ____ *PR Lead* or *PR Manager* notifies *Corporate PR Manager*.

9. ____ *PR Lead* prepares response to query statement, confers with Division management, and obtains approval on statement.

10. ____ *PR Lead* sends statement via FAX to *PR Manager* and to *Corporate PR Manager*.

11. ____ *PR Lead* serves as prime contact for media. *PR Manager* and *Corporate PR Manager* serve as backups.

12. ____ *PR Lead* fields media inquiries and makes follow-up calls to media if necessary.

Communications Procedure for Handling a Major Crisis

Major Crisis:

1. _____ *Division Communications* receives notification from the Fire Dispatcher and compiles the basic facts and chronology of the event (possibly using an Incident Information Sheet).

2. _____ Division Communications representative becomes the *PR Lead* and informs other communications team members.

3. _____ *PR Lead* determines if more information is necessary and if a communicator (*Incident Command Interface*) should be dispatched to incident site to obtain first-hand information. PR Lead also designates another person as *PR Backup*, if necessary.

4. _____ *IC Interface* goes to site and obtains details from Incident Commander (type of incident, when and where the incident occurred, chemical involved and potential chemical reactions, emergency response personnel on site, number of employees evacuated, any injuries, work performed in the building, what is being done to mitigate the incident, and who the appropriate contacts are and how to reach them).

5. _____ *IC Interface* calls *PR Lead* via cellular phone with details of incident. *IC Interface* should also continue to provide updates to *PR Lead* every 15-30 minutes or as circumstances change.

6. _____ On hours, *PR Lead* immediately notifies and confers with *PR Manager* (or backup). Off hours or on weekends, *PR Lead* immediately notifies and confers with *PR Manager* and also notifies the *PR Duty Officer*. The *PR Duty Officer* should notify the *Switchboard Operators* (555-1000) and tell them to direct media inquiries to the person serving as *PR Lead*.

7. _____ *PR Lead* and *PR Manager* agree to key messages and response to query statement.

8. _____ *PR Lead* or *PR Manager* notifies *Corporate PR Manager*.

9. _____ *PR Lead* prepares response to query statement, confers with Division management, and obtains approval on statement.

10. _____ *PR Lead* sends statement via FAX to *PR Manager* and to *Corporate PR Manager*.

11. _____ *PR Manager* informs *PR Operations Manager* and *PR-VP* (or acting PR chief) to review the incident, determine the need for additional on-site support and decide whether the PR news bureau should be opened if it is after working hours. *PR-VP* decides at this point if executives need to be notified.

Communications Procedure for Handling a Major Crisis continued...

12. ____ *PR Lead* or *PR Manager* inform *Internal Communications Manager* who ensures that appropriate internal communications staff will work closely with Division communications personnel in collecting data for a timely report to employees.

13. ____ *PR Lead* and *PR Backup* serve as prime contacts for media. *PR Manager* and *Corporate PR Manager* serve as backups.

14. ____ *PR Lead* determines if on-site media center is needed and designates *PR Backup* to set one up.

15. ____ *PR Lead* continues to receive information from *IC Interface* and updates statements accordingly.

16. ____ *PR Lead*, in turn, provides updates to *PR Manager* and *PR Corporate Manager*.

17. ____ *PR Lead*, *PR Manager* and *PR Operations Manager* confer on whether a press release is needed. If so, *PR Lead* writes the release, clears it with Division management and *PR Manager*. *PR Manager* clears release with *PR Operations Manager*, *PR-VP*, and other senior officials as required.

18. ____ If incident is on hours, *PR Lead* handles follow-up media and employee inquiries and notes incident in report, as necessary.

19. ____ *PR Manager* and/or *Division PR Lead* develops report analyzing communications aspects of the incident and lessons learned. Report is distributed to *PR Operations Manager* and *PR-VP*, *Division Communications staff* and *Corporate PR Manager*.

Emergency Operations Center (EOC) Activation

An Emergency Operations Center (EOC) is a centralized location from which emergency response during a very severe crisis is coordinated and directed. A crisis that would force the site EOC to be engaged would be an earthquake or other incident (an act of terrorism) that causes multiple crises at once. Senior emergency preparedness personnel in the Company contend that site EOCs along with the Corporate EOC would not be fully activated for a minimum of two to three hours after the devastating event (i.e., first tremors during an earthquake).

If the site EOC is engaged, all crisis communications would be directed from that point. For adequate communication response, it is recommended that two communicators should be assigned to the center. One communicator would serve as the Communications Manager who is responsible for coordinating external and internal communications which may include the use of a runner system, in the event all electronic means of communications are out. The other communicator would serve as the Information Officer, responsible for documenting the sequence of events in support of communications and then generating any statements for release either internally or externally.

Each site EOC will be equipped with maps, stationery supplies, white boards, flip charts, viewfoil machines, telephones and numerous other supplies. It is recommended that communicators make sure the following items are either stored in the EOC or are available nearby:

- Pads and pencils
- Laptop computer
- Portable printer or some other printing device
- FAX machine
- Cellular phone(s)
- Radio(s)
- Division Crisis Communications Plan

The procedure for communications response should be consistent with the procedure for handling a major crisis, the only difference being that all communications would be directed from the EOC itself.

Identification of a Spokesperson

After an initial assessment of an emergency, the Division General Manager (or designee such as an outplant general manager) will identify the appropriate spokesperson for the division.

Appropriate spokespeople for most divisions are as follows:

- Division Vice President/General Manager
- Plant General Manager (for other sites under division jurisdiction)
- Division Health Manager
- Division Environmental Manager
- Division Safety Manager
- Director of Facilities
- Division Communications Manager
- Public Relations Manager
- Corporate Public Relations Manager

All releases of information outside the division and company shall be by or through the coordinated efforts of Division Communications, Group and/or Corporate public relations personnel (as noted in the *Communications Procedure for Handling Minor or Major Crises* on pages 5 through 7).

All releases of information within the Division will be coordinated by Division Communications personnel.

Guidelines for Spokespeople

1. **DO NOT SPECULATE.** Always stick to the fact. A more in-depth investigation is required to determine cause.

2. **Focus on two or three key messages to communicate and repeat them during the interview.** Keep answers short and to the point. TV reporters want "soundbites" of no more than 10 to 15 seconds. Try to bridge to your key messages throughout the interview.

3. **Use a technical expert.** There is no substitute for knowledge. If the questions are outside your area of expertise, find an appropriate technical spokesperson within the company.

4. **Speak in simple, common terms.** Avoid jargon.

5. **Remain calm.** Do not be intimidated into answering questions prematurely. You may tell a reporter that you need to clarify an important matter before you can answer questions.

6. **Do not use negative language.** Do not let reporters put words in your mouth.

7. **Consider human safety first.** When human safety or other serious concerns are involved, deal with those considerations first. You can admit concern without admitting culpability.

8. **Do not answer questions you do not understand.** Ask for clarification. Occasionally, this can be used to buy time to think.

9. **Ignore cameras and microphones.** Face the reporter. Don't look away or up at the sky. During videotaped interviews, it's all right to stop your statement and start over.

10. **Make only "on the record" statements.** There are no "off the record statements."

11. **Avoid saying, "No comment."** If you don't know an answer, say so, then bridge to your messages.

Format for Briefing Someone Identified as a Spokesperson for Interviews/
News Briefings

Executives scheduled to talk to the media should be provided a background briefing in advance of the interview. This policy should be followed *even if* the interview is only to be a brief telephone call.

The briefing should include the following eleven items:

- Date, time and location of the interview
- Name of the reporter
- Name of the publication, wire service, station, etc.
- Our experience with the reporter or publication - to help the executive understand the degree of caution needed in this interview and to prepare for the specific reporter's approach
- Subjects/issues/questions to be covered as requested by reporter
- Our position or recommended response and the data needed to discuss these subjects
- **Top three to five messages we wish to make in the interview (not necessarily based on the reporter's suggested topics)**
- List of other executives to be interviewed during this visit, including key topics and messages you suggest the other executives cover
- Issues, if any, that the executive(s) should avoid, and recommendations on how to sidestep them
- Background information/statistics that would be useful in preparing for the interview
- Proposed length of interview.

If possible, this background material should be conveyed <u>in writing</u> so the executive(s) have a chance to review it carefully. Only under exceptional circumstances should you rely on an oral briefing.

In critical situations, it is also useful to prepare a thorough set of questions and answers to define the organization's positions and to be used in rehearsing the executive.

News Release

During an emergency situation it may be determined that a news release should be distributed to the media. The purpose of the news release is to convey written information on the incident and avoid misinterpretation.

Circumstances That May Require a News Release

- An accident, fire or explosion that results in serious injury, death, or considerable property damage

- A health or environmental incident, or discovery of a health or environmental hazard that may affect employees, the surrounding community, or the   environment

- A serious traffic or air accident involving company vehicles, products and/or personnel

- Sabotage, abduction or extortion, bomb threats, or acts of terrorism involving company personnel, products or property

- News of an incident that is likely to be known by employees or circulated in the community and create misleading impressions

- News of an event that is unusual enough to cause concern to employees, nearby residents, or community officials

- Consistently misleading news reports

Writing an Initial Statement for Release

Often, reporters will call before all the facts have been gathered. In such an instance, a simple statement acknowledging the situation is useful. The short statement avoids "no comment" and acknowledges that our company recognizes the need to cooperate with media.

Examples:

"Our company is responding to the situation (or name the emergency). We have trained and experienced people on site working on the situation."

"Our first priority is the safety of our employees and the public. We are gathering information, and as soon as details become available, we will inform the media."

Information Appropriate for Release

During an emergency situation, there will be information that is appropriate to release to employees and to the media. Communications personnel should do the following:

- **Tell what happened**: Give a description of the emergency situation.

- **Tell who is involved**: Report how many employees were evacuated and if any have been taken to the hospital for observation or injury. Report when emergency team members and/or the various city or county fire departments and police arrived on the scene (if applicable).

News Release continued

- **Indicate where it occurred**: Give the street address of the scene of the emergency.

- **Identify when it happened**: Give the time the incident began.

Information That Is NOT Appropriate for Release

Obviously, there will be a lot of information that is not appropriate for release until more is known about the nature of the crisis response and the extent of the impact.

- **Do not speculate** on **why** the emergency occurred or what type of hazardous materials are involved. Likewise, don't make any statement that blames any individual for the accident. (Although the cause of the incident may appear obvious, it cannot be accurately determined without an extensive investigation, nor can the blame be placed on an individual without a thorough investigation.)

- **Do not include "off the record" information** because there is no such information.

- **Do not overreact to or exaggerate the situation.** For instance, during a hazardous material spill, a reporter may ask for the "worst case scenario" of what could happen with the chemicals involved in the accident. It is impossible to determine this until you have specific data regarding the   hazardous chemicals involved. Bridge back to facts and messages.

- **Do not minimize the situation.** Never regard an emergency as a minor incident.

- **Do not release the names of injured individuals**, unless Human Resources authorizes it following confirmation that the victim(s)' family(ies) have been notified.

- **Do not release dollar estimates** concerning the extent of property damage. Normally there is no way to accurately determine this until extensive studies have been conducted.

- **Avoid the "no comment" response** because it often leads the reporter to speculation. If you don't know the answer to a reporter's question or if you can't discuss something, explain why in simple terms.

Writing a News Release

By following a few basic principles when writing news releases, our company stands a better chance of having reporters use the information with only minor changes. **Remember to consult the legal department as needed.**

1.   **Tell the most important information in your lead paragraph.** Your "story" competes with other news and information, so the most important point should be stated clearly in the first paragraph.

News Release continued

2. **Answer four of the five "Ws"--Who, What, Where, and When.** Explain WHAT the emergency is. Identify WHO is involved in the emergency as well as the material and equipment involved. Tell WHERE and WHEN the emergency occurred. Explain WHAT action we are taking to mitigate or respond to the emergency. **Do not** explain WHY the event occurred unless complete information is available.

3. **Attribute information to a qualified source.** A news release is useful only if it conveys credible information.

4. **Write remaining information in descending order of importance.** If the media cuts off the bottom of your story, they will cut information that is least important to the public.

5. **Explain technical points in simple language.** A direct quote can add the human element to otherwise technical information and help explain a situation or event in layman's terms. Tell the real story. Avoid using language that is overly bureaucratic.

6. **Be concise.** A good news release is judged by the quality of information it communicates, not by its length. Stop writing when you've said all you need to.

Messages for the News Media During Environmental Crises

Mention of the following points during interviews may help the company communicate its position on environmental issues.

- Our primary concern is for the safety of our employees, the communities in which we operate, and the public.

- We operate state-of-the-art safety monitoring and control system in our factories and laboratories.

- We are prepared at all times to mitigate a chemical spill or leak.

- We work continuously to reduce our use of toxic chemicals in manufacturing processes and minimize waste.

- Our standards for "worker hazardous materials safety exposure" meet or exceed standards required by the U.S. Occupational Safety and Health Administration (OSHA).

- Our employees who work directly with hazardous materials receive special training in handling the materials safely. It is a mandatory requirement that employees attend such training.

- The company conducts periodic audits of its hazardous materials and hazardous waste installations, equipment and operating procedures to ensure they comply with environmental regulations and permits during normal and emergency conditions.

- As in the past, the company will continue to work closely with state and federal agencies to meet or exceed environmental regulations, comply with test procedures and report results to the Environmental Protection Agency (EPA) and the Department of Ecology (DOE).

Audiences During a Crisis

To effectively communicate your message it's essential to understand who your audience is and how you want your audience to react.

There are two key types of audiences during an emergency.

1. People directly affected by the emergency.
2. People whose attitudes about the company might be influenced by information about the emergency.

These two types of audiences are broken into six categories. Public Relations' objectives in dealing with each of these audiences are listed below:

- **Employees** -- We want employees to know that their safety is the number one priority during an emergency. Employees need information regarding the emergency as soon as possible. This must be accomplished in a manner that assures employees that the company has their best interest at heart and that it can effectively handle emergencies.

- **Community Residents** -- We want to quell any unnecessary fears. We want the surrounding community residents to know that we take quick, effective steps to protect the health and welfare of community residents and the environment. This can be best accomplished by responding quickly to community concerns and need for information.

- **Top Management** -- This group needs to be kept informed in the event of an emergency as well as be accessible as a resource if necessary.

- **Government Officials** -- Key members of this audience need to be kept apprised of the emergency situation, as determined appropriate by the Government Affairs Department.

- **Customers** -- Customers need to know that the company is concerned about crises that impact its operating divisions and may affect production.

- **News Media** -- We want the news media to know that the company is credible, concerned and effective at dealing with emergencies, and that we understand and meet the unique needs of each type of media.

- **Vendors, Contractors and Suppliers** -- We want these audiences to know that we operate state-of-the-art safety monitoring and control systems in our factories and laboratories and that the company takes quick, effective steps to protect the health and welfare of its employees, vendors and suppliers.

How People Receive Information During a Crisis

In order to determine the most effective ways of communicating during an emergency, it's important to consider how each key audience potentially can receive information. The following sources of information for each audience must be considered in communications strategy for each emergency:

- **Employees**
  Direct knowledge of the event
  Other employees
  Intercom and phone systems
  Managers
  Electronic mail
  News Media reports
  Fire department/police/hospital spokesperson

- **Community Residents**
  Direct knowledge of the event
  Neighbors
  News Media reports

- **Top Management**
  Company Security, Communications/PR Manager
  Personal call(s) from concerned employee(s)
  News Media reports

- **Government Officials**
  Government Affairs
  News Media reports
  Concerned or scared citizen(s)

- **News Media**
  Public Relations representative
  Police and/or fire scanners
  Other news media
  Fire department/police/hospital spokesperson
  Eyewitnesses, including employees
  Bystanders with knowledge or hearsay
  First-hand view of the situation
  Outside "experts"

- **Vendors, Contractors and Suppliers**
  Direct knowledge of the event
  Employees and/or management
  News media reports

Tools to Use During a Crisis

The following documents are recommended tools that each communications group can use or adapt to specific requirements. Note that a few of the tools will definitely have to be adapted, such as Site Map(s), Building Facts and Figures, and phone lists for key emergency response contacts.

These tools can prove very useful for documenting information related to incidents and for keeping track of media inquiries:

- Emergency Response Contacts
- Key Division Directors/Managers
- Key Communications/PR Contacts
- Incident Information Sheet
- Telephone Log Sheet
- Initial Release
- Checklist for Establishing a News Conference Center
- Maps of Division Plants
- Building Facts and Figures

Crisis Contacts

	Office	Pager/Cellular	Fax	Home
Key Division Directors				
Jennifer Jones (South)	555-0001	C:555-4892	555-8101	555-9801
Kourtney Johnson (North)	555-0121	C:555-4241	555-8294	555-9123
Rebecca Arnold (East)	555-2127	C:555-4101	555-8711	555-9777
Jeremy Kahlil (West)	555-3122	C:555-4801	555-8222	555-9554
Key Division Managers				
Mary Bland (South)	555-0092	C:555-1121	555-8111	555-9682
John Jackson (South)	555-0013	C:555-6101	555-8221	555-9319
Sarah Yerima (North)	555-1764	N/A	555-8811	555-9276
Jonathan Kyle (East)	555-2809	N/A	555-8611	555-9211
Allison Millet (East)	555-2684	N/A	555-8314	555-9013
Nicholas Michael (West)	555-3093	N/A	555-8781	555-9901
Telephone Operators				
Mary Jackson (Supervisor)	555-2999	N/A	555-8722	555-3994
Katie Marsh (Backup)	555-9057	N/A	555-0092	555-2664
Fire Dispatch				
Adam Yerima	555-8894	C:555-8676	555-9467	555-9276
Duane Troy	555-9075	C:555-0328	555-5541	555-0101
Safety Manager				
Ron Nelson	555-1112	C:555-3434	555-6875	555-0841
Julius Jones, Jr.	555-3756	C:555-4441	555-1954	555-2395
Medical				
Ethan Floyd	555-7864	C:555-3321	555-7764	555-1346
Allyson Bernardino	555-9090	C:555-8341	555-5603	555-7651
Demetria Rudy	555-5642	C:555-2390	555-6678	555-6431
Public Relations				
Ann Davis	555-7490	C:555-4431	555-5505	555-6490
Jerry Brown	555-7456	C:555-2210	555-9898	555-7069
Corporate Public Relations				
Gina Arnold	555-8754	C:555-7890	555-2479	555-0956

Key Communications/PR Contacts

	Office	Pager/Cellular	Fax	Home
SOUTH				
Regina Arnold	555-8754	C:555-7890	555-2479	555-0956
Blair Lissurs	555-0293	C:555-7902	555-2478	555-9154
NORTH				
Kourtney Johnson	555-0121	C:555-4241	555-8294	555-9123
Myrtle Jenkins	555-2123	C:555-4545	555-9045	555-8456
EAST				
Belvia Fulks	555-2345	C:555-7690	555-3147	555-9067
Anthony Floyd	555-0789	C:555-4680	555-4896	555-3558
WEST				
Anne Burford	555-1212	C:555-0097	555-7847	555-0321
O.M. Thornton	555-9557	C:555-4502	555-5575	555-3498

Incident Information Sheet

Complete using ink pen

| Date:_____ Time:_____ | **Initial Report** _____ | **Update** _____ |

Describe the incident (i.e., hazardous material spill, equipment malfunction, serious injury, bomb threat, fire, etc.):

Indicate when the incident occurred and when crisis personnel first responded:

Describe which crisis groups are responding:

Indicate where the incident occurred (Building number, column number, east or west side of building, etc.):

Describe the work performed in the buildings(s) where incident occurred (i.e., machining, office functions, mix of factory and office functions):

Estimate the number of employees evacuated:

Estimate the number of employees evacuated:

Estimate the number of employees injured, nature of injuries (to clarify misleading reports) and where they are being examined/treated (i.e., on-site Medical, local hospital):

Describe what is being done to mitigate the emergency:

Telephone Log Sheet

Priority:_____   Date:_____   Time:_____

Call Received From:

    Name _____
    Organization _____
    Location _____

Message:_____
_____
_____
_____
_____
_____

Call back by:_____

Date:_____   Time:_____

Notes: _____
_____
_____
_____
_____
_____

Example Initial Statement for Release

    At approximately _____ (time) today _____ (date), an _____ (fire, explosion, etc.) occurred on the _____ site of the _____ Division.

    Crisis Response personnel are now responding as well as _____ (other support response groups or local municipalities). Our company's response groups include (list appropriate groups such as fire and security officers, medical doctors and nurses, safety personnel, industrial hygienists, and environmental engineers, etc.).

    Our major concerns are for the safety of our employees and the public and to minimize environmental impact.

    We are now involved in determining what has happened and what is being done to mitigate the situation. As more details become available, we will pass them on to the media.

Checklist for Establishing a News Conference Center

In a major emergency, it may be necessary to establish a news conference center. This will be where the company can conduct briefings or news conferences, grant interviews and issue official statements.

Since time is of the essence during a crisis, communications teams should designate certain locations as potential news conference centers and be prepared to carry out the checklist before an incident occurs.

Preliminaries

1. ____   Check for the best time with company spokesperson.

2. ____   Notify media of time and location.

3. ____   Compile list of names of reporters, editors who indicate they will attend.

4. ____   Compile background information of interest to reporters.

5. ____   Invite outside officials as appropriate.

6. ____   Assign someone to handle the physical arrangements for the news conference.

    ___ Video services to record event?

    ___ Junction box for TV and radio mikes?

    ___ Chairs, tables, podiums as required?

7. ____   Brief staff on the subject, speaker(s) and schedule of events.

8. ____   Prepare opening statement and review with lead speaker.

9. ____   Review anticipated questions and answers with the speaker.

10. ____   Check all sound equipment and tape recorders prior to the conference.

11. ____   Place log sheet in conference room to obtain names and affiliations of attendees.

12. ____   Place all news information and handout materials in conference room.

    ___ News Releases

    ___ Background information, such as fact sheets, maps, statistics, histories, and biographical information

    ___ Copy opening statement and other briefing materials

13. ____   Escort the media to the conference room.

14. ____   Use sign-in sheet.

15. ____   Distribute background materials.

16.____   Have assigned staff member open the conference and establish the ground rules.

17.____   Monitor questions and answers closely. Make any necessary clarifications
           before the end of the event.

Afterward/Follow-up

18.____   Handle requests for follow-up information.

19.____   Monitor coverage received; contact any news organization which has an error in
           its report.

20.____   At an appropriate time when the crisis atmosphere has cleared, contact each
           reporter who attended and ask them what went well in terms of our handling the
           event and what could have been improved.

Big Brothers/Big Sisters of America's Crisis Communications Plan: Crisis Management: Responding to the Media

APPENDIX A
CRISIS COMMUNICATIONS OUTLINE

I. THE CRISIS COMMUNICATIONS SYSTEM

    A. Objectives
- Contain the Crisis Events
- Reduce Risk to Agency
- Respond to Media and Community

    B. Select a Crisis Team
- Board/Public Relations Committee
- Top Management Representative
- Legal Representative
- Medical Experts
- Personnel/Human Resources
- Other

    C. Designate a Spokesperson
- Believable
- Knowledgeable
- Articulate
- Accessible

    D. Prepare a Fact Sheet
- Big Brothers/Big Sisters History
- Information on Programs and Services

    E. Prepare a Contact List
- Board President
- Attorney
- Insurance Agent
- Internal Staff and Board
- Field Managers
- BB/BSA Staff
- Government Authorities
- News Media
- Community Leaders and Supporters

    F. Training Re: Crisis Intervention
- Board
- New Board Orientation Training
- Staff

    G. Networking
- Court System
- Police
- Media
- Social Service System
- Government and CSA Protective Services
- Community Leaders (Recognition and Involvement in Agency)

    H. Select a News Site
- Accessible
- Availability of Electrical Outlets
- Telephones

    I. Get Management Approval
- Solicit Participation
- Obtain Endorsement of Plan

II. WHEN YOU KNOW IN ADVANCE

    A. Evaluate the Situation
- Analyze Options
- Anticipate Reactions
- Develop Strategy

    B. Develop the Strategy
- Include Top Management
- Inform Employees in Advance
- Notify Government Officials
- Contact the Media

III. WHEN THE CRISIS HAPPENS

    A. Assess the Situation
- Confirm the Facts
- Investigate Rumors
- Identify and Locate Witnesses
- Analyze Expert Information

    B. Mobilize
- Take Security Measures
- Adapt Crisis and Media Plans to Actual Events
- Assign Responsibilities

C. Prepare a Statement
    - Release Confirmed Facts
    - Provide Background Information
    - Communicate <u>Positive</u> Actions and Concerns

D. Notify Contact List
    - BB/BSA Personnel
        + Field Manager
        + Director of Marketing + Communications
    - Attorney
    - Insurance Agent (if applicable)
    - Neighboring Agencies
    - Government Officials
    - News Media
    - Community Leaders

E. Respond to Media/Coordinate Coverage
    - Alert Receptionist and all Staff
    - Refer all Calls to Designated Spokesperson
    - Make Press Site Available

F. Inform Volunteers, Parents
    - Changes in Operation or Programs
    - Duration of Disruption
    - Extent of Problem

IV. CRISIS FOLLOW-UP

A. Follow-up Plan
    - Analyze Implications/Responsibilities
        + Legal
        + Financial
    - Resolve Loose Ends
    - Prevent Repercussions
        + Hostile Reactions
        + Negative Actions
    - Anticipate Long-Term Effects

B. Evaluate the System
    - Monitor Responses
    - Assess and Measure Results
    - Refine System

APPENDIX B
BACKGROUND STATEMENT

Big Brothers/Big Sisters of (**Agency**) is affiliated with Big Brothers/Big Sisters of America, and holds the highest affiliation ranking, that of being a Full Member Agency. The Agency's screening and service delivery policies conform to those required by Big Brothers/Big Sisters of America.

This Agency is concerned with the well-being and safety of all children, and therefore, its volunteer selection and match supervision procedures are designed to reflect that concern.

Our screening procedures require an applicant to attend an orientation session conducted by a professional staff member. Each volunteer applicant must complete an application form and provide three references. A criminal history check is conducted, and then each applicant undergoes an in-depth screening interview with a social worker. An additional interview is scheduled in the applicant's home and conducted before any match takes place. The professional staff reviews each case to determine if an applicant would be suitable as a Big Brother or Big Sister. Applicants not meeting the Agency's criteria are not accepted as volunteers in the program.

In addition to having a professional staff, the Agency's service delivery is also evaluated by the Board of Directors. This agency has served thousands of youngsters since 19(XX), and volunteers have helped these youngsters in positive growth and development.

(**If EMPOWER or other child abuse prevention and education program is in place at your agency, include a sentence to that effect here.**)

Our philosophy is to cooperate with agencies and authorities in their efforts to protect the children of our community. We work closely with the parents and children we serve to assure that they find the volunteer/child relationship to be enjoyable and beneficial to the child.

APPENDIX C
SAMPLE CRISIS MANAGEMENT PLAN

TABLE OF CONTENTS

SAMPLE CRISIS MANAGEMENT PLAN:

COMMUNICATION CHAIN

In the event of a crisis, this is the communications route to follow:

1. Contact Executive Director

2. Contact family in person (if applicable)

3. Executive Director contacts President of board

4. Executive Director contacts agency spokesperson

5. Executive Director contacts Field Manager for Big Brothers/Big Sisters of America

6. President of board contacts Executive Committee

7. Executive Committee members contact remaining board members

8. Executive Director contacts local and state authorities as prescribed by law

9. Executive Director and President of board deliberate and determine appropriate action

10. Executive Director contacts agency staff

11. Letters sent to parents and volunteers

12. Neighboring agencies notified

13. Agency spokesperson contacts media in certain crisis situations

14. All media inquiries routed to agency spokesperson

15. Agency spokesperson contacts Director of Marketing + Communications for Big Brothers/Big Sisters of America if media is extensive

SAMPLE CRISIS MANAGEMENT PLAN:

IMPLEMENTATION PROCEDURES

1. Adoption of Crisis Management Plan

2. Selection of Media Spokesperson

    A. Primary: Director of Public Relations

    B. First Alternate: Executive Director of Agency

    C. Second Alternate: President of Board of Agency

3. Staff Orientation

4. Board Orientation

5. Volunteer Orientation

6. Media Orientation

7. Annual Review

SAMPLE CRISIS MANAGEMENT PLAN:

CHILD SEXUAL ABUSE

PROGRAM OBJECTIVES IN THE EVENT OF ALLEGED SEXUAL ABUSE

1. Protect Little Brothers and Little Sisters from abuse and molestation

2. Comply fully with the law

STEPS TO BE TAKEN IN THE EVENT OF ALLEGED SEXUAL ABUSE BY VOLUNTEER

1. Executive Director (or in her/his absence the designated staff person of authority) collects all the facts available from the reporting individual (mother, child, caseworker) or agency (police department, social services department). The staff shall abide by the direction of the Executive Director, or Director's designee, in all actions regarding possible, potential, or actual child abuse cases.

2. As a general rule, the Executive Director notifies the Big Brother or Big Sister involved by telephone or in person, as soon as practical, that a report has been made to the agency that he or she is suspected of child abuse. This verbal report will be immediately followed by a telegram. However, the Executive Director, in consultation with the caseworker and informed Board members, may, in appropriate circumstances, decide not to notify the Big Brother or Big Sister of the report until the authorities have had a reasonable opportunity to investigate the report. In the making of such a decision to do so, the following factors shall be considered:

    (a)   The likelihood of further abuse of the child;

    (b)   The likelihood of threats or actual harm to the child, the child's parent/guardian, or others;

    (c)   The likelihood of additional contact with the child or the child's parent/guardian pending the investigation;

    (d)   The likelihood of attempts to dissuade the child or others from cooperating with the investigating authorities;

    (e)   The likelihood of flight by the Big Brother, Big Sister or others involved;

    (f)   The likelihood that the police investigation will be materially hindered.

3. Executive Director, or designee, notifies the child's family in person, the Board President, agency spokesperson and the remainder of the communications chain.

4. Executive Director, or designee, and the child's caseworker contact the parent/guardian of the child in a personal visit to inquire about the child's condition, verify facts, express concern, extend support and advise the parent and child that the match has been suspended during the investigation and neither the parent nor the child is to have any contact with the volunteer.

5. Executive Director, or designee, notifies the agency's attorney.

6. Caseworker reports the incident to the appropriate authorities, as required by Federal, state and local laws.

7. At this point, the Board President and Executive Director will determine the appropriateness of notifying all Board members of the alleged incident.

8. If any media or police authority contacts the agency concerning the alleged incident, they must be referred to the agency spokesperson, or the appropriate alternate in the spokesperson's absence. Only the agency spokesperson is authorized to make public statements. If any other staff or board members are contacted by the media or police, they are to answer no questions and immediately refer all calls to the spokesperson.

9. In the event that an attorney representing the child or the volunteer contacts the agency, no questions are to be answered and the call must be immediately referred to the Executive Director, or designee, who will refer these calls to the agency's attorney.

10. Executive Director will verbally report incident to the Big Brothers/Big Sisters of America Field Manager. Written reports will follow as needed and requested.

11. Executive Director, or designee, will call the insurance agent concerning the allegation. The Executive Director will follow up with a written notice within 24 hours.

12. Executive Director, Program Director, Caseworker and Board President all thoroughly document their involvement in handling of the incident. The Executive Director will take possession of the Big Brother and Little Brother or Big Sister and Little Sister files. The files will include, but will not be limited to the following:

    Big Brother or Big Sister:
    (a) Application
    (b) Reference letters
    (c) Interview write up
    (d) Supervision contact notes
    (e) Police check results
    (f) Federal Bureau of Investigation check results
    (g) Proof of automobile insurance
    (h) Applicant's driving records
    (i) Documentation of reasons for suspension of match.

<u>Little Brother or Little Sister:</u> (a) Phone inquiry
                                        (b) Application
                                        (c) Information release form
                                        (d) Interview write up
                                        (e) Supervision contact notes
                                        (f) Documentation of reasons for suspension of match.

13.   As soon as practical, and with regard to every case of alleged child abuse, the
      Executive Director or designee shall give the Executive Committee of the Board a
      complete oral report of the case, with such analysis and recommendations for future
      policy as may be appropriate in light of the experience. A written report shall be
      prepared, with direction of legal counsel, as requested by the Executive Committee.

14.   The agency shall assist the parent/guardian and Little Brother or Little Sister with
      referrals to appropriate professional counselors, and, if the agency determines it to be
      necessary, will cover reasonable costs for this independent counseling. The agency
      will not volunteer information concerning insurance coverage, but if asked by the
      parent/guardian, will respond that there <u>may</u> be insurance coverage.

STANDARD RESPONSE TO POLICE INQUIRIES CONCERNING ALLEGED INCIDENTS

"We are very concerned with the welfare of this child, as we are with all our children and we are anxious to fully cooperate with the investigation. Because of the privileged nature of our records, it is necessary for us to request a subpoena in order to release our files."

If asked, the agency's spokesperson can verify that a particular volunteer and/or child are or were members of the organization and the dates of their membership. The addresses and phone numbers will also be given to the police. Upon request, the spokesperson will inform the police of the names, addresses and phone numbers of all Little Brothers or Little Sisters that the Big Brother or Big Sister in question has been matched with.

> [Editor's note: Police will often seek agency cooperation in learning the
> identity of other volunteers brought into the agency by the suspect, as well as
> other Littles the suspect may have been matched with in the past. Local
> counsel should be sought for advice, but it is recommended that the agency
> cooperate, but only through the legal compulsory process of subpoena to better
> protect the agency. When the police requests the agency cooperation in not
> communicating the allegation to the volunteer or in not immediately
> suspending the match (so as to not interfere with their pending investigation),
> such a request should be granted. However, this request should be in writing
> to protect the agency from its responsibility to immediately notify the parties
> and to suspend the match pending investigation.]

STEPS TO BE TAKEN IN THE EVENT OF AN INJURY OR THE DEATH OF A LITTLE BROTHER/SISTER OR BIG BROTHER/SISTER WHILE INVOLVED IN AN AGENCY ACTIVITY

1. Any staff member that becomes aware of the incident is to report it immediately to the Executive Director and the Program Director. If the incident occurs at night or on the weekend, the above mentioned staff members are to be contacted at their homes.

2. The Executive Director, or the Program Director as designee, will collect all additional information from police, hospitals, family members and anyone else involved.

3. The Executive Director will report the incident to the President of the Board, or to the Vice-President in the President's absence.

4. If Executive Director and Board President deem it appropriate and necessary, Executive Director will contact the agency's legal counsel.

5. In the case of a minor injury, if the family of the victim has not been notified of the incident, the Executive Director will attempt to make this contact. In the event of serious injury or death, the agency will _not_ give initial notification to the family; rather, that will be the task of the police authorities.

6. The Executive Director will contact the agency's insurance agent within a reasonable period of time, and will follow up in writing within 24 hours. The Executive Director, or designee, will file all necessary forms.

7. The agency will cooperate to the fullest extent with all police and medical personnel. The Executive Director, or Board President in the Director's absence, will be the only authorized spokespersons to these outside agencies.

8. In the event that the agency is contacted by the media, <u>all</u> questions are to be referred to the agency spokesperson.

9. The Executive Director and all agency representatives involved will thoroughly document for the case files, all their actions related to the incident.

10. The Executive Director, or designee, will follow up with the victim's family in order to offer support. Whatever resources the agency has available, or whatever community resources are available - as covered by the agency's insurance policy - will be offered to the family.

STEPS TO BE TAKEN IN THE EVENT OF MISUSE OF AGENCY FUNDS
BY STAFF OR BOARD MEMBERS

1. If the alleged misuse of funds involves a staff member other than the Director or if it involves a board member, the incident must be immediately reported to the Executive Director, who will then report it to the Board President. In the absence of the Executive Director, the incident is to be reported directly to the Board President. If the alleged misuse involves the Executive Director, the incident must be reported immediately to the Board President or Vice-President in the President's absence.

2. The Executive Director will investigate the incident to the fullest extent possible and will report the findings at a special session of the Executive Committee. If the incident involves the Executive Director, it will be investigated by the Board President or designee.

3. The Executive Committee, and the Executive Director when appropriate, will determine the appropriate course of action, which may include, but not be limited to:

    (a) Suspension of employee, with pay, pending further investigation; suspension of board member.

    (b) Suspension of employee, without pay, pending further investigation.

    (c) Immediate dismissal of employee or termination of board member.

    (d) Informal agreement with employee or board member for restitution.

    (e) Formal filing of criminal charges against employee or board member.

4. The Executive Director or Board President will utilize the services of the agency attorney; the agency bookkeeper; the agency auditor; or the agency's insurance agent, as needed.

5. In the event that the agency is contacted by the police, all questions are to be referred to the person of highest authority not involved in the incident, i.e. Executive Director, Board President, Board Vice-President. No other staff member or board member is authorized to answer any questions.

6. In the event that the agency is contacted by the media, all questions are to be referred to the agency spokesperson. The agency spokesperson is the only person authorized to speak with the media.

STEPS TO BE TAKEN IN THE EVENT OF IMPROPRIETY IN THE RELATIONSHIP OF A VOLUNTEER, AGENCY STAFF OR BOARD MEMBER WITH THE PARENT OF A LITTLE BROTHER OR LITTLE SISTER

1. The alleged impropriety must be reported immediately to the Executive Director. If the director is involved in the incident or unavailable, the incident should be reported directly to the Board President.

2. The Executive Director will investigate the incident to the fullest extent possible and report the findings at a special session of the Executive Committee. If the incident involves the Executive Director, the Board President, or designee, will investigate.

3. The Executive Committee, and the Executive Director when appropriate, will determine the course of action, which may include, but not be limited to:

    (a) Suspension of employee, with or without pay, pending further investigation; suspension of board member or volunteer.

    (b) Immediate termination of employee without pay.

4. Agency's attorney and/or insurance agent will be contacted as needed.

5. Executive Director, or designee, will follow up with the parent of the Little Brother or Little Sister to give whatever agency support may be appropriate.

6. The Board President and Executive Director will determine the appropriateness of notifying all board members of the alleged incident.

7. In the event that the agency is contacted by the police, all questions are to be referred to the person of highest authority not involved in the incident, i.e. Executive Director, Board President, Board Vice-President. No other staff member or board member is authorized to answer any questions.

8. In the event that the agency is contacted by the media, all questions are to be referred to the agency spokesperson. The agency spokesperson is the only person authorized to speak with the media.

9. In the event that an attorney representing the parent of the Little Brother or Little Sister contacts the agency, no questions are to be answered and the call must be immediately referred to the Executive Director, or Board President. The Executive Director or Board President will then refer these calls to the agency's attorney.

10. The Executive Director and Board President will thoroughly document their involvement in the handling of the incident.

STEPS TO BE TAKEN IN THE EVENT OF CHARGES OF RACIAL OR SEXUAL DISCRIMINATION OR VIOLATION OF CIVIL RIGHTS BY POTENTIAL VOLUNTEERS, OR THOSE WHO HAVE APPLIED FOR, OR BEEN FIRED FROM AGENCY STAFF POSITIONS

1. Executive Director, or the Board President in the Director's absence, collects all the facts available from the reporting party.

2. Executive Director or Board President discusses the charges with the agency's attorney.

3. Board President determines appropriateness of calling a special session of the Executive Committee.

4. Executive Director discusses the situation with their Big Brothers/Big Sisters of America Field Manager.

5. In the event that the agency is contacted by the police, or an attorney for the plaintiff, all calls must be referred to the Executive Director, or Board President in the Director's absence.

6. In the event that the agency is contacted by the media, all questions are to be referred to the agency spokesperson. The agency spokesperson is the only person authorized to speak with the media.

7. The Board President will determine the appropriateness of immediately notifying all board members of the charges.

8. All agency personnel and board members involved, thoroughly document their handling of the events.

STEPS TO BE TAKEN IN THE EVENT OF CHASTISEMENT OR SUSPENSION OF FUNDING BY UNITED WAY OR OTHER FUNDING SOURCES

1. The Executive Director immediately makes a verbal report to the Board President and sends a copy of any correspondence from the funding source.

2. The Board President determines the appropriateness of calling a special session of the Executive Committee.

3. The Executive Director, Board President, and - when applicable - the Executive Committee determine the course of action, which may include, but not be limited to:

    (a) The Executive Director and Board President co-author a letter to the funding source explaining the agency's position.

    (b) The Executive Director and Board President arrange a meeting with key people from the funding source.

    (c) The Executive Director prepares all materials that may be necessary for such a meeting.

4. The Board President determines the need to immediately notify all board members of the incident.

5. In the event that the agency is contacted by the media, all questions are to be referred to the agency spokesperson. The agency spokesperson is the only person authorized to speak with the media.

APPENDIX D
SAMPLE MEDIA STATEMENT

Allegation of Child Abuse

We are aware of the recent allegations against a former Big Brother in our Big Brothers/Big Sisters program. We are very concerned about anything that might harm any of our children and we are offering our full support to the family. This agency's primary concern is for the welfare of its children. Our agency is an affiliate of Big Brothers/Big Sisters of America, which sets strict standards for volunteer screening. Our agency is cooperating with the legal authorities to resolve the questions raised by these allegations. Since this is a very sensitive matter, I know that you will understand that I am not free to comment any further at this time.

Volunteer no further information. If requested, only this information can be given:

1. Verification that a particular BB volunteer and/or child is associated with your agency.

2. Historical background statement of BB/BS.

3. Confirmation that there is a screening process and what the screening process entails.

Agency Being Sued

We have been asked to comment on the recent suit brought against our agency. Because of the legal process currently underway, we have been advised not to comment on this pending litigation. We do wish to state, however, that this agency's primary concern is for the welfare of its children. We take great care to provide a safe and responsible service to our community.

Criminal Allegation Against Agency Volunteer/Staff

We are aware of the recent allegations against (a current/former volunteer/board/staff member) in our Big Brothers/Big Sisters program. We have been advised that information regarding this allegation is confidential at this time and we are not permitted to discuss the case. However, we do wish to state that this agency's primary concern is for the welfare of its children and we are cooperating with the legal authorities to resolve the questions raised by these allegations.

APPENDIX E
SAMPLE STATEMENT FOR NEIGHBORING AGENCIES

We have been asked to comment on the recent allegations in a neighboring community. Let me just say that our agency's primary concern is to provide a safe and responsible service to the children of our community. We take great care to screen all individuals who work with the children in our program. Our agency is an affiliate of Big Brothers/Big Sisters of America which sets standards for volunteer screening. We are not, however, in a position to comment concerning matters under investigation in another jurisdiction.

APPENDIX F
SAMPLE LETTERS TO VOLUNTEERS/PARENTS/BOARD MEMBERS

Letter to Volunteers

Dear Volunteers,

You may have heard allegations made concerning a Big Brother who was previously matched in our program. Since you are a volunteer in our program, I feel it is important to communicate to you that we are very concerned and saddened by this charge.

The staff is offering its full support to this child and the family. Additionally, our agency is cooperating fully with the proper authorities in their investigation of these allegations. Because our case files are confidential, we are not able to discuss details of the case.

However, we want you to know that our main concern is to provide responsible and safe services for the children we serve. Nationwide, Big Brothers/Big Sisters is in the forefront of using screening methods with volunteers. As you know, this agency has an in-depth screening process. We believe we do as much as we can to protect the integrity of the Big Brothers/Big Sisters program and to maintain high standards of service. More than (XXX) children were successfully matched with Big Brothers and Big Sisters by the agency in the past year.

Since this is a sensitive legal matter, I am not at liberty to say anymore at this time. However, please don't hesitate to call me if you have any questions or if I can be of assistance.

Be assured of our continued gratitude and support of you and the child you are matched with through our program.

Sincerely,

(Executive Director of agency)

(This letter can be adjusted for any crisis. The important thing to remember is to be honest, sincere, and supportive.)

Letter to Parents

Dear Parents,

You may have heard allegations made concerning a Big Brother who was previously matched in our program. Since your child is involved in our program, I feel it is important to communicate to you that we are very concerned and saddened by this charge.

The staff is offering its full support to this child and the family. Additionally, our agency is cooperating fully with the proper authorities in their investigation of these allegations. Because our case files are confidential, we are not able to discuss details of the case.

However, we want you to know that our main concern at Big Brothers/Big Sisters is to provide responsible and safe services for the children we serve. The children are our clients and we do everything we can to act in their best interest.

Nationwide, Big Brothers/Big Sisters is in the forefront of using screening methods to prevent entry into the program of individuals who may wish to harm children. There is an in-depth screening process that potential volunteers must go through prior to matching. The process consists of character references, an in-depth interview to gather information about personal history, a home assessment and police check. This agency also has in place EMPOWER, the child abuse prevention and education training program developed nationally to provide yet another deterrent, and a way for the children in our program to know how to handle a potentially harmful situation **(if applicable)**. We believe our agency maintains high standards. More than (XXX) children were successfully matched with Big Brothers and Big Sisters by this agency in the past year alone.

Since this is a sensitive legal matter, I am not at liberty to say anymore at this time. However, please don't hesitate to call me if you have any questions or if I can be of assistance.

Be assured of our continued gratitude and support of you and your child.

Sincerely,

(Executive Director of agency)

(This letter can be adjusted for any crisis. The important thing to remember is to be honest, sincere, and supportive.)

Letter to Board Members .

Dear Board Member:

You may have heard of the recent allegation of child molestation concerning a Big Brother. As a member of the governing body, I want to assure you of our support of the family and of our full cooperation with the proper law enforcement officials. Enclosed are copies of letters sent to all volunteers and families.

There is very little more I can tell you at this time. If you have any questions or concerns that you wish to share, or if you are contacted by anyone regarding this sensitive matter, please give me a call. I may be reached at the following numbers: **(phone numbers)**.

Sincerely,

President, Board of Directors

(This letter can be adjusted for any crisis. The important thing to remember is to be honest, sincere, and supportive.)

APPENDIX G
LEGAL TERMS: DEFINITIONS AND PROCESSES

ARRAIGNMENT - The first step in a criminal action after a person has been formally charged with a crime. The defendant is brought before a judge or magistrate and informed of the nature of the charges, his/her constitutional rights, and asked to plead either guilty or not guilty to the charges.

ARREST - The seizing of a person by the police or other law enforcement official in the belief that he/she committed a crime. A person is under arrest whenever not free to leave, and at that time must be given Miranda or constitutional rights.

ARREST RECORD - A listing of all the times a person has been picked up by the police because the police believe that he or she had violated a law. Such records are not generally available to the media or to the public, but are limited to law enforcement agencies. Also known as "rap" sheets.

ASSAULT - An attempt to unlawfully cause bodily injury to another, sometimes combined with battery to actually include an unlawful or offensive touching.

BLANK SUBPOENA - The form which is filled out by the party seeking to compel the recipient of the subpoena to either testify or produce documents. It comes in both subpoena ad testificatum and subpoena duces tecum forms, and can be obtained from the office of the clerk of the court of whichever court the matter is to be brought before.

CIVIL SUIT - The bringing of a claim, usually for monetary damages, to try to right a wrong which has been done to a person or to settle a dispute which cannot be otherwise resolved. The end result is usually an order for someone to do or stop doing something, or to pay money to the person who brought the suit.

CONTRIBUTING TO THE DELINQUENCY OF A MINOR - Making available to a minor that which the law states is illegal for the minor to possess, is contributing to the delinquency of a minor. This includes providing a minor with alcohol, drugs, an automobile and keys (if unlicensed), and in some states, cigarettes and other legal tobaccos; also, seducing a child or statutory rape.

CONVICTION - The finding by a judge or jury that the defendant is guilty of the crime or crimes with which he/she was accused.

CONVICTION RECORD - A listing of all the times a person has been convicted of committing a crime. Such records are generally available to the media and the public.

COURT ORDERED SUBPOENA - All subpoenas are issued by the court, even though the party seeking the particular testimony or documents fills them out and often has them served. However, the court may determine that a particular witness is needed in order to fully adjudicate the matter before it, and will order a court subpoena. Also used where attempts by the individual party to serve the witness have failed.

CRIMINAL SUIT - The bringing of a charge against a person who has allegedly violated one of the criminal laws of the state. The person who is the victim is the complaining witness, and the prosecuting attorney represents the state as the body which has been harmed. The person alleged to have committed the criminal act is called the defendant.

DEFENDANT - In a criminal suit, the person accused of having committed a violation of the criminal laws. In a civil suit, the person accused of having violated a promise or agreement or having done something to harm the plaintiff.

DEPOSITION - A sworn statement by a witness in either a civil or criminal suit concerning the testimony he/she will give at trial. It is often used to discover the facts of a case, or to preserve the testimony of a person who will not be available to testify at trial.

FELONY - A criminal offense defined by society to be serious, the range of punishment going from 1 year and 1 day to life or death, and/or a fine, depending on the crime, circumstances and the state's laws.

GRAND JURY - A group of 12 people selected from the surrounding community or county to sit for varying periods (average is 6 months to 1 year) and listen to the prosecutor's presentation of alleged criminal events which have occurred in the area. If the 12 people believe sufficient evidence exists to prosecute a case, an indictment is handed down. If the evidence is found to be insufficient, a "No True Bill" is issued and the case dropped.

GROSS SEXUAL IMPOSITION - The forcing of someone to perform a sexual act while the person who is exerting the force is unclothed - usually kissing or touching, without rising to rape or sodomy.

INDICTMENT - One method of filing formal charges against a person. It is handed down by a grand jury, who has heard only the prosecutor's evidence. It simply means that the grand jury believes that there is enough evidence against the accused to merit a trial. The indictment states the time and date and place of the alleged violation of the law, and the statute that the person is alleged to have violated.

INTERROGATIONS - The questioning of witnesses or suspects concerning the facts of an incident. This can occur anywhere, but if the person is not free to leave, he/she is under arrest and must be given Miranda warnings before interrogation.

INVOLUNTARY SEXUAL BATTERY - The offense of sexual touching of another when the person who is performing the touching believes the person wants to be sexually touched, but the person really does not.

LEWD AND LASCIVIOUS ACTS - Actions which are intended to sexually excite both the actor and the recipient of the act, such as flashing, oral sex, and sexual stimulation of the actor's or another's sexual organs. Usually used in the context where one of the two (or more) participants have not voluntarily engaged in the activity, either because he/she is too young or otherwise unaware of the nature of the activities in which he/she is a participant.

LEWD ASSAULT - Attempt to cause physical harm by means of a sexual act. Usually an attempt to touch a male's or female's sexual organs, or, less frequently, attempted rape or sodomy. There need be no actual contact for an assault to have occurred - only the intent and attempt.

MIRANDA WARNINGS - Warnings to be given every time a person is under arrest; they include the right to remain silent, the fact that anything said can and will be used against them in a court of law, the right to have an attorney present, and the right to have an attorney appointed if he/she can't afford one.

MISDEMEANOR - An offense defined by society to be criminal, but not nearly as serious as a felony, punishable by from 1 day to 1 year in jail, or a fine.

MOLESTATION - The offense of touching a child's sexual organs, either through clothing or without. Most courts recognize this as always being non-consensual, especially with young children.

MOTION TO QUASH A SUBPOENA - Can be brought on behalf of the rights of the recipient of either a subpoena ad testificatum or a subpoena duces tecum; usually used with a subpoena duces tecum, where the individual or organization served with the subpoena believes that constitutional privacy rights and other rights will be violated if they are required to provide the requested documents. This is the only legal way to challenge and possibly avoid having to comply with a subpoena.

"NO TRUE BILL" - The decision returned by the grand jury when it believes the prosecuting attorney does not have sufficient evidence to prosecute a case.

ORDER FOR CLOSURE/SEAL OF RECORDS - An order by a court sealing the court file of a person so that no one can access the information contained in the court file. Often done in child abuse cases to keep the child's testimony secret, and to protect the child's identity.

PLAINTIFF - The person in a civil suit who claims he/she has been wronged either by the action or inaction of the defendant; in a criminal suit, the state is the plaintiff in the case.

PROFESSIONAL NEGLIGENCE - A wrongful action or inaction of an attorney, doctor or other professional person which thereby results in a harm or damage to the person he/she was supposed to be helping. Also called malpractice.

PROSECUTOR - The person who represents the state and all victims of crimes. Also known as the district attorney, state's attorney, or circuit attorney.

RAPE - The forcible action of sexual intercourse upon a female without their consent. In many states, it can only be performed by a male against a female to whom he is not married, although some states are now recognizing rape within a marital relationship. Rape of one male by another is called sodomy.

SEXUAL BATTERY - The offense of sexual touching of another person without his/her consent.

SEXUAL IMPOSITION - The forcing of someone to perform a sexual act, usually kissing or touching of the sexual organs, without his/her consent. This is usually done while the person being touched is fully clothed.

SEXUAL MISCONDUCT - This is similar to sexual imposition, and it is often used to replace the charge of statutory rape.

SODOMY - The performance of a sexual act termed "unnatural" upon another, or the requiring of another to perform the sexual act. This includes cunnilingus, fellatio, and anal sexual intercourse, as well as bestiality. This does not require force - it can be consensual.

STATUTORY RAPE - The act of sexual intercourse with a female who is under the statutory age for consent. In almost all states, only a female can be statutorily raped. Consent is immaterial; if the female is less than the required age, the man is guilty of statutory rape.

SUBPOENA - An official court document summoning the recipient to appear at a particular time and place to give testimony in person; it can be either for a hearing, a deposition, a trial, or other legal proceeding. Also called a subpoena ad testificatum. Failure to appear as ordered can result in the person so summoned being held in contempt of court and having to either pay a fine or go to jail.

SUBPOENA DUCES TECUM - A court order requiring that on or before a certain date, the recipient, often the custodian of records, provides specified documents to the party issuing the subpoena. This does not require the person so providing the documents to appear or testify, but merely to provide access.

APPENDIX H
SAMPLE MEDIA COVERAGE

Following are samples of publicity received by Big Brothers/Big Sisters agencies. These articles are not chosen to single out agencies having suffered through such situations, but rather to help others learn from their experiences. Some of these samples demonstrate how best to handle crisis situations; the other articles illustrate the wide range of what makes a Big Brothers/Big Sisters agency newsworthy.

II. TYPES OF CRISIS SITUATIONS

While many agencies feel the only kind of negative publicity generated is from child molestation allegations, there are a variety of crisis situations when an agency might find itself dealing with the media. One of the cardinal rules is to "distinguish a problem from a crisis". Take corrective action on problems and remember that both problems and crises can be controlled. Some examples of crisis situations include:

- ◆ Child abuse/molestation allegation

- ◆ Embezzlement of agency funds

- ◆ Sexual or racial discrimination suit/sexual harassment

- ◆ Drug related arrest of staff or youth or volunteer in program

- ◆ Major fire or explosion - wherever matches are together, e.g., at circus or sporting events, bowling centers; could also involve the destruction of the agency's office or property

- ◆ Injury or death of child or volunteer during agency sponsored activity

- ◆ Natural disaster - generally affecting agency offices

- ◆ Suspension of funding by United Way or other funding institutions

- ◆ False allegation about agency.

Each of these situations has caused crisis or emergency dealings with the media for some Big Brothers/Big Sisters programs. It is important to remember that the media considers many issues newsworthy and that your agency should respond by planning *before* the need arises.

These are just some examples of crisis situations that may (but hopefully will not) befall your agency.

VII. POSSIBLE QUESTIONS AND SUGGESTED RESPONSES

Question: **Media:** *"What do you think happened"?*

Response: **Spokesperson:** Refrain from speculation on what or why something happened. It is better to say *"I don't know,"* unless you actually have the facts.

Question: **Media:** *"How much damage was sustained?"* or *"How large a potential suit are you facing?"*

Response: **Spokesperson:** Do not try to estimate any dollar amount. Such guesses can affect amounts of lawsuits or even insurance claims, seldom to your advantage.

Question: **Media:** *"Will you be reviewing your screening procedures after this incident?"* or, *"How will your procedures change as a result of this incident?"*

Response: **Spokesperson:** Never indicate that your current practices could in any way be considered negligent. *"We have no reason to believe our practices or procedures are in need of immediate revision,"* is an appropriate response. Never instigate a program review during a time of crisis. This could be interpreted by the news media as an indication that you were at fault or negligent. Also, be especially sensitive to any staff changes or layoffs during a crisis. This, too, can be taken as an indication of wrongdoing or staff dissatisfaction, which could result in renewed or extended media coverage.

Question: **Media:** *"Will the volunteer be allowed to serve as a Big Brother or Big Sister again?"*

Response: **Spokesperson:** *"The match has been suspended pending the outcome of the allegations. However, you should know that because of the one-to-one nature of the Big Brothers/Big Sisters service, adults who are matched with children in our program are carefully screened. The process is thorough and comprehensive and includes references, police record checks, in-person interviews, and home assessments. The volunteer selection process is designed to assure that the matches made are as appropriate as possible, keeping the child's safety and well-being in mind at all times."*

Question: **Media**: *"Have any rules or regulations been broken that you know of?"*

Response: **Spokesperson**: In answering this question, be honest, but not expansive. If it is known that rules were compromised, your answer should be that, *"It appears as if that may be a possibility, however, the situation is still under investigation."* At this point, most cases of wrongdoing are in the preliminary stages. It is not appropriate to say that situations are more than allegations. Your interpretation of events should not be added to your message to the media - you will be held responsible for what you say if you assign guilt where legally there is none.

Question: **Media**: *"Is the issue of child sexual abuse a major problem for Big Brothers/Big Sisters agencies?"*

Response: **Spokesperson**: This is a tricky question to answer as it addresses a major issue and reflects on the entire Big Brothers/Big Sisters Movement. A suggested response to questions of this nature is, *"The problem of child sexual abuse is not unique to Big Brothers/Big Sisters. That is why Big Brothers/Big Sisters has been in the forefront of requiring screening for adults who work with or volunteer to spend time with children. We also have in place at this agency EMPOWER, a child abuse prevention and education program designed to inform children to report any inappropriate behavior to a trusted adult."* Stressing your agency's prevention and education program will inform the media that you are doing as much as possible about the problem of child sexual abuse.

Question: **Media**: *"How will service be affected due to your agency's recent loss of funding?"*

Response: **Spokesperson**: *"Big Brothers/Big Sisters provides a much needed service to this community. Therefore, we do not anticipate that service will be cut back at this time. We will be looking for alternative funding sources."* If there are questions concerning the possibility of reinstatement of your funding, this could be indicated. *"We have requested a hearing to present our situation for consideration of reinstatement."*

We have previously discussed the issue of *"No comment."* It is being reiterated here in order to get across the importance of not using this phrase. This is an unwise response to **any** question put forth by the media, and is generally interpreted to mean *"I know something but I'm not telling because it is damaging to me"*. The media will continue to dig and pursue when confronted with this simple statement, so use of this hedge will not serve you well. It is far better to be as open and accessible as possible. The facts can be provided with greater accuracy, the story will generally become more positive as a result of your input, and the media will respect you for being cooperative and taking the initiative. You do have the right to refrain from commenting, however, you should explain why you can't comment, eg. *"the case is in litigation and therefore, we cannot comment on the specifics of the case."*

University of Florida's Crisis Communications Plan

AT THE FIRST SIGN OF A POTENTIAL CRISIS OR CONTROVERSY
INVOLVING THE UNIVERSITY OF FLORIDA, WHETHER BEFORE OR AFTER
EXPOSURE IN THE NEWS MEDIA, BEGIN PREPARING FOR A TIMELY, ACCURATE
AND APPROPRIATE RESPONSE.

I.   Assess the situation; take immediate action

    A.   The individual who encounters the situation should determine whether a crisis
actually exists. Quickly gather full, accurate information from appropriate
sources.

    B.   Determine whether an immediate response is necessary. If it is, contact the
public information head of the area in which the crisis exists, the appropriate
vice president or dean, and the University's chief public relations officer (or
those next in line to these individuals). Following discussion among those
administrators, a decision will be made as to who inside and outside the
University should be contacted. If the crisis is of major proportions, the
assistant vice president for information services (the University's chief public
relations officer) will contact the assistant vice president for university relations
and, following consultations with the president and/or provost, the two assistant
vice presidents will contact the appropriate individuals inside and outside the
University. (Telephone lists of University administrators, individuals in
Tallahassee, Washington and elsewhere are attached to this document. Key
numbers listed below.)

Office #   Home #

President John Lombardi

Provost Andrew Sorensen

Asst. Vice President Jack Battenfield

Asst. Vice President Linda Gray

<u>Office #</u>   <u>Home #</u>

(or...Joseph Kays, Associate Director

... Frank Ahern, Associate Director)

VP Student Affairs Art Sandeen

VP Administrative Affairs Gerry Shaffer

VP Research Don Price

VP Development & Alumni Affairs Bob Lindgren

VP Health Affairs David Challoner

VP Agricultural Affairs Jim Davidson

Vice Provost Gene Hemp

C.   If necessary, the two assistant vice presidents (Gray/Battenfield) will, working with the appropriate vice president and/or dean, call together a crisis committee. The composition of the crisis committee will depend on the nature of the situation. (For example, if the situation is student-related, the two assistant vice presidents would work with the vice president for student affairs and dean for student services to convene an appropriate crisis committee. If, for example, the situation involves a research matter, the two assistant vice presidents would work with the vice president for research and director for sponsored research to call together an appropriate crisis committee.)

II.   After the appropriate administrators have been informed of the situation (these would include the area public information officers, the University's public information and university relations officers, the president, provost, and appropriate vice presidents and/or deans), a decision should be made as to what other individuals or agencies should be contacted. The assistant vice presidents for information services and university relations, in consultation with administrators, will determine which of the following offices should also be contacted, if not already involved.

1. Law enforcement or other protective services   <u>Phone #</u>

    -- University Police...   (emergency)

                                          (administration)

    -- City Police, Fire, Medical...   (emergency)

    -- Gainesville Police..   (administration)

    -- Alachua County Sheriff...   (administration)

    -- Gainesville Fire...   (administration)

2. Other appropriate administrators (including any affected deans,

    department chairpersons or program directors)

3. Other campus communications offices and/or members of the University

    of Florida Communications Network

4. Environmental health and safety   <u>Work & Home Phone #s</u>

    -- William Properzio, Dir. of

        Environmental Safety...

5. Physical plant

    -- Robert Cremer (Main Campus)...

    -- John Graves (Health Science Center,

        Chief of Operations)...

6. Legal matters

    -- Pamela Bernard, UF Attorney...

III. After assessing the nature and scope of the situation that has arisen, a plan of action

should be initiated which include some or all of the following components:

A. Plan an immediate response

    1. Designate who will speak for the University. (In case of major crises,

        the president or provost should speak, along with the appropriate vice

        presidents/deans or other individuals directly related to the situation.)

2.   A public information spokesperson should also be designated. In the event of a major crisis, the spokesperson will be the University's chief public relations officer; if the crisis relates to a particular area, a communications spokesperson from that area (i.e., Health Science Center, IFAS, Shands, Athletics) may need to be designated.

3.   Those dealing with the media should review attached list of media relations reminders.

4.   Assign a staff writer to draft a brief initial statement or list of details for use until a more detailed statement or story can be drafted. (News media will expect and demand an immediate response.)

5.   Decide whether a news conference and/or news release is an appropriate means of conveying information to the news media and the public. The University's chief public relations officer or the public relations officer for the area affected will decide logistics of the news conference -- when, where, how the media will be contacted, which media will be contacted, who will supervise the news conference, who will appear, etc. (See attached list of news conference logistical details for review.)

6.   Determine whether the magnitude of the crisis merits establishing a media briefing center. Decide where briefing center should be, if additional phone lines may be needed and other details.

7.   Decide the need to assign videographers and photographers to take pictures of the scene. (This could prove helpful in responding to media inquiries, to possible later litigation, as well as documenting events.)

8.   Decide whether it is appropriate to allow location shooting by TV and newspaper photographers. Determine when, where and who will accompany the media.

9. Discuss need to supply video footage from files. Decide whether to provide TV footage for immediate distribution, via satellite uplink or by handing out tapes.

10. Discuss need to produce taped response for radio or whom to make available for radio sound bytes.

11. Identify any other individuals who may serve as spokespersons or who might be made available to the news media at the earliest time after a controversy or crisis has arisen. Assign a public information staff person to discuss with that individual the idea of making his/her "side of the issue" known to the media. Counsel individual in terms of appropriate ways to deal with the media.

12. Determine what means of internal communications will be used if the crisis affects University students and employees.

13. Alert University main switchboard and any other campus switchboards about where to refer calls pertaining to the crisis.

B. Write a fact sheet and use as a guide to write a statement for the media or preparation for an AP/UPI wire story summarizing the situation. Written material is to be reviewed by the University's chief public relations officer and/or the head public relations officer in the designated area of the crisis, and others as required.

C. After developing a proposed plan of action, with consideration to the elements detailed above, the public information officers should make sure the president or provost and/or the appropriate vice presidents or deans review material to be disseminated and have copies on hand.

IV. At the earliest possible stage, advise public information staff members of the situation. Give secretaries clear instructions in regard to handling telephone calls concerning the situation and alert them that they may be called upon to perform special clerical assignments. Specific assignments may be delegated to members of the communications staff (writing and reviewing copy, running errands, making phone calls, other work).

V.   Discuss alternative or additional means of conveying information. This might include such items as letters to parents of students or selected other constituencies of the University, letters to newspaper editors, consultation with editorial boards or other activity. Other means of communication which may need to be considered include making phone banks available and using ham radios in an emergency.

VI.   Alert individuals handling newspaper and video clippings in the appropriate communications offices to give highest priority to immediately scanning daily newspapers and video reports for stories related to the situation. Deliver copies of these clips or reports to the president, provost, appropriate vice president and/or dean, the chief public information officer or head information officer of the appropriate area. If necessary, arrange for videotaping of any TV coverage.

VII.   Set up information files on the crisis at hand. Material related to the crisis, including clippings, statements, letters, memos and any other documents, should be filed in chronological order.

VIII.   Plan to frequently update staff and appropriate administrators.

IX.   Monitor the situation at least daily. Try to maintain a chronology of events for possible use for fact sheet or historical information later.

X.   Have a follow-up assessment to determine what worked, what did not work, and what changes might be made in the future for improved crisis management. If a crisis team has been called together, that total crisis team should meet after the event has been handled to review and discuss.

LOGISTICAL DETAILS

1. Determine where news conferences/media availabilities can and should be held. (Know sizes of rooms, whom to call to reserve rooms). (See attached list of campus room availabilities.)

2. Assess status of phone lines. Determine whether more phone lines are needed in a crisis event. Determine location of the nearest phones that media can use to call their offices.

3. If a media briefing area or press room needs to be designated, appropriate administrators should discuss where the best place would be to have media gather. Have knowledge of equipment and space. Each communications office should keep an inventory of what equipment and space they have available, where cameras can plug in, where lap-tops can be plugged into phones and where computers can be used in their specific areas.

4. Maintain details on hotels/motels which are closest, best, cheapest. (See hotel information attached.)

5. Determine parking logistics in advance. Where can media park? Specific parking areas may need to be set aside. Campus information personnel should work with the police to determine parking areas. Particular emphasis should be given to determining with police where satellite trucks may park in the event of a major crisis and onslaught of vehicles coming to campus.

6. Maintain a list of available support staff. Clerical, technical back-up people, as well as public relations staff who deal directly with the media, should be reachable.

7. Consideration should be given to the University communications office purchasing a portable power supply. In a natural disaster, such as a weather crisis, computers, faxes and copiers would be useless without back-up power.

MEDIA RELATIONS REMINDERS

1. ALWAYS return media calls, even if they call more than once and even if they are hostile. "Bunker mentality" won't make the problem or the media go away. The more cooperative you appear, the better.

2. Really communicate with media reps when you are talking with them: that means both talking and listening. During crisis time, if you're friendly and don't rush them, they appreciate it. Also, through conversation, the media can provide you with information that is useful.

3. Avoid antagonizing media reps, if possible. A sharp tone at a press conference, during a phone call, or elsewhere can affect your future relationship with an individual and with any other media reps who may hear the conversation.

4. Consider establishing a dedicated call-in phone line that will offer information to media or others who phone in. (Info on news conferences, rumor control info, newly acquired information can be placed on a tape that can be updated. Particularly useful when regular phone lines are tied up with calls.)

5. Consider how information you release to media may affect others. If things you say will result in media calling other agencies or individuals, you need to call them first to warn of impending calls.

6. When talking to media, be sure to give credit to other agencies, groups or individuals working on the crisis, including your staff. (First, because it's courteous and the right thing to do, but it also enhances relationships and reflects well on you.)

7. Try to be pro-active with new information. Even though things may be frantic, if you acquire new information regarding the crisis, reach out to media. Everybody's looking for a "twist" on the story that no one else has. If you can provide some media with a special angle, it can pay off later.

NEWS CONFERENCES AND PRESS AVAILABILITIES

1. When you notify media of news conferences/availabilities, be sure to define what kind of event you are actually having. Usually, if you announce a news conference, media expect you to provide them with information, or to announce something. A press availability can simply mean you are making individual(s) available to answer questions from the media.

2. Don't call unnecessary news conferences/availabilities. If it's not worth their while, the media will only be angered.

3. If holding a news conference, try to tell media in advance some details of what you will be announcing. Being coy will not only irritate the media, but may prevent them from attending your event.

4. Gauge the size of your crowd carefully when reserving a room; better to have too much, than too little space. Make sure microphones, chairs, lighting, and water are in pace at least 30 minutes before an event.

5. Decide format in advance. Who will introduce speakers, who decides when question/answer period ends, and other details.

6. Decide in advance whether or not handouts are needed. If speaker is giving a written talk, you may want to wait and hand out material after the talk, so media will stay and listen. However, it's advisable to tell them you will give them a copy later, so they aren't irritated by having to take unnecessary notes.

7. Check to see what else is happening on campus, in the community. Don't lose effectiveness through time conflicts with other events.

8. Consider whether you need to let other organizations and agencies know you are having a news conference. (You may wish to invite others to attend or participate in your event.)

9. Decide who will maintain control at news conference. Someone may need to be the arbiter as to where camera tripods are set up, who sits where and other details.

10. Try to plan length of news conference/availability, but be flexible. Don't end it when there are still a dozen hands raised for questions.

11. Consider the time of the news conference/availability. If you want to make the noon, 6 p.m. or 11 p.m. TV and radio news, you need to allow time for crews to travel and edit tape. Remember, the time schedule for a news conference/availability can send a signal to the media: sometimes right, sometimes wrong.

12. If you have a satellite uplink or other equipment, be sure to let media know in advance.

13. You may want to pre-plan still photo opportunities.

14. If you are going to set restrictions on an event, try to put it in writing and communicate it to media representatives at least 24 hours in advance.

PERSONAL CONSIDERATIONS

1. In any crisis, try to find out as much information as you can. Even if you are not going to communicate that information, it's probably better to know as much as possible. That way, you avoid inadvertently saying the wrong thing or sending unintended messages.

2. Consider the parameters of your crisis and try to conduct yourself accordingly when dealing with the media and others. Maintaining a sense of humor is important, but inappropriate humor can work against you. Professional dignity is important, particularly in unpleasant times.

3. As the crisis progresses, jot notes for review later. The notes can help you remember things during the crisis and may be useful for later review.

4. If you are on camera, always dress professionally. This may seem like "form over substance," but casual or mussed clothing can send signals to viewers that things are out of control.

5. More common sense -- try to give yourself some down time and sleep time during the crisis. Overwork and no sleep can lead to misstatements, irritability and loss of friends.

6. When the worst of the crisis is over, send notes of appreciation to those who have been of service, outside and inside the institution, including your own staff.

7. Apologize to the folks whose correspondence, projects and other work you may have had to put off because of the crisis, then catch up on that work. Consolation is, much of that work will have taken care of itself.

Then, the following lists:

University Officials

Government Officials

Area hotels and motels (including rates and contacts)

Parking areas

News conference locations

Campus maps

Author Index

Subject Index